By The Editors of Consumer Guide®

Add~A~Room

F A Fireside Book
FIRESIDE Published by Simon and Schuster
New York, New York

Contents

Every home presents a different expansion challenge, and every homeowner has different expansion expectations. It's time to mentally break down walls and dig foundations. Once you understand the options—and how they fit your situation—you can confidently begin the project.

There's more involved in planning than just deciding what to build. Legal factors, economic factors, and personal factors must be debated and resolved. The actual plans themselves must be drawn up, material costs must be determined, and labor needs must be calculated. The planning stage is also where you work out exactly how much you want to do yourself and how much you want to turn over to the professionals.

Louis Weber, President
Publications International, Ltd.
3841 West Oakton Street
Skokie, Illinois 60076

Permission is never granted for commercial purposes

Manufactured in the United States of America
1 2 3 4 5 6 7 8 9 10

Library of Congress Catalog Card Number:
80-65633
ISBN: 0-671-25270-4
        0-671-25271-2 pbk.

A Fireside Book
Published by Simon and Schuster
A Division of Gulf + Western Corporation
New York, New York 10020

Cover Design: Frank E. Peiler
Architectural Renderings: Benson & Benson Design
Technical Illustrations: Clarence A. Moberg
Technical Consultants: Burch, Burch & Burch, A.I.A.

Publications International, Ltd., has made every effort to ensure accuracy and reliability of the information, instructions, and directions in this book; however, it is in no way to be construed as a guarantee, and Publications International, Ltd., is not liable in case of misinterpretation of the directions, human error, or typographical mistakes.

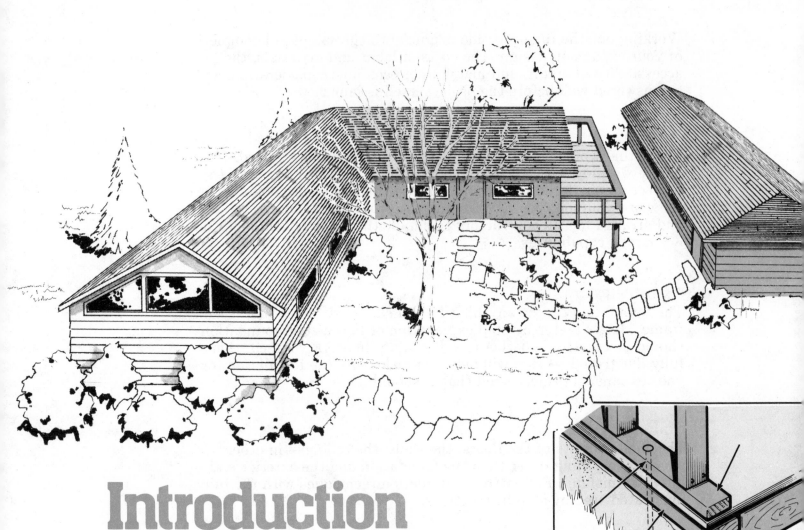

Introduction

One exciting aspect of the current housing confusion is the house addition. People who used to move on in search of bigger and better space are now discovering that their own homes are potentially bigger and potentially better. Turning that potential into reality is what this book is all about. The detail involved in expansion appears overwhelming at first, but with a little know-how, and a lot of enthusiasm, you can get what you want—at a price you can afford.

The Addition

The possibilities for expansion are indeed endless. What do you want from your addition? New bedrooms, extra bathrooms, and larger kitchens fit a practical need. Workshops, patios, and studios are more recreation oriented. This book covers them all, from the simplest sewing room to the more complicated second-floor addition. *Add-A-Room* takes nothing for granted; all various structures—and their possibilities—are discussed in detail. Very few homes are alike, and each addition serves individual needs. This book therefore respects the diverse character of the home—serving you as a guide from which ideas can grow.

Do-It-Yourself?

We suggest you do as much of the work as possible. That means doing what you know you can do, and attempting the unattempted. At times that's not possible, and *Add-A-Room* discusses the ways to hire the best possible, quality help. Although not designed exclusively as a do-it-yourself guide, *Add-A-Room* contains all the necessary structural information, from pouring a foundation to installing the faucets. The trick to getting the most for your money is knowing when to hire professionals and when not to. Sometimes, professional help actually saves you money.

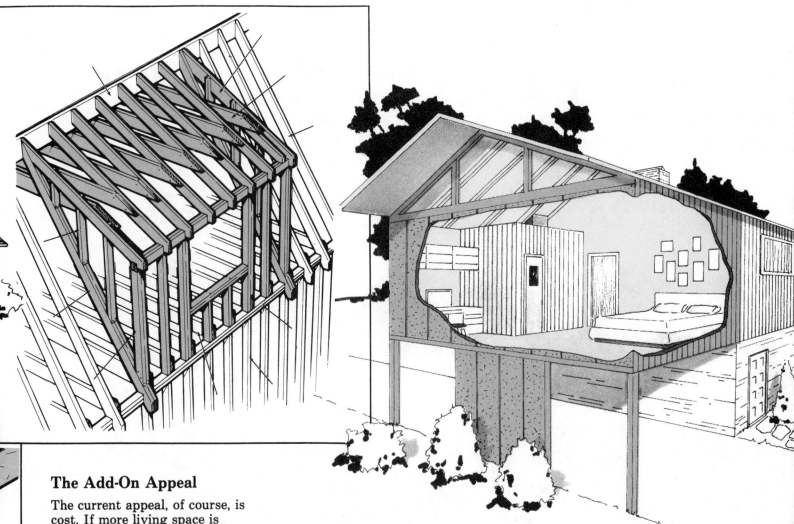

The Add-On Appeal

The current appeal, of course, is cost. If more living space is needed, a room can be added at a fraction of the cost of a new home. Loans for this type of work are more readily available than the mortgage money involved in a new dwelling. And much of the work can be done by the homeowner and the family.

The true appeal of home additions, however, is the sense of accomplishment that accompanies renovation. The house begins to take on the personality of the family. Every addition is built for a purpose—probably signaling a major change in the family's life. And if your own sweat and time is involved, the rewards are immeasurable.

Add-A-Room: The Book

No matter what type of addition you're considering, or how much work you plan on doing yourself,

Add-A-Room will serve you well as a guidebook throughout the project. No book will answer all your questions, but *Add-A-Room* will help you understand the questions—and show you how to get them answered.

One major obstacle to home renovation is the mystery associated with the structural design. The house has become for many a solid, rock-like entity, perfect (or imperfect) as it is, and unchangeable. The first part of this book is geared to get your mind working, to mentally break down walls and dig foundations. Once the house begins to change within your head, the options become truly endless.

The second part of this book discusses the details of planning and economics. This section helps you discover the possible

trouble spots before they occur. Every consideration that should go into the addition, and every agency or professional that should be contacted, is spelled out within this section.

The third part of the book explains the processes of construction, step-by-step. Whether or not you do the work yourself, this section will give you the basic knowledge you need to make sure construction is sound and proper. Fully illustrated, these chapters will enable you to do much of the work yourself.

Adding a room is indeed a major project. It's not going to be easy. It is, however, a relatively painless way to substantially increase the enjoyment of your present home.

Ideas for Expansion

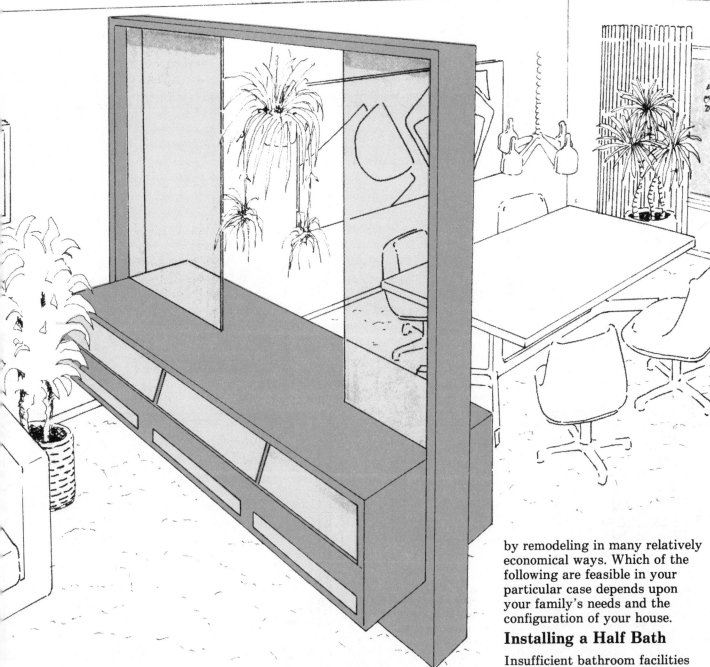

Expansion by Rearrangement

One excellent way to gain additional living space is by remodeling the interior. This might not be possible in smaller homes, where all available space is in use. But in many other residences, especially older homes built when efficient space utilization was less important, altering the interior is a good course to follow.

You can increase living space by remodeling in many relatively economical ways. Which of the following are feasible in your particular case depends upon your family's needs and the configuration of your house.

Installing a Half Bath

Insufficient bathroom facilities is a common problem that disrupts a family's daily home life. This difficulty usually occurs in a one-bathroom residence, but it's not uncommon for homes with two or more bathrooms to need more facilities. The problem doesn't always depend upon the number of people in the household. In many cases the need for a second bath stems from inconvenient accessibility, as is the case when a bathroom is placed so that you must walk through a bedroom to reach it.

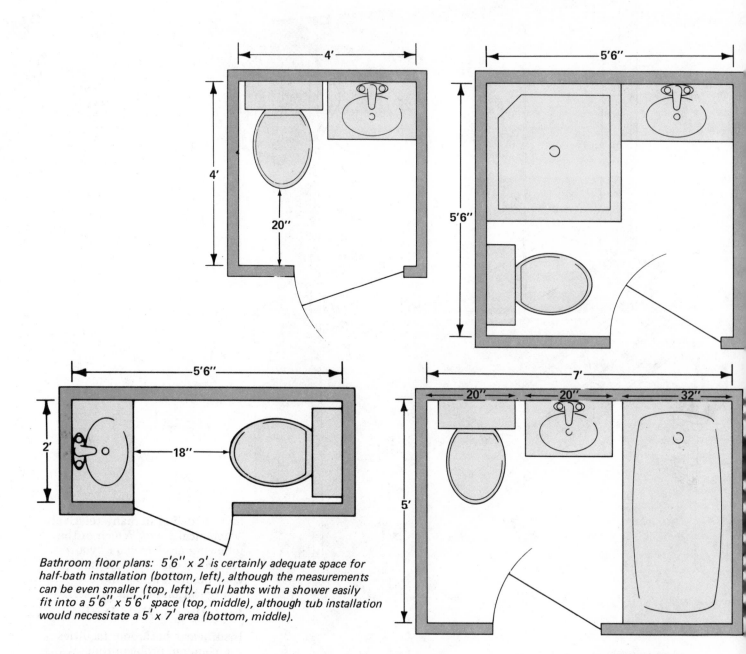

Bathroom floor plans: 5'6" x 2' is certainly adequate space for half-bath installation (bottom, left), although the measurements can be even smaller (top, left). Full baths with a shower easily fit into a 5'6" x 5'6" space (top, middle), although tub installation would necessitate a 5' x 7' area (bottom, middle).

Often, a simple solution to the problem is to install a half bath.

Due to the small amount of space required for a half bath, one or more of them can be installed without too much difficulty or expense. A half bath consists of a wash basin and a toilet, and you can install these fixtures in a space as small as 2 x 5½ feet. By judicious selection of fixtures, these dimensions can sometimes be reduced to a mere 20 x 62 inches! This means you can

often convert a small closet into a practical half bath.

Although a half bath is often built into an extra closet, there are other suitable locations. Any nook that can be easily enclosed is a possible site—like the wasted space under an open single stairway. A room corner or any other place that can be enclosed by partition walls presents possibilities. Done properly, such an enclosure will be unobtrusive and may even enhance the overall interior.

A half bath should be installed close to water supply and drain pipes. Otherwise, the plumbing required will be prohibitively expensive. A location without windows is acceptable, and may be preferable considering the placement of the existing plumbing system or the presence of long, cold winters.

Installing a Full Bath

When a half bath falls short of meeting a family's needs, a new full bath is the only alternative.

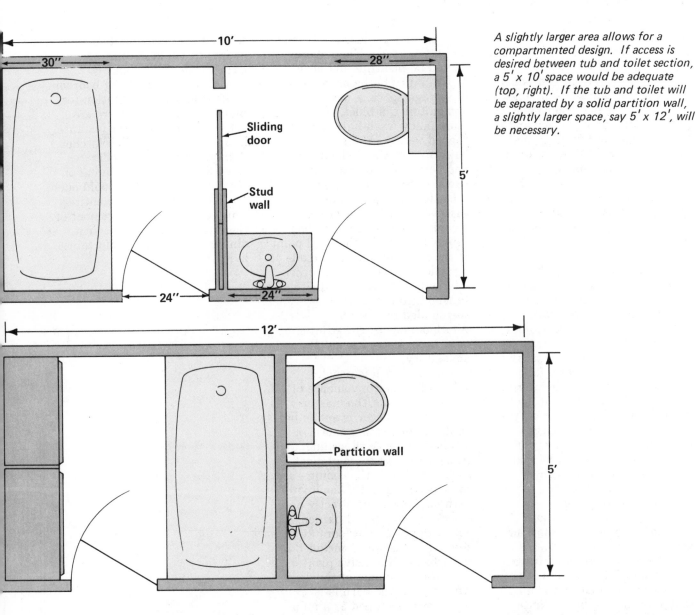

A slightly larger area allows for a compartmented design. If access is desired between tub and toilet section, a 5' x 10' space would be adequate (top, right). If the tub and toilet will be separated by a solid partition wall, a slightly larger space, say 5' x 12', will be necessary.

For a slightly higher cost in space and dollars, a full bath can significantly increase a home's liveability. Full baths can be built in a wide range of styles, from simple to simply opulent.

The Functional Bath

A simple and functional full bath requires the space of a room about 5½ feet square. This allows adequate room for a full-sized wash basin, a standard toilet, and a shower stall. If a bathtub is substituted for a shower stall, the space would need to be at least 5 x 7 feet. Of course, a full bathroom need not be these specific dimensions. They're just rules of thumb. Bathroom fixtures come in a wide variety of sizes and configurations, so all the needed fixtures could possibly be installed in space like 3½ x 8, and 4½ x 9½ feet.

Expanding the area slightly—to 5 x 10 feet for example—affords the possibility of a compartmented bathroom. This arrangement allows two people to use the bathroom at the same time in privacy. In such a bathroom, the tub area and lavatory section could be separated by a stub wall and sliding door. And each section has a separate entrance door.

Another compartmented design allows no access between the two sections; they're separated by a solid partition wall. The lavatory—in effect a half bath—is in one small room. The tub, and perhaps dressing table and storage shelves, is in another. Depending on the size of the room, other fixtures could be added, like a bidet, shower stall, and an extra wash basin.

Placement of the full bath follows the same guidelines as those for a half bath. Any location is theoretically possible, but it's best to stick close to existing plumbing lines. Even if the location chosen is below the lowest point of a house's drainage system, proper equipment can allow for bathroom waste drainage.

Sometimes a full bath can be installed in a small extra

bedroom or in an unused storage room. By moving or rearranging partition walls, you could convert two adjacent bedrooms into a larger master bedroom with a master bathroom. This gives adults more privacy and convenience, and frees up the house's original full bath for other family members.

It doesn't matter on which floor of the house the new bath will be built. Almost any floor can be beefed up to support heavy bathroom fixtures. An installation on the ground floor of a house built on a poured-concrete slab foundation can be difficult, but is quite possible.

Some homes have certain rooms that are too large to be fully utilized. You can make good use of the wasted space by erecting partitions for a full bath. Sometimes, in the interest of good interior design, it may be necessary to partition off the entire side or end of a large room. If so, the bathroom can occupy one portion of the space, and the other portion can be turned into an office, den, sewing room, or closet.

When planning a full bath installation, you must consider your family's traffic patterns and the room's potential usage. For example, a bathroom at the far end of a recreation room that's a considerable distance from other activity centers would be inconvenient. A bath intended for both family members and guests should not be situated so that users have to parade through the kitchen, a bedroom, or living room to reach it. And, ideally, the bathroom should be located adjacent to the guest bedroom. Of course, attaining these goals isn't always easy and compromises are often necessary.

The Luxury Bath

Three main factors set the luxury bathroom apart from a standard bathroom: size, extent and type of fixtures, and lavishness of furnishings and decor. A luxury bath is at least the size of a standard bedroom, and often larger. The fixtures should be plentiful and posh. Most luxury baths have plenty of storage space, a modern design toilet, a bidet, two or more fancy wash basins, marble-topped vanity cabinets, a hairdressing and makeup unit, and perhaps a special shampoo basin. Often, a chaise longue and other furnishings not usually associated with a bathroom are included, too. A large, stylish tub is likely to be the focal point of the room. It's usually made of ceramic, marble, or some other interesting material, and either sunken into the floor or surrounded by decking. Whirlpool baths, either integral or as separate units, are almost mandatory.

A luxury bath is usually located for the convenience of the occupants of the master bedroom. Its decor is apt to be opulent, with rather exotic or emphatic floor, wall, ceiling, and trim. Large expanses of glass—perhaps even on the ceiling—are common. Frequently the luxury bath may open out directly onto a deck or landscaped garden, with indoor and outdoor sunbathing facilities included in the scheme. Extensive planters may also form part of the decor. And, part of the bath is sometimes equipped as a mini-gym—complete with exercise equipment and a massage table.

When planning a luxury bathroom, it should be viewed as a retreat, where the user can retire to seek solitude and relaxation. Often, the character of this room has little in common with the remainder of the house.

Partitions

Some houses have too many partitions, and some have too few. By removing unnecessary partitions and adding new ones, you can increase the amount of a home's useful living space.

For example, a large bedroom could be converted into two children's bedrooms. Or, by removing a partition, two small bedrooms could become one large master bedroom.

Although readjusting bedroom walls is a common solution for many homeowners, there are other possibilities. For instance, in a house with a small kitchen, dining room, and a moderate-sized living room, removing or rearranging the walls could open up the area partially or entirely. This could allow enlargement of the kitchen, more convenient dining and a more comfortable living room area.

When converting one large bedroom into two smaller rooms a closet partition wall utilizes space very efficiently. The closets open into both rooms.

If a more formal dining area is desired, partitions might be erected in a suitably situated, large family room. The remainder of the family room might then be converted to a more formal living room.

Removing partitions is simple. There are two types of partition walls: nonload-bearing and load-bearing. The former can be eliminated by removing the wall section carefully, piece by piece. Remaining gaps and rough places are covered and matched to blend with the existing decor. Done properly, no one will ever know that a wall stood in the location. Load-bearing walls, however, must be approached with caution, because they help support parts of the house. This means that new permanent structural members must be

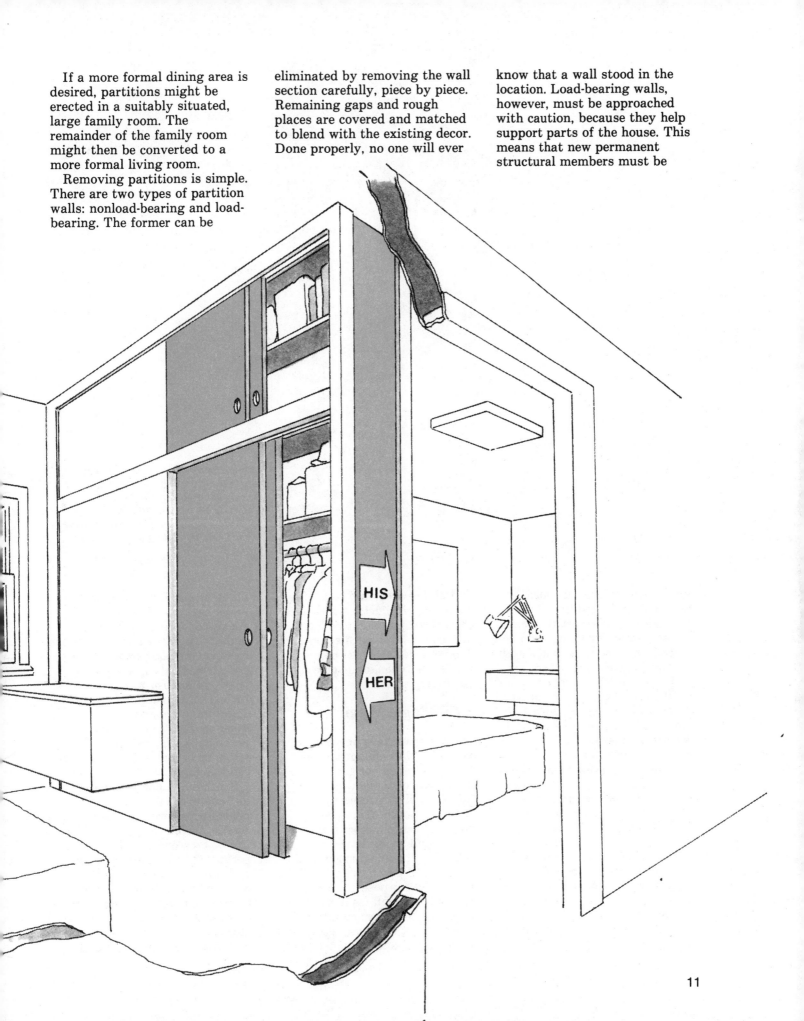

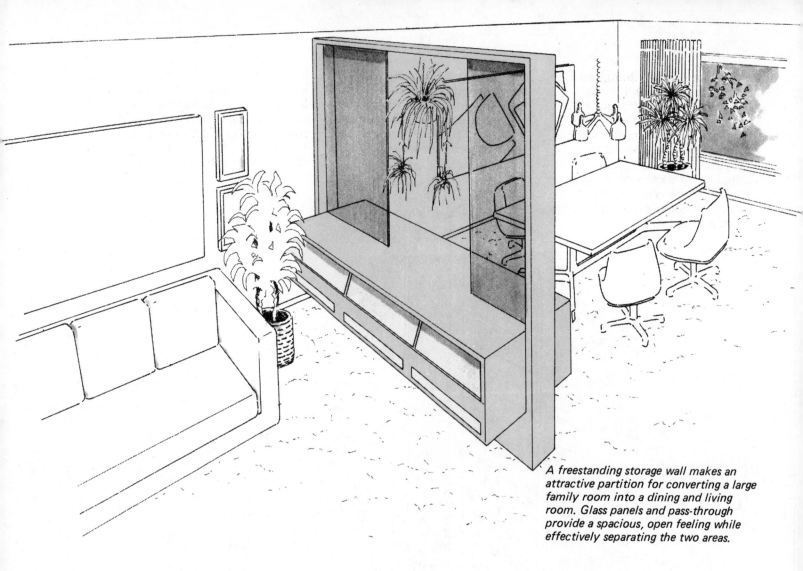

A freestanding storage wall makes an attractive partition for converting a large family room into a dining and living room. Glass panels and pass-through provide a spacious, open feeling while effectively separating the two areas.

substituted to bear the load formerly supported by the wall.

Building a new partition wall is also simple. The most common procedure is to frame a new wall of studs, covering the framework with a suitable wall covering and finish. Trim is added to suit the decor. In many cases, wiring, piping, or perhaps even ductwork must be enclosed within the new wall.

Instead of a stud wall, a closet wall could be built as a partition. This kind of wall contains a closet for each room. It's a good way to put all available space to work.

A floor-to-ceiling storage wall can also serve as a partition. It could include bookshelves, display cases, magazine racks, desk, and file drawers. A freestanding divider wall could also be built between a kitchen and dining area, and consist entirely of cabinets and shelves. Pass-throughs might be located at counter level, with some cabinets and shelves opening into the kitchen, and some into the dining room.

Enclosing a Porch

Many homes have porches or verandas that enhance neither the appearance nor the liveability of the house. But a porch doesn't necessarily have to remain a porch. It can be converted into a more useful, year-round living space.

With some imagination and planning, a porch can serve a number of purposes. For instance, a small front porch might be transformed into a formal front entryway—complete with clothes and storage closets, planters and indirect lighting. A small back porch could be converted into a mud room, laundry room, or storage space for sporting equipment. A larger porch, particularly with a southern exposure, can be turned into a sunporch, solarium, plant room, or greenhouse. Properly located, a porch can also serve to expand a room, or become an entirely new room in itself.

Enclosing a porch is usually an easy project, because the basic framework is already there. Conventional stud walls can be erected around the perimeter to enclose the porch, with doors and windows installed as desired. In some cases, the porch floor framing and foundation may need to be strengthened. A subfloor can be laid over the original porch floor,

Converted to a plant room, this porch becomes an integral part of the residence. Standard wall-framing techniques can be used to enclose the porch and make it weathertight. Large expanses of glass let in plenty of light and give the feeling of being outdoors.

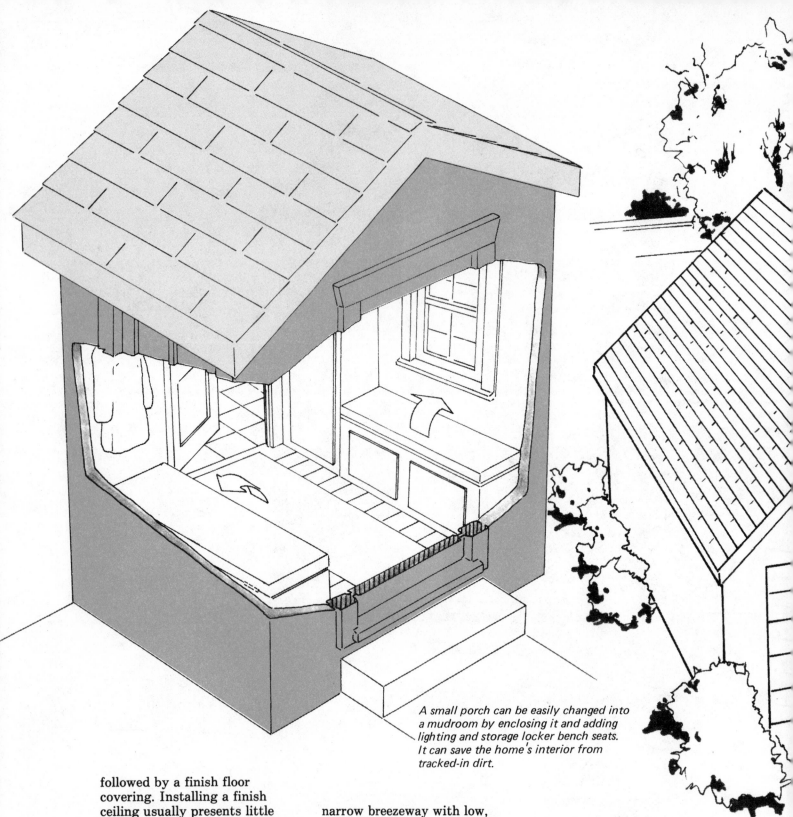

A small porch can be easily changed into a mudroom by enclosing it and adding lighting and storage locker bench seats. It can save the home's interior from tracked-in dirt.

followed by a finish floor covering. Installing a finish ceiling usually presents little difficulty, and by extending the house's utility systems into the porch as necessary, the conversion can add greatly to the house's liveability.

Enclosing a Breezeway

Breezeways can be enclosed and converted, too. Fitting a long, narrow breezeway with low, solid walls, topped with large expanses of glass turns it into an excellent plant room. A larger breezeway could become a full-scale greenhouse, or be used to expand a room of the house.

The construction of a breezeway is the key to its relative ease of conversion. Most are built with post-supported roofs and poured concrete, slab-on-grade floors. So, the hard work is already done. Conventional stud walls can be framed into the openings between support posts. If

Breezeways are easy to convert to living quarters because they usually have a foundation and roof. Framing in the walls and installing windows changed this breezeway into a comfortable T.V. room.

necessary, these walls can be set atop low concrete-block perimeter walls to keep the wood members away from ground level. The wall framing, built with suitable windows and doors, can be sheathed and covered to match the house's exterior.

The interior can be finished in the same fashion as an enclosed porch. And except for a converted garage, a wood stove or fireplace can be more easily installed here than in any other area of the house.

15

After removing the garage door and replacing it with a windowed wall, an attached garage can be transformed into a spacious family room. The interior is remodeled using the same methods as for a basement conversion, and utilities connections are usually very easy to make.

Converting a Garage

Many garages offer space that lies virtually unused. Even if the garage is used for sheltering a car, the space might be better utilized by converting it to living quarters. Whether the garage is attached or unattached makes little difference in most cases.

Attached Garage

An attached garage may be joined to the house by a common wall section. Or, it may be built a few feet away from the house, and connected by a breezeway, covered patio, or other arrangement. In many cases, it is actually an integral part of the house structure—built into one end of a single-level home or beneath a multi-level house.

A garage area that's within

with other activity areas. Careful planning, however, can usually eliminate such problems. Access doorways could be rearranged, adjoining portions of the house could be altered, or a small addition could be built to connect the garage to some other part of the house.

Converting the garage itself is a relatively simple job, especially since most are constructed with conventional wood frames. Usually, the walls and ceiling have already been covered with wallboard, to meet local building codes, but insulation may not be present. The conversion process consists of adding heat, lighting and electrical outlets, and adding insulation, if needed. Then the garage door is replaced with a stud wall and covered to match the existing walls. Windows and doors can be installed, enlarged, or rearranged, and a fireplace or other amenities put in as desired. The final step is to apply a finish covering to the floor and apply finishes to the walls and ceilings. A two-car garage provides ample space for a living room, family room, or recreation room. And a smaller, one-car garage can be adequate for a workshop, kitchen, study, or library. In many cases, part of the garage's attic space can be used for storage.

Converting a garage that's attached to the house by a breezeway requires basically the same techniques. The main difference is that it may be slightly more difficult to provide adequate heat and electrical capacity. Also, the connecting structure between the house and garage may need reworking. This would probably be more important if the garage were converted to a family room, than if it were redone into a workshop. The breezeway or other structure could be made into another living area, like a solarium or greenhouse. Or, the garage might be made an integral part of the house by an extensive new addition.

A garage that is an integral part of the first-floor or ground-level section of a house poses slightly different problems. This is the case when the garage is incorporated in the overall house shell, or attached at one end by a common wall. Most often, access to the garage from the house is gained through the kitchen or from a utility room adjacent to the kitchen. This could lead to some inconvenient traffic patterns and interfere

the house shell and is an extension of a basement or lower-level living section is probably the easiest to convert. The attaching area within the house is usually compatible with your plans for the new space. All that need be done is the actual remodeling of the garage.

Unattached Garage

An unattached garage is a separate building, some distance from the house. It's converted just like a garage with a breezeway, but lends itself to some types of rooms particularly well. Because it is somewhat isolated from the house, it can be ideal as a workshop, office, artist's studio, or other type of room for activities that are best kept separate from those in the house.

On the other hand, there are plenty of possibilities for joining the garage to the house by way of an addition. This might be as simple as adding a covered breezeway, or as complex as building an ell or a new series of rooms. This way, not only is the garage converted, but it's incorporated fully in the structure of the house.

An unattached garage makes a fine candidate for conversion when you desire a room that's isolated from the normal house activities. In this case, a garage was remodeled to create an artist's studio. Note the skylight in the roof.

Converting an Attic

Most newer houses have small attics. High construction costs, modern construction methods, and efficient roofing materials make larger designs wasteful. But still, many older homes, and a few newer ones, do have attics that offer a lot of potential living space. Granted, most attics look dreary at first glance, but imagination and planning can work wonders.

Regardless of the attic's width and length, if the ridgepole is at least seven feet above the subfloor, the space can be converted into living quarters. The higher the ridgepole, and the greater the floor space, the larger and more comfortable the living space can be. And while an attic conversion isn't a one-weekend job, it isn't as difficult as most people believe, either. Of all the possibilities for expanding a house internally, the attic is perhaps the best remodeling option—especially for the do-it-yourselfer.

Access may be the first problem when dealing with an attic. Especially in old houses, there's no stairway—just a trap door or a push-hatch in the ceiling, reached by standing on a tall ladder. Or, there may be a folding stairway that swings down from the ceiling with the pull of a cord. Either situation is unsuitable. If there's room to build a staircase or stairway on the floor serving the attic, all is well. To do this, a 2½ x 10-foot space is needed on the serving floor—longer if the ceiling height is greater than eight feet. The same space (although a space eight feet long could be adequate in some circumstances) is required on the attic floor level. Plus there must be sufficient headroom above the stairhead to allow a six-foot person to step up without banging his head on the attic's roof.

It's often the case that space of that kind is not available. If it's not, don't despair. You can install a vertical, spiral staircase. Such units can be bolted to the serving floor and spiraled straight upward through an opening in the attic floor. The smallest of these staircases occupy a four- or five-foot square space. Of course, you don't have to place this kind of staircase in the existing hatch opening. You can set it up in any convenient spot.

When you've licked the access problem, you can begin planning the attic conversion. If there's no subfloor, one must be installed. Then, if the ridgepole is more than seven feet high, a ceiling can be installed. This is optional, but it will close off the extra space in the peak of the roof, provide something to staple insulation to, and provide support for the finish ceiling. If a ceiling isn't desired, the roof rafters will support the insulation and wall covering.

This stage of the project is the best time to install dormers, skylights, or roof-windows for fresh air and sunlight. It's also the time to consider changes or additions to gable-end windows. If the existing ones are insufficient, you might want to add more or substitute larger units. And, if a freestanding wood stove or fireplace is part of the plan, now is the time to install the chimney. In short, any construction work involving the gable ends or the roof itself is best done at this stage.

Then, utility lines can be run into the attic, and its interior can be finished using the procedures which appear later in this book. Although, instead of full-size walls, short, stub walls, called "knee walls" are built to enclose the eaves.

Converting a Basement

Most basements are damp, cheerless places, cluttered with ducts, pipes, electrical cables, and many years of accumulated odds and ends. Since the space is usually grossly underutilized, it might as well be put to some worthwhile purpose. Remodeling a basement isn't all that different from converting an attic, and it may even be easier in some respects.

Before you do anything else, you have to inspect the basement and clean it up. This might require arranging some temporary lighting, so you can see what you're doing. Once this is done, you can inspect the area and ponder the conversion possibilities and problems.

Examining the basement walls is a good starting point. If they're smooth and relatively clean, like a fairly new poured concrete or concrete block construction, you may be able to merely paint them. In most cases, however, it's better to attach vertical wood strips to the walls at intervals. These furring strips provide spaces for placing insulation and serve as nailing strips for securing wall covering. If there's any sign of dampness or seepage through the walls, this must be corrected by applying a special waterproofing paint. Make sure outside footing-drainage systems around the foundation are in good shape. Most basement floors are made of poured concrete. But if only packed earth is present, a concrete floor will have to be installed—a fairly sizeable and expensive job.

If the concrete floor is smooth and in fairly good shape, it might be painted. Or, you can lay paving stone, brick, floor tile, sheet vinyl floor covering, or carpeting. Depending upon the material used, an underlayment might have to be installed first. A raised floor may be possible if there's sufficient headroom. This is done by laying wood sleepers on the concrete floor in mastic, raising the floor level several inches. Then a plywood subfloor can be attached to the sleepers, and virtually any kind of finish floor covering can be applied to it. Raising the floor is a good method to use if the original floor is rough or cracked, and it lets you install thermal insulation beneath the finished floor.

In most basement areas, it's necessary to build partition walls that screen off utilities. And partition walls can be used to create one or two new rooms, like a laundry room, darkroom, or workshop. These partitions, however, must be carefully integrated into the overall remodeling scheme and into your work-flow schedule. For example, there would be no need to extend a built-up floor into the area housing the furnace.

The flooring should stop at the partition wall line.

Basement ceiling construction is likely to cause the most problems. When there's sufficient headroom, a dropped ceiling is the best bet. Such a ceiling can be constructed by nailing a wood ceiling frame of strapping and supports to the floor joists, or by hanging a metal grid with removable ceiling panels. Either way, pipes and wiring will be hidden from view.

In cases where a dropped ceiling isn't feasible, you can nail lengths of strapping directly to the bottoms of the floor joists, and attach ceiling tile or wallboard to the strapping. One problem, however, is that all electrical junction boxes, plumbing valves, and pipe clean-outs must be left accessible. This means you have to frame in ports with removable covers. Also, all existing lighting fixtures must be removed and the fixture boxes must be capped. They can, however, be used as connection boxes for new fixtures located in or on the ceiling.

Pipelines can cause trouble, too. Often, there are pipes that extend a considerable distance below the upper-floor joists. They can't be moved without a major replumbing job, so you must box them in with boards or an auxiliary framework covered with wallboard, tile, or paneling. The same is often true of ductwork.

Some basements have a few small windows set high in the walls, while others have none at all. And even if windows do exist, they usually admit little light. Unfortunately, unless the exterior grade level is exceptionally low, there's not much chance of enlarging basement windows or adding to their number. So, the installation of lighting fixtures is an important part of basement conversion.

The new electrical wiring system for the basement is usually quite extensive. In addition to lighting fixture outlets, there must be plenty of duplex receptacles. Switches to control ceiling or wall lighting, and perhaps a few receptacles as well, should be conveniently located.

In situations where a bathroom, laundry facility, or wet bar is part of the project, plumbing must also be considered. But this is usually simple, because in most basements a good portion of the plumbing system is open and accessible. Pipe runs can be short and direct. The usual procedure is to run pipes through the ceiling cavities and down through the walls to desired locations.

Drainage connections, however, can be difficult. This is because the house drain frequently exits a basement well above floor level. Connections to the new plumbing fixtures must be made at points from below floor level to slightly above. In this case, a sewage-ejector system is required, so collected waste can be periodically pumped upward and into the house drain. Of course, if the drain happens to lie at a point somewhat lower than the lowest fixture drain to be connected, there's no problem. The connection is just made in the usual fashion.

To heat a basement adequately, you must be sure it's weathertight. This means caulking and tightly covering perceptible air leaks in above-ground portions of the basement, and at the joints between the walls and the building sills. A vapor barrier installed over the furring strips on exterior walls will also help prevent air infiltration. Insulation, of course, is necessary in cold regions to minimize heat loss.

From this point on, the conversion process is relatively standard, and it is discussed at length in later chapters of this book.

Expansion by Addition

Sometimes a house's living area can't be increased by remodeling the existing space. This may be due to architectural or structural considerations, or just because all the available space is presently used to its fullest. In either case, there are only a couple of alternatives—sell the house and buy another one that's larger, or build an addition that increases the home's living space.

Fortunately, building an addition to an existing structure is almost always feasible, and considerably less expensive and bothersome than buying another home. Often, a knowledgeable do-it-yourselfer can handle part, or even all of the project, which makes the idea even more attractive.

There are a number of options, and sometimes two or more can be combined for a major expansion project. And, in many cases, expansion by addition is often accompanied by some interior rearrangement.

Installing Dormers

One possible course is to add one or more dormers. This can serve a number of purposes. Small dormers can provide additional daylight, and usually ventilation, for an attic converted to living space. Although small dormers don't actually add much living space, they do make a small attic appear larger and add to the overall decor. Plus, they allow greater freedom of movement and give you more options for arranging furnishings. Large dormers give you the same advantages, and also add greatly to the amount of useable living space. And, regardless of size, dormers change a house's exterior appearance considerably.

There are three general types of dormers: single, double, and full. The single dormer is generally narrow—only about four or five feet wide—with a

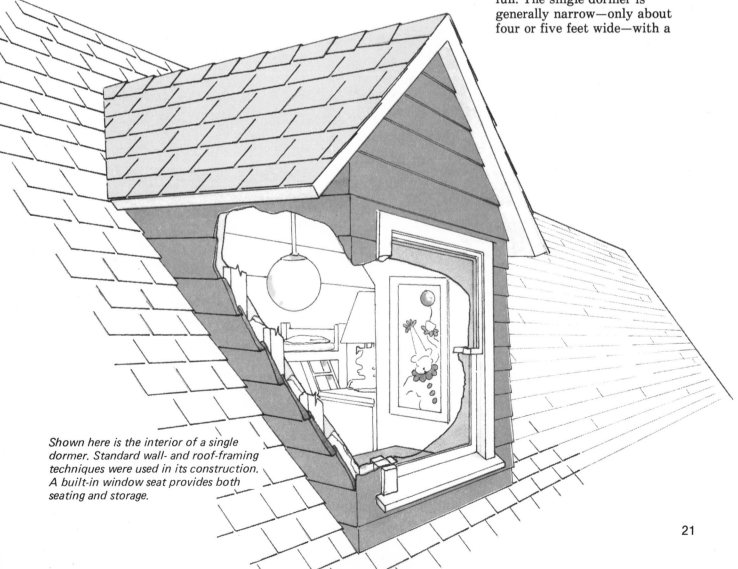

Shown here is the interior of a single dormer. Standard wall- and roof-framing techniques were used in its construction. A built-in window seat provides both seating and storage.

single window occupying nearly the entire face. A double dormer is usually over six feet in width; it frequently contains a matched set of windows. Either type of dormer can be used singly or in multiples. The full dormer is much wider, and may span nearly the entire length of a roof.

The two most common dormer styles are the gable dormer, featuring a small pitched roof, and the shed dormer, with a shed-style roof. Of the two, the shed style is the easiest to build. But there are also many other styles. For example, a dormer with an arched roof and arch-topped window could be built. This could be done to match existing arched roof lines or arch-topped windows located beneath the dormer. Whatever the case, you should plan the dormer so that it's in proportion with the size of the present structure and compatible with the structure's design.

Dormers are generally most attractive and useful when built into a roof with a fairly steep pitch. When only one single or double dormer is constructed, it's usually placed on the roof's vertical centerline. A pair of dormers can be positioned so that each is as far from the edge of the roof as they are apart from one another. Or, they might be placed equidistant from the roof edges, with a wider space between them. Three dormers might be equally spaced, or the outside pair could be located equidistant from the roof edges with the third centered between them. A full dormer usually takes up nearly the entire roof.

Full dormers span almost the entire length of the roof. They add a great deal of living space, fresh air, and sunshine to an attic room.

This series of small, single dormers enhances the exterior appearance of the house and makes the attic room much more livable.

23

A double dormer works well with this house because it allows matching the roof style to that of the house.

Framing and installing a dormer isn't particularly difficult or expensive. It's best to install them when the attic is still unfinished, but adding one to a finished attic isn't much more trouble. Of course, dormers can be installed on either side or both sides of a pitched roof.

Basically, installing a dormer involves cutting out a section of the roof—including the weather surface, sheathing, and portions of rafters that lie within the opening. A certain amount of roof reframing is necessary to regain structural integrity. Then you frame up the dormer sides, face, and roof and nail them into position. Exterior sheathing, siding, and roofing is applied, along with the windows. The joint where the dormer butts the original roof must be flashed, and the roof weather surface

around the dormer replaced. Then you finish the dormer interior.

Installing a full dormer is a more ambitious project, because

you have to remove so much of the original roof. A considerable amount of reframing and temporary bracing is usually necessary. The dormer's roof

essentially becomes a substitute for the original roof. And, although weather-tightness isn't a big problem during the quick construction process of building a small dormer, it is a major concern when building a full dormer.

Raising the Roof

Before deciding to build a large, full dormer, the homeowner should consider the alternative—raising the roof. This takes about the same cost and effort and can also result in a larger amount of living space and even strengthen the structure at the same time. This is typically done on a gable-roof house that has a fairly steep roof pitch. Of the many variations, two are basic. One is to elevate one entire side of the roof. In effect this involves raising the lower edge of the roof as though it were hinged at the ridgeline, and then installing a new exterior wall beneath the eave. The other possibility is to create a new roof line on each side by moving the ridgeline so that one roof half is steeply pitched, while the other is only pitched slightly. Either method can provide a great increase in living space.

As you could guess, this is no

Raising one side of a house's roof can create a very spacious attic room. Extensive wall and gable end reframing is required in a project of this kind.

26

*If desired, both roof sections can often be raised. In t.
case, the conversion created an entirely new roof line,
with one side steeply pitched and the other pitched
only slightly.*

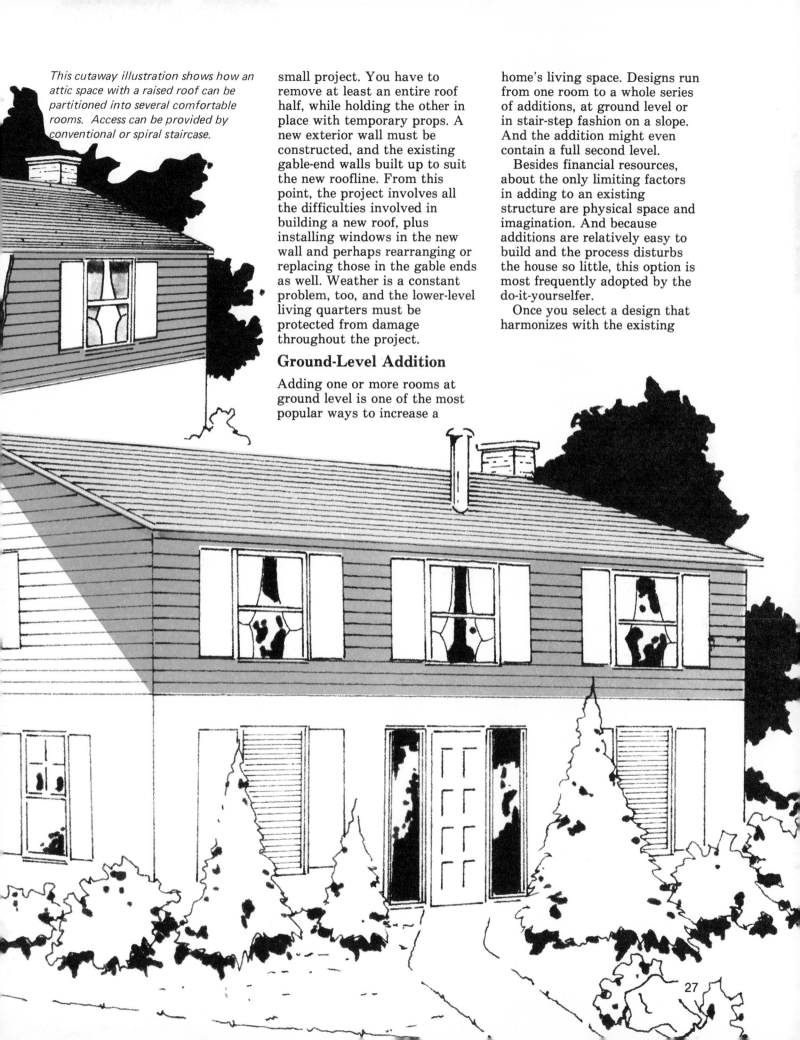

This cutaway illustration shows how an attic space with a raised roof can be partitioned into several comfortable rooms. Access can be provided by conventional or spiral staircase.

small project. You have to remove at least an entire roof half, while holding the other in place with temporary props. A new exterior wall must be constructed, and the existing gable-end walls built up to suit the new roofline. From this point, the project involves all the difficulties involved in building a new roof, plus installing windows in the new wall and perhaps rearranging or replacing those in the gable ends as well. Weather is a constant problem, too, and the lower-level living quarters must be protected from damage throughout the project.

Ground-Level Addition

Adding one or more rooms at ground level is one of the most popular ways to increase a

home's living space. Designs run from one room to a whole series of additions, at ground level or in stair-step fashion on a slope. And the addition might even contain a full second level.

Besides financial resources, about the only limiting factors in adding to an existing structure are physical space and imagination. And because additions are relatively easy to build and the process disturbs the house so little, this option is most frequently adopted by the do-it-yourselfer.

Once you select a design that harmonizes with the existing

house, basic platform-framing methods and materials are used to build the addition. The first part of the job is to build a suitable foundation, which is matched and joined to the present one. The floor, walls, and roof of the addition are framed, and utility systems are installed as needed. Then the exterior is finished to be compatible with the existing house, although the old and new exteriors needn't be identical. For instance, an addition to a brick house can be sided with clapboards, with good results.

Rearranging a home's interior may also be involved in the building of an addition. Many additions are planned to gain more space in an existing room. A 15-foot extension might be added to a living room to make it larger and more enjoyable. Or, a kitchen wall might be moved out 10 feet to gain more counter space and a breakfast nook. Sometimes, one or more rooms are added for new functions—a family room, recreation room, or woodworking shop.

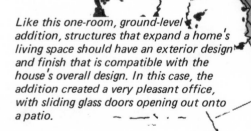

Like this one-room, ground-level addition, structures that expand a home's living space should have an exterior design and finish that is compatible with the house's overall design. In this case, the addition created a very pleasant office, with sliding glass doors opening out onto a patio.

Above: Built on a slope, this ground level takes good advantage of surrounding land contours. The raised deck doubles as a convenient carport.
Below: The large expanses of glass and the attached deck of this ground-level addition built on a slope make the room look even more spacious than it actually is. Exposed-wood ceiling beams complement the wood of the outdoor deck.

Second-Story Outward Addition

Additions can also be constructed outward from second-story levels. It makes little difference whether there's a portion of the house below the proposed addition or not. Either way, the job can be done in an attractive fashion.

Building an addition to a second story on top of an existing first story is relatively simple. If both sections are the same shape, all you need to do is remove the roof section from the first-floor level, build a floor frame, construct walls and a new roof, and attach the addition to the existing second-story framework. If the addition is smaller than the structure below, a portion of the existing structure is fitted with a floor of the necessary size, while the

remainder is left as a roof.

Building out over open space is a different proposition. Sometimes it's possible to cantilever small additions, such as a short extension to a bedroom, directly outward with no need of external support. This would be much like a small balcony. Slightly larger additions would require the support of angle braces, running from the outside edges of the addition, back to the existing structure's wall. Outward additions of any substantial size, however, need to be supported by posts, columns, or narrow wall sections. These are placed at appropriate points along the outside perimeter and extend to a ground-level foundation.

When built over an existing first-story, these types of additions are usually large

enough to create a full second floor, matching the rest of the house. This is because there's little difference in cost between building a full and partial addition.

Small second-story additions that extend outward are generally built just to expand living space without disrupting the remainder of the home. But larger ones that require support are usually also built for architectural emphasis and to gain more semi-enclosed space at ground level. The addition might serve as the roof of a carport, patio, or deck. Or, the addition's support posts might be screened off to create a ground-level summer room. Actually, the area beneath the addition could be fully enclosed to form another room. Of course, if this were the plan, the first-story addition

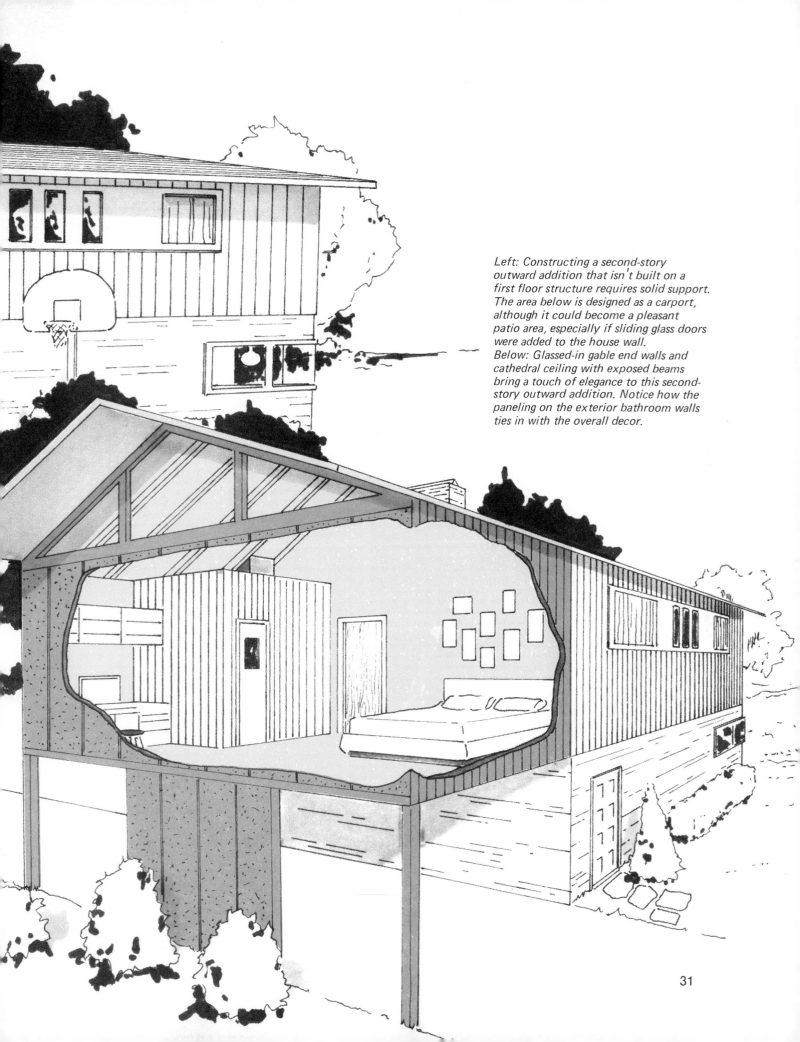

Left: Constructing a second-story outward addition that isn't built on a first floor structure requires solid support. The area below is designed as a carport, although it could become a pleasant patio area, especially if sliding glass doors were added to the house wall.
Below: Glassed-in gable end walls and cathedral ceiling with exposed beams bring a touch of elegance to this second-story outward addition. Notice how the paneling on the exterior bathroom walls ties in with the overall decor.

would be built first.

Building a second-story addition is likely to be more troublesome than constructing a comparable one at ground level. Due to the height involved, the work is more difficult and time consuming. It's also more difficult to make the correct engineering assessments in the design, and to make the new structure harmonize with the house. For these reasons, it's recommended that you enlist the services of a competent architect for all but the simplest second-story outward additions.

After you work out the aesthetic and structural details, the addition is framed and joined to the existing structure. Standard platform framing is generally used, with slight variations as necessary to provide solid attachment and ample support. The roof lines are conjoined if necessary, exterior siding, and trim are applied,

utilities are installed and the interior is finished.

Adding a Second Story

You can also add a full second story to a home, although not all houses take kindly to this treatment. This can be particularly worthwhile if you have a relatively small single-floor house. A second story can also be added to a larger house, covering the first floor partially or entirely. This, however, is a major undertaking with a number of problems.

It's frequently difficult to achieve a pleasing design. A full second story added to a small and basically rectangular house can result in a large, ugly box shape. This is often remedied by additional first-level construction to make the entire structure more attractive. Such construction can take many forms, such as a single or double garage, extra rooms, open or

32

Above: When adding a second story, avoiding a boxy looking exterior is often a problem. By making this second-story addition smaller than the first floor, this problem is overcome. Left: In this case, making the second-story addition larger than the first floor enhances the appearance of the front of the house. Without the second-floor overhang, the house's front would look plain and boxy.

33

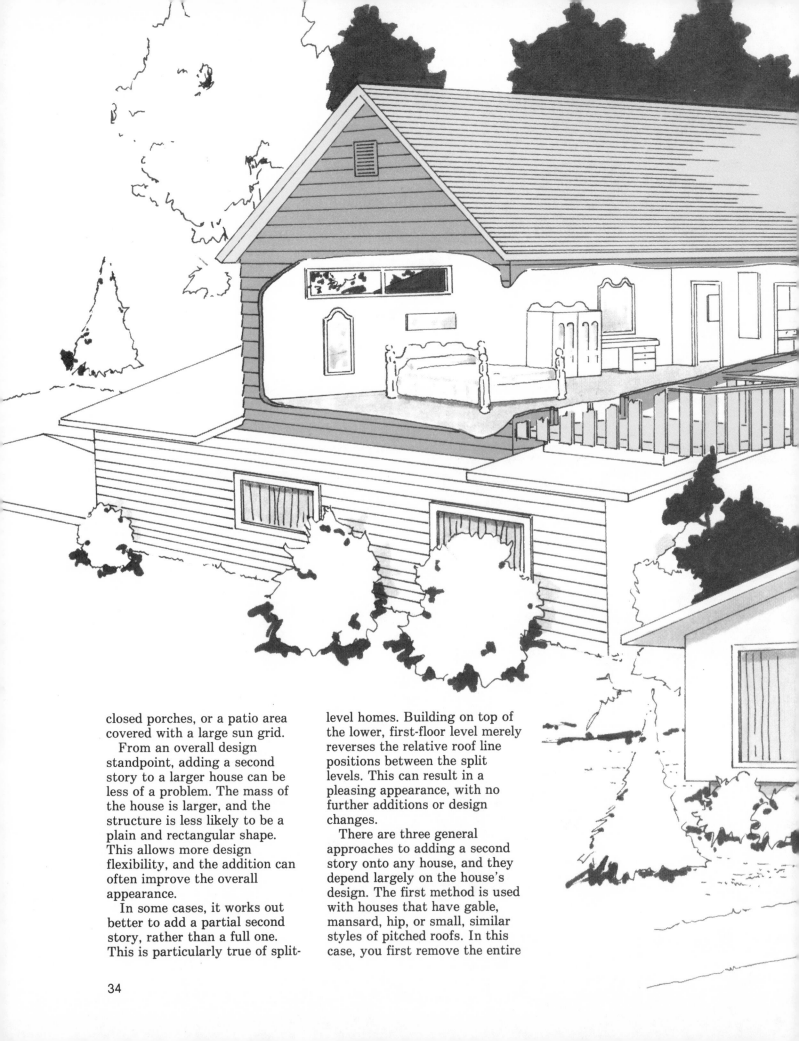

closed porches, or a patio area covered with a large sun grid.

From an overall design standpoint, adding a second story to a larger house can be less of a problem. The mass of the house is larger, and the structure is less likely to be a plain and rectangular shape. This allows more design flexibility, and the addition can often improve the overall appearance.

In some cases, it works out better to add a partial second story, rather than a full one. This is particularly true of split-level homes. Building on top of the lower, first-floor level merely reverses the relative roof line positions between the split levels. This can result in a pleasing appearance, with no further additions or design changes.

There are three general approaches to adding a second story onto any house, and they depend largely on the house's design. The first method is used with houses that have gable, mansard, hip, or small, similar styles of pitched roofs. In this case, you first remove the entire roof structure piece by piece. The dimension stock in the roof framing, and perhaps some of the sheathing and other odds and ends, can be cleaned and reused. This process also involves dismantling chimneys, waste and vent stacks, ventilation ducts, and similar items. Then, if no flooring exists in the attic area—now wide open to the weather—a floor has to be put down to make a work platform. The second-story walls, usually both interior and

exterior, are framed up and set in position. Joists follow, and then a new roof frame is built, sheathed, and covered with a weather surface. Chimneys, stacks, and ducts are extended through the new roof. Utilities are run in and the interior is finished.

If the house isn't too large, and the upper story is to be essentially a continuation of the first, a different system can be used. This involves cutting the entire roof assembly away from the first-floor framing, and leaving it in place in one piece. Chimneys, stacks, wiring, and

things of that sort are removed. Exterior and interior partition walls are framed up on the ground, and a miscellany of other items prepared, so once begun, work can proceed at a rapid pace without delays. Then, a crane lifts the entire roof assembly off the house and holds it suspended while work crews quickly set all the new second-floor walls. As soon as they are up, the roof structure is lowered down on them, and the roof is resecured. Aside from the interior and exterior finish and trim work, the actual changeover can take only a matter of hours for a small house.

Buildings with flat, shed, or other gently pitched roof styles can be added to without removing the roof or disturbing the first-story living quarters greatly. With a flat-roofed house, a new floor frame is built right on the old roof, and the second-story walls are framed up and erected to continue the first-floor walls. Then an entirely new roof, either flat or some other style, is built on top.

A variation of this method is used for a shed-roofed house. In this case, the new floor frame is attached directly to the original structure only at the high line of the roof. Stub walls are built to compensate for the slant of the roof and to hold the floor frame level. And, various supports are placed between the new floor and old roof as needed. Construction goes upward from there.

With both shed and flat roof styles, access to the second floor is planned ahead of time, but cut through and built after the addition has been closed to the weather. Utilities extensions have to be pre-planned, too, so they can be installed easily later. At this point, there's some disruption of the first-floor living quarters. But it usually doesn't matter much, because changes are often made on the first floor as a result of the house's overall increase in living space.

Expanding a Partial Basement

Many old and new homes have only partial basements. A house with a partial basement has a perimeter-type foundation that extends all around the outside borders of the structure. But only a small part of the total area is excavated to full headroom depth. The remainder is only a shallow crawl space. In older homes, this crawl space is open to the rest of the basement, although in newer homes it's likely to be closed off or connected by a small access hatch. Partial basements of older homes are sometimes completely finished in concrete, but often the walls are of stone or brick, and the floor may be dirt. More modern houses usually have poured-concrete or concrete-block foundations.

Whatever the case, partial basements can often be expanded to take advantage of a considerable amount of under-house space. The expense is potentially low for the amount of

A partial basement or crawl space can be converted to a full basement. The job requires a great deal of excavation, but it can double your home's living space. In this case, the room gained was used to make a spacious workshop.

square footage gained. The cost in sweat and energy, however, can be considerable if you decide to do the drudge-work yourself.

Few technical difficulties are involved in expanding a partial basement. The job is basically just a lot of hard work. There are at least two approaches. One is to excavate the crawl space by hand to within about three feet of the foundation wall. At that point, a new retaining wall is built. The area behind it is filled in with dirt, and the space between the new wall and the old is capped with poured concrete. This forms a shelf at approximately the height of the original crawl-space floor.

Another method involves expanding the area all the way to the original foundation wall, removing that wall in sections, and placing temporary support columns to hold up the house. After removing the old wall, excavation can be continued to below-floor depth. Then a new footing is poured and a new foundation wall is built up to sill level. If the temporary support columns are made of steel, you can leave them right in place, imbedded in the concrete. Or, concrete blocks can be built up around them. The last step is to pour a new concrete floor.

Converting a Full Crawl Space

It is possible to convert a crawl space to a full basement. This is true whether the house rests on a full perimeter foundation of stone, concrete block, or poured concrete, or if it's perched on a

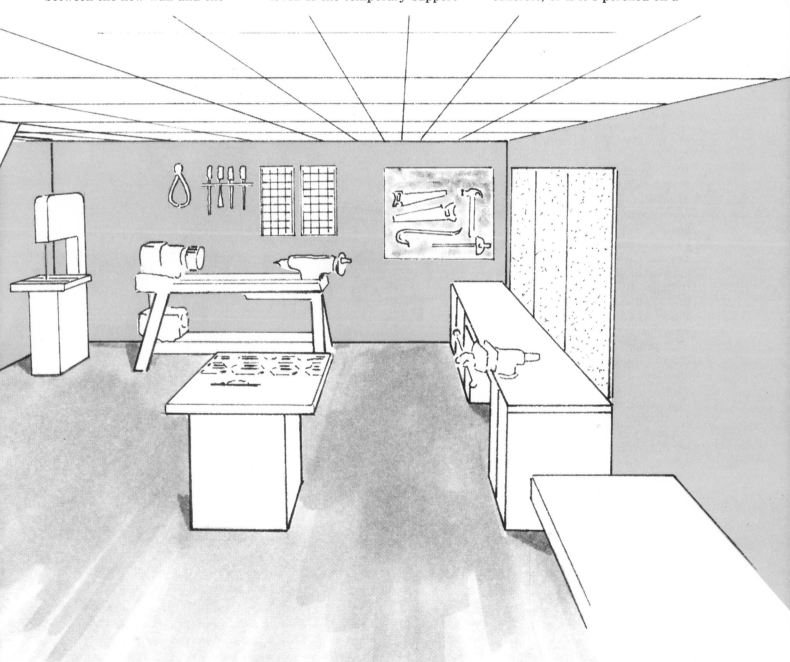

series of piers or posts sunk into the ground. The surface of the crawl space may be relatively level, but in many instances, this kind of foundation is built on sloping or rough ground, with the foundation height above ground level variable.

There are several ways to do the conversion, but the easiest is to hire a house mover and a building contractor. They'll disconnect all utility lines and ductwork, slide a few huge steel beams under the house and jack up the building. Then the space beneath the house can be excavated to full depth with power machinery. Foundation walls and floor are put in just as though the house wasn't there at all. When the construction is finished, the house is lowered onto the new foundation walls, the beams are withdrawn, and the foundation holes filled.

Using another method, the house is left on the existing foundation walls. A section of one wall is removed at some convenient point where access is easiest. Then, as much area as can be reached conveniently beyond the access point is excavated. Temporary props are installed to hold the house up, and the remainder of the wall is removed and replaced with a new, full-height foundation wall. This procedure is repeated all around the house—removing sections of original wall, excavating as much as possible, and installing full-height foundation walls. Interior floor-support piers must be replaced by temporary props as excavation continues and the original piers are removed. The temporary props will be replaced later by support columns or perhaps by heavy girders run under the floor. Once the new foundation is completed and arrangements are made for permanent interior support, a concrete floor can be poured. Windows, vents, bulkheads, and the like are installed as the job progresses.

A third possibility—a good one for the do-it-yourselfer—is to leave the perimeter foundation wall or piers alone and concentrate only on building into the central area beneath the house. This works particularly well with a house set on piers or posts and built against a relatively steep slope. In this case there are no foundation walls to cope with, and at one point the ground level may be so low as to afford nearly full headroom.

If there is sufficient room, excavating can be done by machine, but pick and shovel is usually the best way. The object is to remove the earth to within about three feet of the house perimeter in all directions, leaving the original perimeter foundation undisturbed and well supported by plenty of earth. Two or three temporary supports are placed next to each interior support pier to bear the loads when the piers are removed. When the entire area has been excavated, new walls of concrete, concrete blocks, or wood foundation panels are built

38

to enclose the area. After pouring the concrete floor, utilities are put in and either a conventional or spiral staircase is installed to provide access to the upper level. Then the project can be finished in any style desirable. On completion, the house gains a substantial amount of living space and an exceptionally sturdy double foundation as well.

Making a Daylight Basement

A daylight basement has one or more exterior walls or wall sections that open out onto grade level by means of doors and windows. This conversion creates a ground-level living area from at least one vantage point, even though much of the total exterior foundation wall remains below-ground.

Under the right conditions, a basement can be daylighted as part of a project to increase useable living space. Or, it can be done while converting a partial basement or crawl space to a full basement. The only prerequisite is that there must be a section of full-height foundation wall that's large enough for a door and at least one good-sized window. And this

A daylight basement, such as this one, is created by removing earth away from one or more walls of a full-basement foundation. The additional light provided by the windows and sliding glass doors makes the basement conversion much more versatile and attractive than it would be otherwise.

part of the foundation must be exposed down to floor level, or be capable of being exposed.

A house foundation built on a slope can be ideal for this treatment. The foundation wall that lies at the downslope position and is most fully exposed is the obvious one to rebuild. Another likely candidate is a full foundation with one or more walls buried only a few feet deep, that can be excavated easily. This is especially true if the earth has been bermed against the wall simply as a matter of protection or landscaping. You can even uncover walls that are deeply buried, provided only that the immediate terrain can be recontoured into an effective landscaping design.

The job is tougher if you're dealing with a full-basement foundation with all walls deeply buried in an essentially level building site. Here the feasibility of the conversion depends upon sufficient space adjacent to one or more foundation walls. In this case, you can't just remove dirt from the wall. A great deal of soil must be removed from a large area, and the entire grade level must be lowered several feet and recontoured into a sunken terrace or similar arrangement. Although expensive, the project can enhance the appearance, liveability, and value of the property.

A daylight basement conversion provides much more liveability and interior design options than an ordinary basement conversion. Most of the entire basement can be converted to one or several multi-purpose rooms, complete with outside access. It creates a new traffic pattern that increases flexibility and privacy, while decreasing congestion in the house's upper level. The new living space usually looks larger than it actually is, because it provides attractive views, daylight, and fresh air. Also, a terrace or patio, deck or gardens

can be made part of the overall design.

Although sometimes the job can be done by hand, an excavator usually must be hired to do the digging, recontouring, and soil removal. A set of plans should be drawn up specifying door and window arrangements, exterior treatment of the exposed foundation wall, and interior arrangement and decor. Then, rough openings for doors and windows can be made in the wall. Or, if substantial portions of the wall are to be removed, it may be easier to just remove the entire wall. Then you can replace it with a new one of standard wood-framing construction, mounted on the original foundation footing.

At this point, door and window bucks can be fitted in the rough openings, the ragged wall edges filled in and repaired

where necessary, and the door and window units installed. If a new wood-frame wall is used, the doors and windows are framed into place and installed as reconstruction progresses. The new wall can be finished in a number of ways. It's common to apply exterior siding and trim that matches the rest of the house. Or a different, but compatible type of siding can be used. For example, stone or brick veneer could be used to contrast with existing beveled siding.

Completing the exterior phase of the project involves a variety of items—such as building

40

retaining walls, laying a patio or making a deck, recontouring the surrounding area, and planting shrubs or gardens. A barbeque, patio cover, screened summer room, or other projects could be built, too. As for the interior, it's finished much like an ordinary basement conversion.

Creating a Cluster Home

The cluster-home concept is neither new nor widely popular, but it bears mentioning because it has the potential for making some homes exceptionally attractive and practical. The concept is usually applied to leisure homes—many leisure homes are built with this in mind—but it's equally workable with certain types of primary residences.

You start with a small, but completely self-contained living unit. For example, the unit could consist of a kitchen, small bath, and combination living room/bedroom. Later, another unit is

Cluster homes are very versatile because they can be added to many times. This cluster addition is butted to share a common wall with the main residence.

41

added, perhaps containing two bedrooms. Still later, a third unit, maybe a family room, joins the group. These units are freestanding buildings. They may be butted up against one another to share common walls, or they may be set some distance apart and connected by open breezeways or glassed-in hallways. All units may be on the same level, or they might stair-step up a slope, or be set at random levels.

A small, conventional house can also be used as a starting point. To this central core, you could add successive units—a living room, bedroom, recreation room, garage, and so on. The units are arranged in a cluster, which is often dictated by surroundings and topography. They may face a central compound or courtyard, or face outward, toward a scenic view. Although cluster units are often

similar in appearance, they can be different as long as the overall design is pleasing to the owner.

The versatility of a cluster

42

Left: Cluster additions need not be connected directly to the original house. In this case, a stair-step slope is the connecting feature.

Below: This cluster addition is connected to the original house by a glass-walled hallway. All structures in a cluster home arrangement must be very similar to provide a good overall appearance.

home is amazing, and only limited by imagination and available space. Although most conventional homes are not suitable for this concept, there are exceptions. They mainly include cottages, cabins, small Cape Cods, and similar styles. Whatever the style, the original building must be small enough so that the cluster units aren't dwarfed. The units must be able to match the original structure's style at a reasonable cost, and yet be large enough to be practical. And, of course, there must be sufficient room for expansion, and the project must

Cluster additions can be arranged to form a courtyard. In this case, it is complete with a hot-tub area.

unit disappears, you can convert it to another purpose, dismantle it, or even sell it and have it moved to another location.

Adding a Module

Some house styles are not suitable for adding a new room or ell. This is particularly true of the increasingly popular round, hexagonal, octagonal, and geodesic-dome houses. Ordinary additions are just not practical or attractive in connection with these styles. In many cases, a much more pleasing addition can be made by adding a module—another unit of similar or identical design, essentially freestanding, but connected to the original unit.

For example, you could expand an octagonal house by building an octagonal module nearby. It should be of similar design, but not necessarily of the same dimensions as the original structure. The two units could be connected by a gallery, hallway, greenhouse unit, or covered swimming pool. You could add as many modules as you need, connecting them to the original building, another module, or both. Tiny, but similar units could also be added to the larger ones, perhaps interconnected by open walkways. These smaller units could serve as a sauna, private studio, storage shed, or childrens' playroom.

This treatment can be adapted to some more conventional style homes, too. For instance, the A-frame style home has become conventional over the past few years, and is usually expanded by extending the front or rear of the structure. A module alternative to this is building a second A-frame of identical size next to the original, and connecting the two by a broad passageway under a gable roof. Or, the original might be flanked on both sides by smaller A-frames.

Even some older designs, like the standard Cape Cod house, can be expanded with a module.

be permitted by local building codes and zoning.

If the conditions are right, the cluster-home style offers a lot of advantages. It is by far the most easily expandable in a wide variety of ways at the lowest cost. Starting with a small central unit adequate for immediate needs, you can expand over a period of years—as demands arise and finances permit. The investment at any given time is not large, and taxes, upkeep, and expenses are always commensurate with your current financial situation. And, if the need for a particular

When it's difficult to add an ordinary addition to a home, such as this one of geodesic design, a module of the same design can expand the living space. This module is connected to the original house by a glass hallway.

Of course, you could expand such a house with a standard room addition or ell. But there's also no reason why an owner couldn't double the home's living space by adding a second, full-sized Cape Cod module directly to the end of the original. Or, a second Cape Cod might be constructed directly in line with and opposite one end of the first, with the two connected by a wide, gable-roofed passageway or room. Other house styles can be treated in the same way—this is a natural for a low-posted log cabin design. The only danger is you could end up with something that looks like an ordinary duplex house. But this can be

avoided by careful planning.

The interior of the added module can be anything the homeowner desires. It might contain additional bedrooms or some living areas not existing in the original structure—like a gameroom, workshop, or library. You could divide the module into separate rooms, or leave it completely open, as in the case of a recreation room. Or, the original unit could be remodeled to contain only a living room,

A-frame houses lend themselves to the module concept very well. Here, a smaller A-frame structure was built on the side of the original house.

48

dining room, and kitchen. And the rest of the house's functions could be incorporated in the module. Many combinations are possible, and one of the advantages of the modular arrangement is the privacy it affords by separating family activity areas.

Erecting an Outbuilding

Outbuildings are often constructed after remodeling a house's interior, to compensate for loss of storage space. For example, converting a full basement would probably create a need for a new place to store lawn and garden tools and other home maintenance items. Building a small garden or tool shed could take care of those needs. A similar storage problem could result from the conversion of a one-car attached garage. Or, you might want a new, freestanding garage to replace the original.

An outbuilding can also be erected for other reasons. A substantial outbuilding is an ideal site for a large woodworking shop—noise, activity, and fumes do not affect the house. The privacy afforded by an outbuilding also makes it a good place for an office or study.

Whatever the intended use, erecting an outbuilding is not difficult. Most are small and simply made—good do-it-yourself projects.

Many different kinds of outbuildings are available in kit form. They're made of metal or wood and hardboard. Although most are of the garden shed variety, not all are small. All have full headroom, and sizes range from about 6 x 10 feet to as large as 12 x 18 feet, with wide doors at each end.

But, buying a kit really isn't necessary, because you can easily construct an outbuilding with ordinary building materials and platform-framing methods. The building might be erected on a wood-platform floor set on sleepers or skids, or it could be

Connected by a gable-roof hallway, this module greatly increases the living space of a Cape Cod style house. Notice the close match between the module and the house.

49

The log cabin style home is another design that can be expanded with a compatible module.

permanently anchored to a poured-concrete slab. There may be little difference between the cost for a kit and a scratch-built structure. The advantage, of course, is that when you build from scratch you can design the building to meet your specific needs. And, you can match its architecture and exterior finish to that of your house or other surrounding buildings.

Kits are also available for wooden structures the size of a one-car garage, and even larger. Garage kits are available in many sizes and designs. You can buy most of them without overhead doors, so they can be easily modified for other

purposes. Exterior design and finishes can also be modified to suit your needs. The available kits for larger steel buildings are mainly designed for storing farm and commercial equipment. But, because so many different styles and sizes are offered, it can be worthwhile to consider them as well.

The pre-cut leisure-home industry also offers some kits

that may be applicable. Many firms specialize in building prefabricated kit structures. Of course, you couldn't use their complete-house packages, but some smaller models they offer may be useful. These are intended as cluster-home modules or complete add-ons to existing structures, and might serve as outbuildings without modification; others can be

easily adapted.

Remember, outbuildings can expand living space, but they can also serve to expand a family's activities and enhance its lifestyle. For example, they could be used for starting a kennel, or for housing a riding horse or two. The possibilities for outbuildings are nearly endless.

Creating Indoor/Outdoor Living Areas

When outdoor living areas, such as porches and patios are designed and built properly, they actually expand a house's living area into the outdoors. The same is true of greenhouses and solariums attached to a home, or built in a way that provides convenient access to the main house. As we discuss the many possibilities for indoor/outdoor living areas, keep in mind that an area can be partially or even wholly enclosed and still give the feeling of being in an outdoor environment. It all depends upon careful planning and construction.

Porches

Whether or not your present home has a porch matters little, because one can be added easily to almost any home. Almost any porch of adequate size can be converted into a living area by adding a good level of lighting and comfortable furnishings. Depending upon the porch's design, you may also be able to enclose it with screening or wall-framing with substantial amounts of window area. The functions of a well-arranged porch are limitless, as are the furnishing and decor possibilities. A lot, however, depends upon how weatherproof you make the porch.

Decks are a popular do-it-yourself project. Most decks are planned with direct access to the house, such as these sliding doors.

Decks

Decks, which are basically just inexpensive wood platforms, can be added to virtually any house. Since they require no roofing, and only a modest amount of support and foundation, even large decks can be built by the homeowner himself. A large deck could have lighting fixtures, electrical outlets, deck furniture, barbeque, exercise equipment, planters, and much more. With convenient access to the house, a deck can greatly enhance the quality of family homelife.

Patios

While a deck is made of wood and raised from several inches to many feet above grade level, a patio is built at or on grade and can be constructed of many materials. Patios can be made of stone, masonry, gravel, and other materials, either singly or in combination. Some portion of the patio is generally placed just slightly below the house's entrance level, but overall it can be constructed on several levels.

Planters, border strips, gardens, shrubbery, and trees are easily integrated into a patio's design. It can also accommodate freestanding and built-in furnishing of all kinds, plus barbeques, garden pools, fountains, and such. Lighting of many types can be installed easily, and a portion of the patio can be covered with roof, sun grid or other arrangement.

Access to the patio can be through a single door. But a better idea is to install one or more sliding glass patio doors, flanked by sizeable expanses of fixed glass at several locations. This provides free and easy access from all major interior areas of the house, and opens up the home to the outdoors. If a great amount of glass is used, the interior and exterior environments can seem to be one uninterrupted expanse.

Greenhouses

Obviously, a greenhouse has a single main function. But by using a little imagination, even a detached greenhouse can be used for more than just growing plants. By rearranging the interior structure, a greenhouse

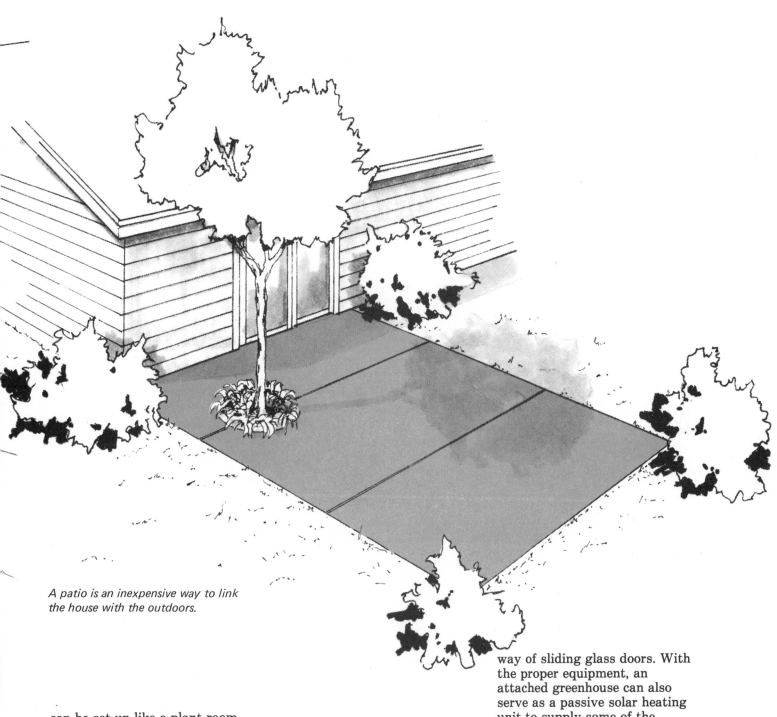

A patio is an inexpensive way to link the house with the outdoors.

can be set up like a plant room. Part of it can be devoted to plants, and part can be carpeted and furnished. A greenhouse transformed in this fashion makes a marvelous spot for reading and quiet contemplation. You could also use it as a part-time dining area or year-around sunbathing spot. A large greenhouse could even be used to enclose a small swimming pool.

Attached to a house, a greenhouse has even more

flexibility. It could be used to extend a room of the house, like a living room, by 20 feet or more. You could devote a portion of the greenhouse to plants, and use another portion to complement the house's interior—perhaps by adding sunbathing lounges, a dining area or game tables. One end or side of the greenhouse could open out to a deck or patio by

way of sliding glass doors. With the proper equipment, an attached greenhouse can also serve as a passive solar heating unit to supply some of the home's heating needs.

Solariums

A solarium is a bit like a greenhouse without the plant-growing equipment. Glass walls and ceiling sections admit the sunlight. The primary purpose of a solarium is to provide a place for therapeutic sunbathing, but you can also use it as a reading room, dining room, or even as an enclosure for a hot tub or small indoor pool. It can be either

Greenhouses make excellent passive
solar-heat systems, when built with
that idea in mind.

The hot tub is no longer considered
a strictly therapeutic devise. The
above hot tub combines with an
unattached deck.

54

This solarium, which encloses a swimming pool, expands the dining room by a large amount of space. A requisite for a solarium, of course, is a large expanse of glass.

attached or separate from the main house. An attached solarium can become an extension of a room, such as master bedroom or bathroom, with delightful results.

Hot-Tub Areas

Hot tubs are one of the newest home accessories intended for indoor/outdoor living areas. Essentially, a hot tub is a huge wooden vat that holds a great quantity of hot water. The smallest models, which are too big for the interiors of most houses, easily hold two people; larger models have ample room for several persons.

In some cases, hot tubs are placed indoors, within a shelter or outbuilding. But most often it's placed at an outdoor location convenient to the house. Usually, a special foundation is required, because of the tub's size and weight. And, although these tubs sometimes stand alone, they are most often the focal point of an attractively arranged and landscaped deck or patio. These installations are even becoming extremely popular in areas where winters are long and severe, especially resort areas. There's no danger of a tub freezing up as long as its heaters remain on. And, the experience of a steamy soak in a hot tub while the temperature hovers around 20 degrees is an interesting one. Indeed, getting out can be a particularly exhilarating experience!

Assembled hot tubs are heavy and bulky and not easily handled by one person. Two or three people can set one up, but the dealer frequently takes care of this. Hot-tub kits are also available for the do-it-yourselfer. In fact, a homeowner could handle the entire hot-tub area project, although plumbing and electrical connections might have to be done by professionals to stay within local building codes.

Atriums

An atrium is an architectural feature developed during Roman times. It comprised a large open or partially open ground-floor central hallway in a Roman house. The modern atrium retains the same general idea, but it is an open patio, usually rectangular, and surrounded entirely by the structure of a house.

Atriums are not common in this country, and building one is an ambitious project requiring a lot of planning. Usually, one or more additions must be made to an existing structure to form the enclosed atrium area. However, there are some older designs that lend themselves to this construction, and some newer ones as well. Some Spanish style homes and certain types of cluster homes are good examples.

Pergolas, Gazebos, and Belvederes

A pergola, sometimes called a sunscreen or grid, is a kind of arbor that consists of an overhead horizontal trellis, latticework or grid arrangement, which is supported by columns or posts. The number and design of these posts varies, and sometimes they have vertical trellises mounted in the interstices. Or, a series of decorative columns might be installed at regular intervals along one or more sides, forming a modified colonnade.

A gazebo is a small, roofed

structure with full headroom. It's open on all sides and built on a slightly above-ground wood-decked platform. The traditional shapes are hexagonal and octagonal, although a gazebo might be built round or square. Low openwork railings or solid sides are generally built between the roof support columns, with one section left open for access. Bench-type seating may be

permanently built-in, but ordinary lawn furniture works just as well and is more comfortable. Full screening could be installed on all walls if conditions warrant, and although glass is seldom used, it can be installed.

In style, a gazebo is reminiscent of Victorian times, and these structures are frequently fitted out with

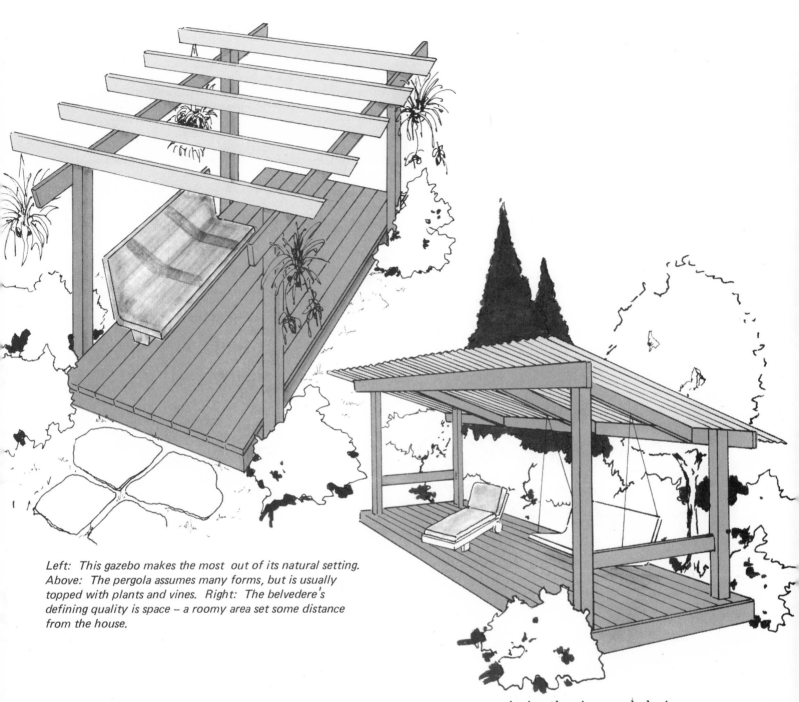

Left: This gazebo makes the most out of its natural setting.
Above: The pergola assumes many forms, but is usually topped with plants and vines. Right: The belvedere's defining quality is space -- a roomy area set some distance from the house.

gingerbread, carvings, and assorted furbelows. However, it also could have a modern motif. Size varies from six feet across to as large as 20 feet in diameter. Construction is perfectly straightforward and employs standard building materials, so a gazebo makes a fine do-it-yourself project.

The term "belvedere" is somewhat general, and can refer to any small outbuilding that's designed to take advantage of pleasant surroundings or a striking view. A screenhouse would be an example. These structures can be permanent structures, or portable units in kit form. A tiny shelter of standard wood construction could also be a belvedere, if it were of open design. It could serve as a place for relaxing and enjoying the view, card playing, entertaining, or warm-weather dining.

A pergola, gazebo, or belvedere can serve nicely to increase living space in pleasant weather. Any of the three might stand alone. Or they can become the focal point of interesting landscaping or serve as adjuncts to decks or patios. The pergola, in particular, is extremely effective when used in this manner.

Planning the Addition

When you understand what your expansion options are, you can begin the sorting-out process. You must now put the appealing options to the test, in relation to personal and practical factors. First, the expansion must fulfill your family's need for more space, and it must be reasonable in terms of degree of inconvenience, loss of grounds, and perhaps property value return on your investment. Second, it has to be practical from a construction and architectural standpoint. And, third, the project must be legally and economically feasible.

Personal Factors

To begin the planning process, gather the family together for a series of round table discussions.

Find out what all family members expect the project to do for them individually; explore their present and future needs. Discuss each point, however minor it may seem; iron out potential difficulties and make compromises where necessary.

A multitude of questions can arise. Will a one-room addition be sufficient, or should you build two rooms? If you convert the garage to living quarters, should you include a workshop? Would it be a good idea to renovate the bathroom when you build a second-story addition?

This preliminary part of the planning process is extremely important, because once the project is underway, changes are expensive. And once it is completed, further expansion in

the immediate future may be financially impossible. The project must remain practical over a span of many years if you are to get full value for your extensive outlay of time and money.

Other expansion related considerations affect the whole family, too. For example, there is bound to be some degree of inconvenience during the construction. Everyone may have to tolerate air filled with plaster dust, sawdust on the floor, and a certain amount of noise and commotion. A normal household traffic pattern may be disrupted, and you may even lose the use of an entire part of the house for a time. In some cases, it could be better to move out of the house while the work

is in progress. At least some of these inconveniences should be expected, and everyone should be aware of what is involved before the work begins.

Loss of grounds is another topic for family discussion. Outward expansion of a house inevitably reduces the amount of open space around it. This space may include gardens, shrubbery, lawns, and even full-grown trees. Money and effort gone into landscaping may be negated, and a new landscaping program may have to be initiated on completion of the project. Even adjacent areas of land—not related to the work—can be damaged by trucks and other equipment. You can, however, keep this to a minimum by instructing the contractor or equipment operators as to which areas are off limits. It's also a good idea to include a damage penalty clause in any building contract you sign.

Once you have discussed all the preliminary aspects of your project, and come to conclusions about what it will be like, make some rough sketches. These

sketches of the interior and exterior of the expansion will help you during the succeeding phases of planning.

Structural Factors

Primarily, structural considerations involve the existing building—rather than the expansion project itself. Sometimes there's a question as to whether a building is physically able to bear the weight of additional construction—at least without further structural alterations.

For instance, if you are to add a full second floor to your house, the foundation must be able to bear almost twice the present weight. If it can't, the added load could cause foundation damage or subsidence of the entire building. The foundation isn't the only structural aspect you have to consider. Items like lightly framed first-floor sidewalls, and light and widely spaced ceiling joists can also cause problems. Of course, you can usually revise the original foundation and framework to take the added weight of the

addition. The question is whether the complicated process required to revise the original structure is worth the effort.

All expansion projects require structural evaluation. For example, a new full bath includes many heavy plumbing fixtures, and the floor frame beneath the bath area must be capable of supporting the extra weight. In the case of attic conversions, floor joists must be sturdy enough to accept the weight of the new flooring and the loads imposed upon it. And, when an internal load-bearing wall or a large section of exterior wall is removed, new load-bearing structural members must be employed to retain the house's structural integrity.

Stiffness is another structural factor to be considered. The structural framework in the area of the expansion must be stiff enough to handle the new load without excessive vibration, deflection, or springiness. Also, you must check whether removing original framework, or adding to it will have any ill effect on the structural integrity.

Making determinations about these structural factors should usually be left to a professional in the building trade. Arriving at a conclusion about structural matters is often difficult because so much of a house's framework is hidden from view. So, enlist the aid of a competent homebuilder, general contractor, remodeling contractor, architect, or structural engineer for your answers during early planning stages. If structural changes are needed, they should be approved by an architect or structural engineer in order to secure a building permit.

Utilities Factors

Electrical, plumbing, and heating systems can also pose a threat to the practicality of your project. At the start, you must evaluate what effect your expansion project will have upon the various utilities.

Electrical

Unfortunately, a large proportion of homes today—including many new ones—have undersized and sometimes outmoded electrical systems. Often, there is neither physical space nor electrical capacity to serve any new living areas. Suppose, for instance, you plan to convert a large basement—adding several new circuits for lighting, convenience outlets, and auxiliary heating units. An older 60-ampere service entrance could never handle this added load, and chances are that the more common 100-ampere service entrance would be inadequate as well. To prevent an overload you would have to replace all of the service entrance equipment— along with the service drop and perhaps even the serving pole transformer (the power company will do the work). You should also expect to do a certain amount of internal rewiring too. Of course, depending upon the project's size, the electrical system's modifications may not be so extensive. But it's wise to check out the electrical system during the initial planning stages of any expansion project—however small.

Plumbing

In homes connected to municipal water and sewage systems, plumbing problems seldom develop. However, if your water comes from a private well, or if waste disposal is by means of a septic system, expansion may lead to operational difficulties.

For example, let's say you wish to add several new water taps to a house supplied by a private well. Adding these new taps could mean lowered pressure or volume to all the taps in the house—especially if the new ones are installed in a second or third-floor location. Generally, the septic system will not be affected by additional drainage outlets, but if the amount of daily waste is increased, the septic tank may need to be enlarged. If your expansion project will also add occupants to your house, the increase in waste could overload the septic tank or leaching field capacity, rendering the system ineffective or completely inoperative—and possibly in violation with local codes and ordinances. When examining the adequacy of your plumbing system, don't forget to look into local codes. Some require adding septic tank capacity when you add bedrooms and bathrooms to an existing structure—unless the septic system is oversized to begin with. If you have any questions concerning your septic tank, check with the local plumbing inspector from the building department.

Heating

If your living-space expansion takes place within an adequately heated area, you can breathe easy on this point—unless you make adverse changes in the thermal insulation value of exterior wall sections, or install a large expanse of glass. But expanding into an unheated attic or partially heated basement can spell trouble. The original heating system may not have sufficient capacity to handle the additional load, and this could result in leaving the entire house inadequately heated. The situation can even be worse when additions are made to the building, and extensions to the existing heating system are installed to serve them.

Heating problems can arise because most home heating systems are matched very closely to the needs of the original house. If more heating capacity is needed, you must replace the original heating unit with a larger one, add a second central unit to serve the new addition—as in the case of a complete ell—or install individual auxiliary heating units in the new areas.

Legal Factors

Just because an expansion project can be done from a practical and technical standpoint, doesn't mean that it can be done from a legal standpoint. In most parts of the country, building projects must meet certain legal standards. Although this is not always the case, you should always assume that your remodeling activities will be regulated—until you determine otherwise.

Zoning

Not only do zoning regulations vary widely throughout the country, they may be somewhat arbitrary and even capricious. Where these regulations are in force, they may establish setback requirements—how close to your property line you can build—and establish view planes and density standards. They may also restrict building height and square footage, govern the type of construction allowable in a given location, and impose other rules to follow.

Building Codes

Some areas have no codes at all, but in others the national building codes may be followed and local codes may take precedence. Codes specifically govern items like construction requirements and techniques, and allowable designs and materials. For instance, a building code may require that a certain amount of glass installed in a building or addition must be openable. It may also prohibit the use of cedar shingles as a roofing material—unless they are fireproofed—or require certain minimum thermal-insulation values.

Covenants

Regulations known as protective covenants are often found in subdivisions or housing developments—especially where zoning regulations are weak or nonexistent. Even though you may not know about them when buying your house, signing your property deed usually obliges you to abide by them. These regulations are usually general: establishing property line setbacks, governing property usage, limiting garage size, disallowing outbuilding construction, and specifying placement of driveway curb cuts. But some of the regulations may be quite specific and may concern design and construction of all property improvements.

Architectural Control Committees

These regulatory bodies are often established by homeowner groups, tract developers, and more recently by community governments. Their purpose is to regulate and control all construction within their jurisdiction. Generally, the primary concern is with exterior appearances—such as design and finish—rather than internal construction or arrangement. They often delineate exactly what a homeowner can and cannot do in these areas. For example, they may dictate or suggest the size and location of a building on a particular lot, control the erection of outbuildings and fences, prohibit the use of certain building materials and exterior colors.

Permits and Inspections

Wherever regulations are in force, one or more permits for various aspects of the expansion job must be obtained, and you may have to pay certain fees—which can be substantial. You or your contractor must also arrange for periodic inspections during the course of the project. In most cases, a building permit involves four inspections: foundation, framing, insulation, and a final inspection on completion of all work. And if permits for utilities work are needed, inspections for each type

---

Legal Requirements

No matter where or what you build, some legal matters must be cleared before construction takes place. One of your initial trips should be to the local building department. Bring along your very basic ideas. Someone will be able to tell you what you can and cannot do. The chart below outlines the various legal obstacles. You probably won't be affected by all of these regulations, but you no doubt must abide by some.

Law or Regulation	Possible Restrictions or Requirements	Control Body
Zoning	setback requirements, view planes, density standards, building height and square footage, type of construction	local
Building Codes	construction requirements and techniques, designs and materials	national/ local
Covenants	property line setbacks, property usage, garage size, outbuilding construction, placement of driveway curb cuts	subdivision/ housing developments
Architectural Control Committees	exterior appearance, size, location, materials	homeowner groups/ tract developers/ community governments
Permits and Inspections	foundation, framing, insulation, utilities, final inspection FEE CHARGED	city/county building dept./homeowners associations
Do-It-Yourself Regulations	what you can and cannot do yourself	local
Other Regulations	health regulations, electrical, plumbing	local/ health department

---

of work are usually required. Often, such inspections are made by mutual agreement, but unannounced spot checks may also take place. Obtain details about permits and inspections from agencies such as city or county building departments and homeowner's associations.

Do-It-Yourself Regulations

In many areas, homeowners are allowed to do any or all of the construction and finish work on their own property. As long as they are not acting as contractors for hire and are the owners of the property on which

they are working, they can go right ahead.

On the other hand, other areas—particularly urban ones—restrict homeowners from performing work on their own property. For example, a plumbing installation might have to be made by a licensed plumber. The same holds true for electrical installations.

But there are variations on this theme. Often, it is possible for knowledgeable do-it-yourselfers to make arrangements to do the bulk of the work themselves—under the guidance of a licensed professional. Or the licensed contractor and the homeowner can work together as necessary to fulfill legal requirements.

Other Regulations

You may be faced with other rules and regulations in addition to those mentioned. Even where zoning or building codes don't apply, health department requirements usually do. So if you're thinking of installing, modifying, or upgrading private water supplies or septic tank systems, be sure to check with the health department. In many areas the state or county oversees all electrical wiring installations—generally following the National Electrical Code as well as local codes.

Economic Factors

Before drawing up final plans, you should have a rough idea of what the project will cost you now and in the future. This can be divided into three facets: construction costs, possible diminished property values, and ongoing expenses.

Construction Costs

Before you draw up final plans, it's only possible to look at the broad cost picture for the project. Unless cost is no object, you should determine how much you really wish to spend for expansion. Then develop several sets of figures—based on modifications of your initial plan—to see how they measure up to your finances.

At this time, you should have a rough idea of your start-up costs—which include items like permit fees and engineering or architectural services. Use the rough sketches you made in the early planning stages to help you prepare a list of the principle bulk materials that will go into the project. A visit to the local lumberyard can give you the cost of those materials; add them all up and tack on 20 percent for the items you may have overlooked.

If you plan to do all the work

yourself, add your start-up and materials costs plus about 10 or 15 percent for contingencies. If you're going to hire a contractor, double the materials figure and add another 10 to 20 percent. This will give you a rough figure that can be used as a guideline. Or you can use the alternative method of calculating the floor area (in square feet) of a new addition and multiplying by the average per-square-foot residential construction costs in your area. In either case, if extensive utilities work is included in the project, make substantial allowances for that as well.

Diminished Property Value

Also, now is a good time to explore the possibility of diminished property value. It's a mistake to think that property value increases automatically in proportion to money spent on additions, improvements, and renovations. For example, if dramatic changes in your house make it fall outside the norm for your area, it could become a white elephant in the marketplace. The same goes for changing a $40,000 cottage into a $100,000 residence. If your new "palace" is surrounded by modest cottages, you're pricing yourself out of the housing market for your area. The intrinsic value of the completed house may be there but the marketability and actual value are not.

The amount of increased market value you can expect from your investment depends a lot on what type of work is done. Spending $10,000 on interior rearrangement and redecorating, painting, carpeting, appliances, and lighting fixtures will probably not increase the house's value by an equal amount. However, spending the same amount on a new ell, may—plus enhance the building's marketability. If increased market value is your primary goal, you're better off investing in a $5,000 tennis

court. Although this may limit potential buyers to tennis players, the court would probably increase your property value by about $10,000!

The subject of dollars-returned-for-dollars-invested is tricky and variable. The most specific determinations are little more than educated guesses. And these determinations can only be made by balancing facts of individual cases against the current and projected local real estate markets. It's best to discuss the matter with an architect, local banker, property appraiser, real-estate agent, tax assessor, or another expert.

Ongoing Expenses

Besides the initial dent in your wallet from construction costs, expanding your living quarters may increase your family's monthly expenses in other ways. These expenses may include utility expenses for heat, light, and air-conditioning, as well as maintenance costs, periodic replacement of furnishings, and taxes. Add these projected ongoing expenses to your estimated monthly payments for financing the construction. If all seems reasonable and within your family's budget, all is probably well. If the ongoing costs seem like they will put you in a financial crunch, perhaps you're overexpanding. In this case, you may want to reassess the scope of your project.

Final Planning Stages

These last steps in the planning process include assessing the practicality of your idea—based on information you have gathered and the drawing up of formal plans. After this is done, you can launch your idea into reality.

Assessing Practicality

By way of your preliminary assessments, you should now have a good idea of whether or not your project is feasible—but is it practical? Only you can decide just where the line between practicality and impracticality lies. The judgement you make will depend upon how badly you want to see your intended project through to the end—without further compromises, modifications, or alternative ideas.

For example, you may decide that your original idea is impractical because an engineer told you that your house's existing structure must be extensively altered. Or local building codes or zoning regulations might be such that you face a long fight in seeking a variation to allow your project. Is the effort and possible high expense justifiable? Perhaps your family has vetoed your expansion idea because it eliminates space for gardening. Do you want that struggle on your hands? These are questions you have to ask yourself before drawing up final plans and proceeding with the project.

Final Planning

Assuming you have jumped the hurdles already discussed, now you can plan the project in detail. This involves making an extensive series of measurements and juggling the elements of your project so that everything balances out. At the same time, the plans must be successfully integrated with the existing structure, architectural design, and decor.

Plans. Begin your final planning with a new series of rough sketches that show all measurements and details. These can be either refined sketches or informal drawings, but they should be done in considerable detail and preferably to scale. Of course, the larger the drawings, the easier they are to work with. Be sure to include all the principal elements of the project, such as: wall placement; locations, types, and sizes of doors and windows; built-in furnishings, such as cabinets, counters, and shelves; and placement of plumbing fixtures,

appliances, and fireplaces. Remember to note dimensions on the plans wherever necessary.

These plans can be drawn up in a number of ways. A floor plan is the first requirement so you can work out correct placement and proportions of the various elements. Interior or exterior elevations—which are simply detailed drawings of a single plane of the structure as viewed head-on—are also helpful. If you wish, you can also make detailed drawings showing how the framework will be put together and covered, as well as enlargements of particular construction areas, like window or door installations and trim treatment.

Utilities drawings, such as those showing electrical and plumbing extensions, are usually drawn out symbolically on a basic floor plan. With all of the plans, don't skimp on construction details or specifications. The object is to create plans that can help you work out problems in advance of construction—and that you can use for reference as the job progresses.

Specifications. As you work out the final plans, you should also establish specifications for the materials, hardware, and equipment needed. You can note these specifications directly on the plans or on separate lists. For instance, decide what type and brand of shingles, exterior siding, interior wood paneling, finish floor covering, lighting fixtures, and other materials you would like to have. Give these items careful thought to avoid time consuming changes and misunderstandings later.

Bill of Materials. After you've dealt with the plans and specifications, make a list of all the items that will go into the construction of the project. This bill of materials should be checked against the plans and/or specifications lists several times to make sure nothing is omitted.

Formal Plan Sets. It may be possible to use your informal

plans to begin the construction—without arranging for formal plan sets. This is the case when the banker, building department, or architectural control committee you're dealing with will accept informal plans. If you are going to do the project yourself or if you hire a competent contractor and explain your plans to him, the informal plans may be adequate, too.

However, even if you don't need formal plan sets to get the okay from banks and regulating bodies, arranging for detailed and formal blueprint sets is a wise move. You'll find that they can be invaluable for minimizing potential problems throughout the construction period.

If you're a competent draftsman and familiar with construction blueprints, you can probably do the job yourself. Even if you're not knowledgeable about blueprints, you could attempt the job with the help of the many books available on the subject. But the usual course followed is to hire someone for the task. A reputable architect or engineer can draw up formal plans from the information you've accumulated. Or a free-lance engineering or architectural draftsman can make blueprints for an hourly fee. In any case, be prepared to spend some time explaining the details of your project.

Be careful to check first with your building department if structural changes to your existing building are necessary or if the dollar expenditure falls within certain requirements. You may be required to have your plans sealed by a licensed architect or engineer before a permit is issued.

Also, don't make the common mistake of having "a friend who can draw" make plans for you only to find out later that you can't get a permit with them. If you get professional help initially, you will find that you will save time and money.

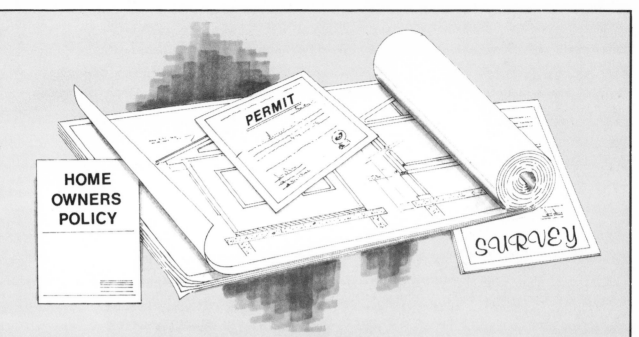

Professional and Legal Considerations

The trick to getting your money's worth is knowing when you need professional and legal help and when you don't. Unless you are skilled in a variety of structural arts, you'll no doubt need some guidance somewhere.

Building Department

The local building department should be contacted during your initial planning stages. Codes and regulations vary drastically between states, counties, and towns. The free advice available here covers everything from the necessary materials to the exterior appearance. One regulation you should be immediately aware of are setback requirements. These requirements designate the point to which you can build on your own property. In other words, you may not be able to expand as far as you want to. If the building department is contacted initially, obstacles such as setback requirements can be incorporated into the final design. Building departments also specify the necessary building permits, inspections, and fees.

Insurance Agent

Contact the agency that handles your homeowner's insurance policy. If you will be acting as the general contractor, worker's compensation insurance will be necessary. Other policies that can supplement your homeowner's policy are available, such as "Builder's Risk" insurance. There are construction liabilities not necessarily covered in your homeowner's policy. Therefore, contact your insurance agent before hiring any labor.

Architect and Structural Engineer

Local codes may require the signature of an architect or structural engineer before building permits are granted. It is a good idea, in any case, to talk with one of these professionals before building. They can act in an advisory role, guiding you through the maze of structural specifica-

tions. This is usually done on an hourly-wage basis. Or they can completely take over the project, from designing the addition and obtaining the permits, to hiring the contractors and inspecting the work. This is usually handled on a percentage basis, say fifteen percent of the total cost. Two functions these professionals should be strongly considered for are drawing up the plans and inspecting the work. Once the plans have been drawn up, they can serve as a legal basis for the work done. In other words, all workers must abide by the plan, as long as that is built into the contract. Considering an architect's and structural engineer's knowledge of building materials and methods, it's a good idea to have them inspect the project, making sure the proper materials are used and the proper methods employed. Contact your local American Institute of Architects or your State's Society of Engineers for lists of professionals in your area.

General Contractors and Subcontractors

A general contractor will assume the responsibilities of your entire project. Insurance policies, labor, materials, permits, and inspections will be under the contractor's direction. If you plan on working under these conditions, make sure the general contractor is reliable and able. Talk to as many people as possible: neighbors, government bureaus, banks, and any others who may have knowledge of the contractor's work. Make sure the contractor is adequately covered as far as insurance is concerned. That means both worker's compensation and automobile insurance. The National Remodeler's Association should be able to suggest contractors in your area.

If you want to save a good sum of money and work as your own contractor, somewhere along the line you'll probably need a subcontractor. Subcontractors handle specialty skills, such as plumbing, roofing, and electrical work. Great care should go into the hiring decision, just as with a general contractor. It is also important to give your subcontractors ample warning as to when they should appear. When working with subcontractors, it is especially important to have standard plans from which they can work.

Economics of Expansion

Before the onset of the expansion project, it's imperative that you investigate actual costs and financing arrangements. And for the duration of the job, you must keep tabs on all financial details. Fiscal problems can bring a half-completed project to a shuddering halt, and can even stop a project before it gets started.

Job Estimates

A job estimate is generally arrived at by adding together the estimated costs for materials, labor, and any other costs related to the project. There's nothing to guarantee that a figure for a job estimate will be firm—nor even accurate. But it should be a reasonably definitive total figure from which further calculations and judgements can be made.

Material Cost

The computation of material costs begins with a materials takeoff. This is a list of all parts, materials, and supplies you will buy *personally*. Don't include materials that professional subcontractors will use; they will provide you with a total cost estimate for their individual jobs that you will add to the job estimate later. You must make the takeoff as complete as possible—noting the quantities of each item. Wherever there is a question, make allowances on the plus side.

When the takeoff is complete, some legwork is required. Visit lumberyards, hardware stores, and other suppliers to get the current unit price for each item, and multiply by the quantity needed. Be sure to include any freight charges, sales taxes, or other charges.

Labor Cost

In other than purely do-it-yourself projects, materials probably account for only half or less of the total job cost. The balance is mostly labor charges. You only need to figure the cost of labor if you hire casual labor for parts of the job—since there will be no cost if you do all the work, and professionals will supply you with their own bids or estimates.

If you decide to hire casual labor, you need to calculate the number of hours each particular job will take. Then multiply the time by the hourly rate you're willing to pay for the work. There may be several hourly rates involved depending on skill levels and the trades of the workmen. Be aware that if a considerable number of hours is involved, you may be subject to state and federal taxes as an employer, and you may have to acquire workmen's compensation insurance.

Other Expenses

To arrive at a total job estimate, you must add together the cost of labor, materials, and all the other expenses you will incur for the project. These other expenses may include subcontractor costs and fees charged for surveying, permits, inspections, legal counseling, and other types of consulting. Initial charges made by moneylenders should be figured in too.

Soliciting Bids

If you are going to hire a general contractor to do all the work, it's best to have him work on the basis of a firm bid rather than an estimate. There are many advantages to soliciting bids from contractors, and it is generally accepted as the most foolproof course to follow in all but the smallest construction projects. A contractually accepted bid price is legally binding—an estimate is not. If you're stuck with a grossly faulty estimate, you seldom have any recourse. But you do have legal recourse with a bid price and its accompanying contract.

To reap the benefits of this system, the bids must be solicited correctly. The first step is to acquire a complete and accurate set of construction blueprints drawn up according to current conventional practice—with all construction details, material schedules, and job specifications. Any special restrictions—alternate methods or materials, unusual job conditions, or job deadlines—must also be included. Materials takeoffs can be supplied, but many bidders prefer to make up their own.

The next step is to make as many full sets of this information as you'll need for the solicitations. This could be several to a dozen, depending upon your preference. It's best to get names of prospective bidders from personal references. Your bank can help, as can friends and neighbors who have had projects completed recently. Other reference sources include the local chamber of commerce, building supply houses, real estate agents, architects, and engineers. You can also contact the National Remodelers Association (50 East 42nd Street, New York, NY 10017) for a list of participating members in your area. The members are experienced specialists in the home improvement industry.

It's a good idea to call prospective contractors first—since some will decline to make bids. Then send the solicitation sets to those who showed interest. If you didn't cover applicable bidding conditions—the due date and other such details—in your phone conversation, send along a cover letter with this information.

If you are going to act as your own general contractor, you can solicit bids from subcontractors in exactly the same way. You can reduce the solicitation packages to include only that part of the job that is applicable to the particular subcontractor. But it's wiser to provide a subcontractor with information for the entire job so he can understand how his work relates to the whole project.

When you plan to tackle a fairly large project all by yourself, soliciting bids for materials may save you time and money. It's possible to get a better price on materials if you buy everything from one supplier at a firm bid price, which may also include a discount. The same procedure can be followed if you're acting as your own general contractor. In this case, you state in your bid to subcontractors that you will supply all materials. However, many subcontractors look askance at this procedure.

Reducing Costs

Paying more than you need to is just plain foolish. The key, however, is to cut costs without affecting the project's quality or scope. Here are some possible ways to do this.

Doing It Yourself

Of course, one of the most obvious ways to reduce costs is to do all or part of the work yourself. But this is not always possible depending upon your skill and amount of free time. You can, however, at least prepare the site so the workmen can start without having to move furniture, chop down shrubbery, or move the woodpile. And you can clean up after the job is done to save dollars spent on labor.

Substitutions

As you draw up your plans, ask yourself, "What materials or methods could I use to save money without affecting the project's quality or level of effectiveness?" For example, let's say your original specifications called for prefinished, ¾-inch oak parquet tile flooring, laid on ⅝-inch exterior-glue C-D plywood subflooring. This is a common and workable combination, but it can be changed in order to save money. One of several ways would be to substitute an interior-glue C-D plywood put down an underlayment of ⅜-inch particle board, and top it with ⁵⁄₁₆-inch oak parquet tile. If you make substitutions like this in several areas of the project, they could add up to a considerable savings overall.

Smart Buying

Rather than buying materials from one or two suppliers on a day-to-day basis, you might consider comparison shopping. There are ample opportunities to do this in the building materials field. Some possible sources include large hardware and supply discount houses, and cash-and-carry supply warehouses. Other potential sources for savings are special manufacturer's sales, sales on distressed materials and equipment, mill-end runs, obsolete or discontinued stock, warehouse inventory clearances, and materials or hardware auctions. You can also obtain good, used materials from various sources—and even buy leftover stock from building contractors.

Although this may all sound terrific, you do have to keep in mind that it's easy to get stuck. To be successful, remember these three points. First, saving money this way requires ingenuity, judgement, and knowledge of building materials and their potential uses. You must know the difference—at a glance—between good quality materials and hardware, and junk. Second, you must have a good grasp of standard retail prices of the materials you wish to purchase. And third, buy only what you need, and pass up buying unnecessary items that seem to be real bargains. You can save money by looking for bargains—but it takes a lot of knowledge and willpower.

Simple and Modular Construction

Simple construction means sticking with ordinary building materials and standard framing, finishing, and trimming practices. Items to be avoided include exotic materials, special order goods, materials shipped from a distance at extra freight costs, any specialized items, or any items difficult to install. Straightforward construction practices must be followed, too. Everything should be basically rectangular to avoid extra labor expense in fitting curves and tricky angles.

Modular construction involves using standard size building materials with as little alteration as possible. For example, wallboard comes in standard 4 x 8-foot sheets, so your walls should be eight feet high. Standard stud spacing is 16 inches, so you should use four framing members for each piece of sheathing. By adjusting wall sizes to these standard dimensions, construction is easier and cheaper—with no waste. This holds true for all aspects of your expansion project. You can save labor and material by planning to build with unaltered, standard size materials as much as possible.

Kits

Purchasing kits of materials and adapting them to your construction needs can often result in considerable savings. Frequently, the kit can be purchased—freight included—for less than the cost of raw materials, plus labor for cutting, and fitting and assembling the pieces locally.

A number of manufacturers of kit homes make units or modules that can be used as additions to existing structures. And there are a number of other possibilities. Garden shed kits of wood and metal are inexpensive and easy to erect. Unassembled, unfinished kitchen cabinet kits may suit your needs. All sorts of furniture and furnishings are available in kit form, as well as items like intercom sets, fire alarms, and security systems.

Financing: Cash or Borrow?

There are a lot of "maybes" involved in an expansion project, but there is one thing you can count on for sure—you are going to spend money. Even before the project gets underway, you have to decide how much you can afford—and where and on what terms you will obtain funds. Only you can decide how much you can afford to spend, but here's some information on the other economic aspects.

There are two basic ways to pay for your project. One is to tap your own cash reserves by dipping into savings accounts or converting stocks, bonds, certificates of deposits, and other investments into cash. There are no strings attached to your own funds, and you can do with the money as you please. The alternative is to borrow from a lender or lending institution. In this case, your use of the money may be restricted. And, of course, you are also under strict obligation to repay according to the terms of the loan.

Using Your Own Cash

Generally, using your own funds is the best course to follow. It gives you complete control over construction and expenditures—and you don't have to worry about paying the money back with interest. If you plan to perform all or most of the work yourself, your own funds may be the only money available. Do-it-yourselfers don't enjoy high favor in banking circles.

Furthermore, if you have money tied up in low-yield investments, you might realize a better return over a period of time by funneling those funds into the expansion. For example, let's say you pay for the project by withdrawing funds from a six percent annual yield savings account. If you're expansion project is well designed and will result in nearly a dollar-for-dollar increase in property value for the funds invested, you can come out ahead of the game. Depending upon the appreciation rate of property values in your area, you could realize an annual rate of 7 to 15 percent or more on the funds used for expansion. Of course, assets tied up in improved property are not as liquid as those in a savings account. But you can still convert them into cash if the chips are down.

Borrowing Possibilities

There are circumstances, however, under which borrowing is more advantageous. This depends upon many factors, such as your tax bracket, the nature of your investments, and your need for tax shelters. For instance, if you could get a five percent loan to finance your project, it wouldn't make sense to remove money from a 15 percent annual yield investment you have. Aside from circumstances similar to those in this example, there is only one other big advantage to borrowing: it gives you the use of money you couldn't otherwise attain. Since this is common in these days of high inflation, let's explore some of the ways you can borrow money for your project.

Personal Sources. If you're lucky enough to have friends or relatives who are willing to supply expansion funds, they could be your best source of financing. Interest rates are usually low or nonexistent, agreements are friendly and simple, and your commercial credit rating is of no consequence. The only hitch is that borrowing from friends and relatives sometimes strains good personal relationships. So be cautious, but don't rule out the possibility if it exists.

Life Insurance. The loan value of a whole life insurance policy depends upon the amount you've paid into it. If the policy is reasonably substantial and you've had it for a long time, you could borrow up to several thousand dollars on it. Contact the insurance company or your agent to find out the loan value of the policy and the repayment terms. Interest rates vary, but they are usually below current commercial rates—and you may not have to pay back the loan at all. But this invariably destroys part of the policy's value.

Commercial Loans. The following are the basic commercial sources of financing for expansion projects. Before making a decision as to which is best for you, be sure to explore several categories and contact a few lenders in each—since comparison shopping can save you a bundle of money.

If you need a minimum of about $10,000 and you own your property free and clear, a *first mortgage* could be considered. Besides current interest rates, you also incur closing costs and perhaps even "points." Closing costs are fees for legal services, contract writing, any necessary surveying, and other services. Points is a term for a surcharge. It means that a certain percentage of the loan must be paid when the loan is closed. A one-point charge on a $50,000 note would amount to one percent of the total, or $500. This would be immediately deducted from the loan proceeds so you would actually end up with $49,500 for your project.

Another possibility is *remortgaging* a house that already has a first mortgage. This can only be done if there is sufficient property equity to borrow against. Property equity is the difference between the unpaid mortgage balance and the appraised value of the property. You gain this equity by either repaying a substantial part of your first mortgage or by

having your property appreciate considerably—due to rising property values. Like a first mortgage, remortgaging is only practicable when a sizeable amount of money is needed—and perhaps not even then.

Remortgaging is done like this. You take out a new first mortgage on your property and use the proceeds to pay off your smaller, old first mortgage. Then you use the funds left over to pay for property improvement. It's beneficial to remortgage when interest rates are low and expected to rise, or when the current rate is lower than or the same as the original first mortgage rate. It would be foolish to do the reverse—exchange an old 6-percent mortgage for one of 10 percent. A point to remember if you're considering remortgaging is that bankers are often not receptive to the idea—especially if they won't benefit from it.

Taking out a *second mortgage* is a common procedure today, although conservative financial advisors frowned on it in the past. In this case, you leave the original first mortgage alone and take out another, smaller mortgage against the equity value of the property. The chief drawback to you is cost. As a rule, you can expect an interest rate four to five percentage points higher than that of your first mortgage. Partially, this is because whoever gives you the second mortgage is in a position of higher risk. He is in second place to the first mortgagee in event of default. As with first mortgages, the term of the loan usually extends at least 10 years.

If you don't need a great amount of money—and can pay it back in a short period of time—an *installment loan* is a good possibility. Lending institutions sometimes call this a home improvement loan, but it's basically the same kind of loan used to buy appliances, furniture, and vehicles. Generally, these are one to eight

year loans for amounts up to about $10,000. Maximum interest rates are set by law. They vary widely, but they're usually higher than those for real estate mortgages.

A *personal note* is a workable alternative if you have an excellent credit rating and have a good working relationship with a lending institution. Personal notes can be made for any amount, but they are usually taken out for a few thousand dollars. The payback period is varied to suit the requirements of both parties. Such notes are usually renewable on an open-end basis. Let's say you have a six-month, $4,000 note. You might pay off the interest and $1,000 in principal, and "roll over" the balance for another six months. Then you could continue this procedure every six months until the note is paid off. Interest rates on personal notes are generally comparatively favorable.

If you're part of a company or group that has a *credit union*, consider yourself lucky. Credit unions offer loans for home improvements at reasonable rates and with good terms. Amounts loaned are generally limited to $5,000 or $10,000, but if you don't need a great deal of money it may be a good idea to take advantage of this service.

Loans obtained through *finance companies* are generally of the high-interest, short-term variety. For this reason, you should exhaust all other possibilities before considering a finance company as a source of funds. Some of them have programs dealing specifically with home improvements—but don't look for any bargains here.

Approaching Lenders

Basically, the procedure for approaching prospective lenders is not complicated. You make an appointment, present your case, provide all information requested, and wait for a decision. If you have an established credit rating, it will be checked. If you don't, you'll probably run into difficulty and need to establish one. The lender will also want to know your current financial status, future prospects, potential earning capacity, and other relevant information. In some cases, you may have to provide additional collateral for your proposed loan, or you may have to find a person with a high credit rating to cosign the note for you. This person accepts full financial responsibility if you default. Sometimes lenders also require a full set of plans and specifications for your project that they must approve before giving you the loan. Each case is different, and there's no sure way of outlining exactly what will occur when you approach a lender. It does help to have a confident attitude. If a lender turns you down, don't be discouraged—just go to another one. The reason for rejection by one lender may not even enter the picture with another.

Borrowing Costs

Although points and closing costs—which we've discussed—account for some of the expense of borrowing, interest is the biggest expense. The interest that a lender charges on the unpaid balance of the principal can amount to a tremendous sum of money.

For example, let's choose an interest rate of 10 percent—an easy figure to work with—and assume you want to borrow $20,000 with a payback period of 10 years. Your payments would be $264.31 per month for 120 months. That comes to $31,717.20 to pay off the entire loan. So the cost of borrowing the $20,000 would be $11,717.20—a good sum of money. In other words, you have bought a $20,000 expansion project for your house at a cost of almost $32,000. In the case of a 20-year loan for $20,000, the figure jumps to over $46,000!

You should also realize that the principal—$20,000—of the loan is not paid off on a straight-line basis. When you reach the 10-year mark of a 20-year loan, you have not paid off half the principal; you've paid off just a bit over a quarter of it. When you begin making payments, the amount that goes toward the principal is very small and slowly rises over the years. The amount that goes toward interest payments is initially high and diminishes slowly.

This means that it's not often beneficial to pay off a loan in the early stages. Let's take the example of our $20,000, 10-year loan. The $11,717.20 total interest cost—your charge for use of the $20,000 for 10 years—is almost totally paid for after five years. If you pay off the total loan at that time, the total dollar amount you pay will be less, but you're essentially paying the lender almost $11,000 for only five years' use of the money! There may also be a penalty charge for paying the loan off early. Since you've basically already paid for the use of the money, it's often better to do just that—use it. Take the $15,858.60—the balance of the payments for the last five years—and invest it in some type of liquid, interest-yielding account. From this account, you can make your monthly payment on the loan, while receiving interest on the balance.

Inflation also effects the actual cost of a long-term loan. Just how much it will effect the cost of a particular loan isn't easy to figure out, but here's a very simple example of what happens.

Any calculation that attempts to project the effect of inflation on a long-term loan is based on the fact that each year the dollar has less buying power. It takes about two dollars now to buy the same amount of goods that one dollar could buy in 1967. Let's say you take out a 10-year loan for $10,000 today at a certain interest rate. One year later, let's surmise that inflation stands at nine percent. In this case, you have made the year's payments in dollars that have successively diminished in value over the months. The next year, the inflation rate is eight percent and the dollars you use to pay the loan are worth still less than those you borrowed two years ago. If inflation continues, the dollars you're using to pay the loan at the end of the 10-year period might have only half the buying power of those you borrowed. This is like paying back 50 cents on the dollar. Under these conditions, your "real" interest cost in terms of constant dollars could be only one or two percent. Since you're paying off the loan principal in increasingly cheaper dollars, you could conceivably end up "making money." This is a difficult concept to grasp, but it's worth investigating—perhaps with the aid of your banker or accountant.

Borrowed Fund Restrictions

Frequently, a loan contract will impose various restrictions on the borrower. This is less true of installment loans and personal notes for small sums, but for other types of commercial loans it is common. Primarily, these restrictions involve repayment schedules, paying bills attributable to the expansion project, methods of funds disposition, construction inspection, right of approval of construction techniques and materials, and similar items.

In many cases, the lender has the final say about all aspects of the project. The loan contract may also specify that the lender has the power to shut the job down completely at any time, to stop further funding, or to call the note in altogether.

Restrictions are sometimes difficult to avoid. You can always try to have them deleted before you sign the contract, but they are often non-negotiable. If they must remain, be wary of them and make certain that you can live up to the contractual obligations without difficulty.

Launching the Project

When you've drafted your final plans and secured financing, it's time to get the project rolling. This is your last chance to make changes. Final decisions must be made before the project gets underway to avoid delays, confusion, and extra expense.

Checking Your Plans

Review all project plans and sketches, specification sheets, material schedules, and takeoffs. Make sure they are correct and require no changes—not even minor ones. Examine cost estimates and update them if they are affected by recent price changes. Review all bids to make sure you're actually getting what you require for the stated price, and make adjustments where necessary. Double-check your financial arrangements, too. All parties must clearly understand the agreement, funds should be sufficient, and you must be sure you can comply with any restrictions.

Your Personal Plans

Determine what part you will play in the construction work. This could range from picking up the phone and telling the contractor to begin tomorrow, to doing the entire project yourself. Whatever your role, be certain you're properly prepared and that other workers understand all arrangements. Above all, you must be sure that you can handle your own part of the job effectively with respect to available time, skills, tools and equipment, and general knowledge and expertise.

Plans for Contracted Work

At this time, also contact anyone who will be helping you with the work—contractors, subcontractors, or casual laborers. Verify that they know what role they will play and which parts you will play. If you are going to be deeply involved in the project and hire casual labor, plan their part of the project now. Once the project begins, you should be able to direct the workmen to get the most value for their wages.

Scheduling

When the expansion job is small and you are the sole worker, scheduling may not be important at all: you just keep working whenever you can until the project is finished. Larger projects, however, will require at least a small amount of both time scheduling and work programming. For instance, you may want to create a schedule that lets you finish the job in a reasonable time without cutting into your social activities. Or maybe you'd like to do a large part of the work during your vacation days.

Work programming is a matter of establishing a flow pattern for various phases of the job, so tasks can be done sequentially and without interfering with one another. This is particularly important if you'll be using subcontractors or casual labor. You must arrange for workers to appear when needed so they can do their tasks efficiently. Few things are more exasperating than having a crew waiting because they lack materials or the job is not quite ready for them. And the workers don't like this kind of situation either. In particular, subcontractors' jobs should be worked into the time program carefully. They should be notified when they will be needed far in advance. Also, you should keep them informed about the progress of the project—especially if you find yourself ahead of, or behind, schedule.

General contractors will take care of their own day-to-day scheduling. But it's your responsibility to tell a contractor exactly when to begin, periods when you don't want workers around, and the completion date.

Few projects, especially large ones, run on schedule without problems. So make your schedule flexible to allow for problems like delayed material deliveries, bad weather, illness, or absent workers. When a schedule is too tight, it's inevitable that the finished project will be of lower quality than originally desired.

Dealing with a General Contractor

A general contractor—or a "general"—can be either an individual or a sizeable company. The general is responsible for every part of the job from start to finish. Most generals supply their own crew for all carpentry work, and hire subcontractors for utilities installation—and sometimes for insulating, drywalling, and roofing. They buy all materials and supplies, arrange for permits and inspections, schedule the workers, and take care of the final cleanup. A general contractor is the job supervisor and is responsible for virtually everything. But if you want satisfactory results, you have some responsibilities, too.

Selecting a General Contractor

Whether you have narrowed your choice of contractors by soliciting bids or simply by recommendations, you must do some checking before making a final decision. You must consider the contractor's reliability, honesty, experience, and financial responsibility. By checking with the contractor's customers, your bank, the local chamber of commerce or Better Business Bureau, and local building offices, you should get a good picture of each candidate. It's also a good idea to have a personal interview with each candidate. But be aware that a person's personality may not reflect his or her ability to do the job well. Also remember that the contractor who offers the lowest bid or estimate is not necessarily the best choice. What you're looking for is the lowest *qualified* bid.

The matter of the contractor's financial responsibility is especially important to consider. The laws of most states make it legally possible for a party to put a lien against your project for materials or wages owed by the contractor. Some contractors may be bonded, but if the bond amount is less than the contractor's debts, you may still end up footing the bill. There are procedures offered by states to protect you from such liens, so check with your state licensing agency.

Establishing Ground Rules

In most situations, a written contract is drawn up between the homeowner and the contractor. Included in the contract will be the basic contract information: work involved, payments, payment schedules, warranties, completion dates, adherence to plans and specifications, guarantees, final inspection checklist, disposition of change orders, and other specifics. These are binding agreements between both parties.

The general ground rules, however, may be either written or verbal, and may not be legally binding. Often they are verbal and cover a wide variety of instructions. For example, you have to instruct the contractor as to which trees and shrubs must be saved, where vehicles can be parked, and where bulk materials can be unloaded and stored. You may want the construction to cease on weekends, or not begin until a certain time in the morning. There may also be a period of time during which you will be away from home and you may want operations to stop for that period. If you plan to have any direct involvement in the work, or if you intend to assume any authority concerning the workers' daily activities, you should let the contractor know about it.

All these issues should be covered well in advance. Inevitably, some unforeseen points will pop up during the job, but the more potential problems you resolve ahead of time the better the job will go.

Checking the Contract

Although some contracts are short and simple, most are fairly long and complicated. A standard form may be used, but often the contract will be modified or specially written to specifically cover your particular project. Either party can write the contract—with the aid of a lawyer and architect. But regardless of the document's origin, never sign it until you are absolutely sure that it is correct and that you thoroughly understand and agree with every point.

Before you sign, discuss the contract with your lawyer, and if you have a friend in the contracting business, get his opinion, too. You might also want to discuss the contract with an architect or another person knowledgeable about building contracts, who is not involved in your project. If contractual points need to be negotiated—or argued—it is best done between you and your lawyer and the contractor and his legal counsel. And remember that if a moneylender is involved, he may also want to have his say.

Personal Inspections

No matter how competent your contractor is, you can't take it for granted that the job will be done correctly, according to your specifications. The contractor or supervisors can't be everywhere to catch mistakes or poor craftsmanship by workers. So to make sure you ultimately get what you paid for, personal inspections must be made as the work is in progress.

You may feel knowledgeable enough to perform these inspections yourself, but in most cases, it's much better to seek the services of a reputable architect. If an architect drew up the original plans, he is the obvious choice because of his complete understanding of the project. Otherwise, any good architect who has the time can perform inspections for you. This is frequently done on an hourly rate basis.

If you plan to make the inspections yourself, make sure you don't get in the way on the job site. The proper way to oversee a construction project is with your eyes open and your mouth mostly closed. Make your inspections before or after working hours. Look everything over carefully and note the progress made since your last inspection. If there's anything you don't like, don't understand, or have a question about, jot it down in a notebook. When an opportune moment arises, discuss your notes with the person in charge on the work site—never with a worker. And unless you wish to complain about the foreman, supervisor, or other person in charge on the site, don't call the general contractor's office. You won't get much satisfaction dealing with people from the office because they aren't aware of the day-to-day details of the job. And by going over the foreman's or supervisor's head, you may inadvertently get the person into unnecessary trouble.

Above all, never make a nuisance of yourself on the job site. Workers don't like having homeowners peer over their shoulders while they work. It ruins their concentration and can result in low morale and faltering production. Beyond a wave and a cheerful "good morning!" it's a good idea not to talk to workers at all while they're on the job. Save comments or questions for lunch breaks or after hours. Never engage the workers in idle conversation, or ask that they make a change or assist you with something that's not their job. After all, the general contractor is paying the workmen to do a job under his direction and time schedule. Your interference is nothing more than meddling. Not only can this practice cause dissension and slow production, but it can also give a contractor a legitimate claim for extra expenses incurred by virtue of lost time and other problems.

Your interference can also destroy the working relationship between you and the contractor. And there are many ways that a contractor can retaliate against an obstructive and uncooperative homeowner. The contractor holds most of the cards, so be nice and helpful.

Your own safety is another reason to make yourself scarce at the job site when work is in progress. It's easy to get injured while wandering around the job site. Falling through a hole in the floor isn't going to help your image as a reasonable person; nor is it going to enhance your rapport with the contractor.

Things to Check. You should concern yourself with the materials, craftsmanship, and adherence to the plans and time schedule. Check the materials being installed and those stockpiled for future use, against your original specifications. If you discover substitutions, inferior materials, or those not specified, find out the reason for the discrepancy.

Inspect the construction work to make sure the materials are being put together and installed properly. This does take some knowledge of construction techniques, but poor workmanship and mistakes are usually obvious. For example, if a stud is held in place by only one nail, you can assume that the installation is incorrect. Check for tight and true fits between structural members; for neat, clean joints; and for proper application of sheathing, finish covering, trim, and similar items. Also review the plans and time schedule and check that the job is being done as planned—and on time.

Incidentally, as you make your inspections, never disturb anything on the job site, and don't do any cleaning up. Inevitably, the chunk of "scrap wood" that you throw away will turn out to be the piece that a worker set aside for the next day's work. But do insist that the workers keep their work areas neat, clean, and orderly.

The Punch List. Whether you or someone else makes inspections during the course of the job, you should take responsibility for one or more final inspection when the job is completed. This is known as making up the punch list. Although the contractor will make a list of his own and take care of the items listed, he should look to you for the final punch list. The contractor's job is not officially complete until he deals with the items on your list to your satisfaction.

To compile the punch list, carefully inspect the job and note any items that you feel are not up to par and that must be corrected. The problems you find may be simple to resolve, such as a sloppy bit of painting or a missing piece of trim. But they can also include major defects, such as a malfunctioning light switch or a cabinet placed in a wrong location. It is best to make your dissatisfactions known at the earliest possible moment, in fairness to the contractor.

The contractor is usually obliged to make all corrections at his expense, but sometimes disputes make compromises necessary. According to the contract you signed, you are entitled to have all the items on the punch list corrected to your satisfaction—if they appear to be the contractor's fault. But often no one can be clearly blamed for the problem, so be fair and keep an open mind.

Acting as Your Own General Contractor

It is possible for you to save money by assuming the role of a general contractor yourself. But this is a very complicated, time-consuming task that takes plenty of expertise in construction techniques, and the management of money and personnel.

To begin with, you may have to obtain worker's compensation insurance; register as an employer; acquire all permits; pay necessary fees and make inspection arrangements; undertake land surveys, engineering specs and any other requirements. It's also your responsibility to establish a time-flow schedule for the whole project, to purchase all or nearly all materials and supplies, and coordinate their delivery so they arrive when needed.

Insurance

The standard homeowner's insurance policy does not cover on-the-job injury to your employees. You need to obtain a special worker's compensation policy to cover your liability connected with worker's injuries on the job site. This is a comprehensive policy that generally pays all costs resulting from an injury—from hospital bills to lost wages and even burial expenses. And in the majority of states, the policy also protects you from lawsuits claiming negligence on your part. Worker's compensation insurance is available from insurance companies and brokers, and sometimes from a state fund. You can take out the policy for any period of time you wish and extend it while the work is in progress if you're running behind schedule.

You pay for the policy before any work is done. The premium cost is calculated on the basis of work hours necessary to complete the project, the pay scales of the workers, and the degree of risk involved in the jobs. After the project is finished, you may end up paying additional insurance money if you find that your payroll amounted to more than you anticipated. On the other hand, you could also get a refund if the payroll was less than you estimated.

Make sure that any subcontractors involved in your project have worker's compensation insurance on their employees. Another insurance you should definitely consider—whether or not you are the contractor—is "Builder's Risk" insurance. This protects you as an owner against loss or suit for accidents on the job—whether or not they are work related. Talk with your insurance agent about "Builder's Risk" before the work begins.

Employer Registration

If your project calls for hiring people directly and for paying them above the state minimum, you must also register as an employer with the federal and state governments. In this case you also have the responsibility to withhold taxes, remit them to the governments, pay insurance covering disability, and pay social security.

Hiring Labor

You are in charge of hiring all skilled tradesmen, either individually or through subcontractors, and all casual laborers. Every phase of the job can involve specialized help—from framing to insulation, finish carpentry, roofing and painting. There's a specialty contractor for every aspect of the building construction field. Of course, where specialists are not available, particularly in smaller communities, you must hire men who are skilled in several areas.

Working with subcontractors is usually done by bid and contract, although both are sometimes eliminated. A contract is sometimes used in hiring individual skilled tradesmen, but often it is worked out on an hourly, weekly, or per job basis at a certain rate. Hiring and firing is verbal. Finding satisfactory casual labor is simply a matter of seeking out conscientious workers who can follow directions and work with a minimum of supervision. In the case of large-scale projects, you may have to hire some unskilled workers, too, to act as laborers.

Coordinating and Expediting

When acting as your own general contractor, your biggest job will be to keep the work running smoothly. This requires two skills—coordinating and expediting. The first, coordinating, consumes the greatest amount of time and effort. It involves scheduling the project so that the tradesmen, materials, and supplies appear at the right time at different phases of the job.

To accomplish this, you need to make a work-flow chart and a materials-flow chart. The work-flow chart shows the sequential phases of the project, broken down into specific operations. When the work-flow chart is complete, you can devise a materials-flow chart that shows the materials and supplies needed at each stage. You can also make up a third chart that shows the type and number of workers needed at each phase. The charts can then be translated into a timetable. In most cases, continual revision of the charts will be necessary to account for minor delays or speed-ups in the job. You should allow some extra time in the beginning, but even this can be insufficient.

The second skill, expediting, is a matter of being the job's overseer and ramrod. You must make sure everything is on schedule according to established flow charts, and speed up progress if necessary. This also means keeping a close watch on all aspects of the job, anticipating delays, forestalling difficulties, and generally keeping everything on an even keel.

Avoiding Problems

Throughout the course of the project, you should watch for small problems that could snowball into big disasters—like liens, work stoppage, and lawsuits. Always be alert for the following red-flag indicators of impending trouble.

Changes. Substantial changes should be viewed as warning signals. These include changes in materials, workers, payment schedules, and contract agreements. Whenever a change is suggested or requested, carefully examine the reasons and consequences. Making a change is a problem in itself, and could lead to further difficulties. Of course, some changes can be beneficial.

Low Morale. Strife between individual workers or low morale in general can spell trouble for everyone. Whatever the cause for the discord, deal with it immediately. If the workers themselves are the problem, get rid of them. If the cause lies in job conditions, pay scales, or something of that nature, resolve the difficulty quickly and satisfactorily. Productivity will suffer and more problems will arise if you don't.

Job-Site Safety. Be on the lookout for safety hazards and eliminate them immediately if they appear. Do everything you can to assure the safety of the workers. By making it clear that you're concerned for their safety, you'll develop good rapport with the workers and help keep morale high.

Fiscal Difficulties. Failure to keep money matters straight can easily result in liens or lawsuits. Keep close track of financial records, abide by agreed-upon payment schedules, and pay all bills promptly. If you are unsure of your abilities in this area, hire a part-time accountant or bookkeeper-secretary to handle the business details for you. But remember—the ultimate responsibility is yours.

Disputes. Look out for disputes between subcontractors and between you and those people you hire. Even if you're not directly involved, you might find yourself in the middle of a lawsuit—just because of your connection with the job. Try to quell arguments quickly and arbitrate as necessary.

Delays. Delays, whatever the cause, result in more delays, disrupt schedules, and create all-around havoc. Many can be avoided by simply staying on top of the job. Even unforeseen delays can be shortened by fast action on your part. Always be aware of them and don't let them get out of hand.

Do-It-Yourself Building

If you're skilled and ambitious, you may want to do as much of the expansion work as possible by yourself. Some people may be able to tackle the entire project from start to finish. But most hire specialists for those parts of the job requiring special skills and equipment. It may boost your ego to say you did it all yourself. However, remember that some tasks, like electrical work, can be extremely dangerous, and that some jobs can actually be done more economically by hiring a tradesman. If other workers will be involved in the project, be sure to review the material previously discussed about outside labor. Much of it is applicable and important. In any case, whether you do the work solo or with help, here are a few matters that you must attend to before the job can get underway.

Site Preparation

In general, site preparation involves getting rid of anything at the work site that will hinder the job. For an interior remodeling job, this includes taking up carpeting, removing furniture and other items in the room. This, incidentally, is always the homeowner's responsibility—even if a general contractor is to do the remodeling.

Tools and Equipment

Before the project begins, all tools and equipment that will be needed—except rental tools—must be on hand and in good condition. If you already have a good selection of tools and know how to use them, this part of the job is easy. But the neophyte do-it-yourselfer will have to determine what will be needed, buy it, and learn how to use the items before attempting any work.

An average-size home workshop usually contains all the basic tools needed for an expansion project. You need a wide selection of carpentry tools: saws, hammers, measuring and leveling devices, drills and bits, squares, and screwdrivers. Finish work calls for a miter box and saw, nail sets, planes, wood chisels, and such. Power tools make the job much easier, and for most projects, you should at least have a portable circular saw and an electric drill. Additional items like a saber saw, table or radial arm saw, pad sander, power planer, and perhaps a router can be helpful, too. Depending upon the nature of the job, you might also need a pick and shovel, sledge, screw-jacks, wheelbarrow, and crowbar.

Besides the general tools, more specialized items may be necessary if you plan to do electrical work, ducting, roofing, and other tasks yourself. In any case, check to see that you have everything you think will be needed, and establish a cash reserve for purchasing or renting additional items.

Laying In Materials

Obviously, a certain amount of material must be laid in before you can start the project. But you must decide whether you want to buy all the materials before you begin, or whether you wish to have the materials arrive as needed. Both methods have advantages and disadvantages.

Provided you have a clean, safe, and dry storage area, you may want to buy everything in advance. With such a major delivery, you may save money, and you may save time spent visiting suppliers and waiting for materials to arrive. And you reduce the risk of a supplier running out of something just when you need it. This procedure also lets you view all the materials as a whole, and plan to make any minor adjustments due to irregularities in type or size. In particular, it's always wise to have all trim, specialty, and finish hardware items on hand. Then you can alter the construction specifics to suit them, rather than visa versa.

Stockpiling large quantities of materials, however, is not always the best course to follow. This is especially true if suitable storage facilities are not available, or if vandalism or pilferage is a problem. If your supplier maintains large stocks of materials, it may be best to buy only what you need for each few days' work, and let him take care of the storage problem. Also, buying materials only as you need them is a good idea when the project will be done bit by bit over a long period of time. In this case, there's little point in tying up large sums of money that could be earning interest, and cluttering up your grounds with huge stacks of materials.

The Foundation

Construction of an addition begins with the foundation. This portion of the structure must be designed and built to match the addition's design and specifications exactly. It serves to keep the structure off the ground and distributes the weight of the structure over the ground to prevent settling. And, in many cases, the foundation also encloses additional living or storage space.

Foundation Construction

You can choose from several types of foundations, and the type you select doesn't necessarily have to match the existing foundation. Since they're all about equal in their ability to support the structure, your final decision should be based on the building design and construction, job site details, costs, ease of construction, and similar factors.

Slab-on-Grade Foundation

A slab-on-grade foundation is simply a flat pad of poured concrete, supported at the edges by concrete grade beams and over the remaining portion by undisturbed soil. Most codes require positioning the slab so that there is six inches from the top of the concrete to the grade. The slab serves as both foundation and first floor, and is the type of foundation usually used for garages, small outbuildings, and ground-level additions where no basement or crawl space is desired.

There are three common approaches to constructing this type of foundation. The first method is generally only used for detached buildings, due to code restrictions. It consists of making a monolithic concrete pour. The footings, shallow sidewalls, and slab are formed up as a unit, reinforced and poured all at once. You begin the job by digging the footing trenches carefully—often by hand—into undisturbed native soil. The area beneath the slab must be smooth, free of all vegetation and topsoil, and covered with a layer of compacted gravel or sand. It's very important that you never pour concrete on black dirt. Side forms must be constructed around the outer edges of the excavation to contain the concrete. Lower portions of the footings can be poured directly into undisturbed soil trenches.

If the climate warrants, rigid insulation is installed around the below-ground perimeter of the slab to full depth. A vapor barrier goes under the slab on the gravel or sand. The bottom of the footing should rest

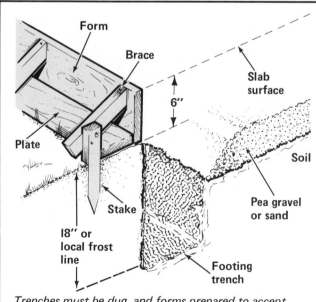

Trenches must be dug, and forms prepared to accept the monolithic concrete pour. This foundation method is used generally for detached buildings.

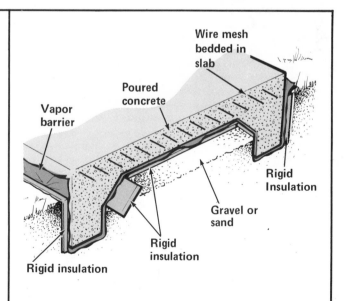

Rigid insulation, vapor barriers, wire mesh, and steel reinforcing rods are appropriately placed. Then the ready-mix concrete is poured.

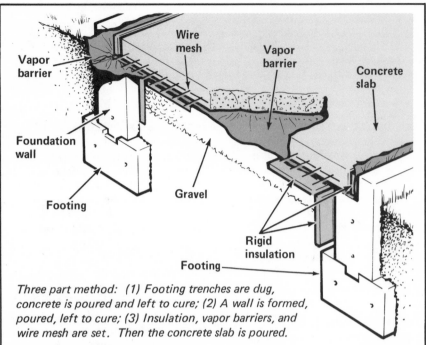

Three part method: (1) Footing trenches are dug, concrete is poured and left to cure; (2) A wall is formed, poured, left to cure; (3) Insulation, vapor barriers, and wire mesh are set. Then the concrete slab is poured.

approximately 18 inches below grade, or at or below the local frost line; the top of the slab should extend at least six inches above finished grade level. Steel reinforcing bars are often placed in the footings. On each side, one bar is placed about two inches from the bottom, and one is placed about two inches from the top. Local codes may require different arrangements. Reinforcing mesh is bedded within the slab itself. The entire foundation is poured of ready-mixed concrete, leveled with a screed and darby, finished and cured.

Another method is to construct the foundation in three parts. First, you dig footing trenches, form up the footings,

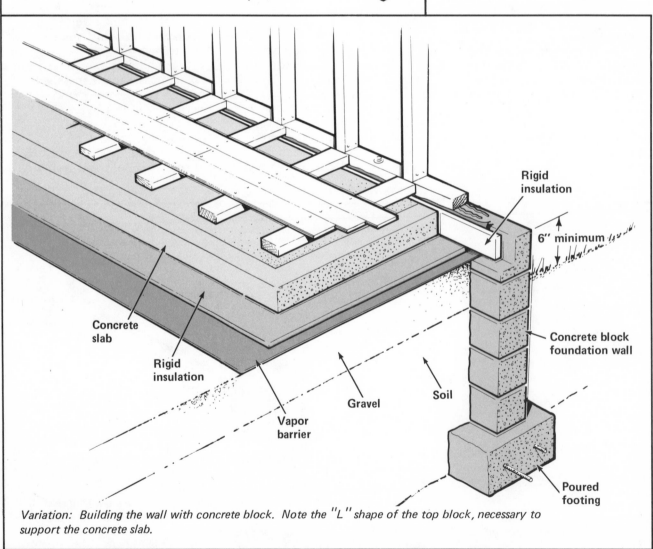

Variation: Building the wall with concrete block. Note the "L" shape of the top block, necessary to support the concrete slab.

and pour them. After the footings have cured, a shallow wall is formed, poured, cured, and stripped of forms. Backfill is set around the wall/footing combination, the slab area is smoothed off, and a cushion of gravel or sand emplaced and compacted under the slab. This is followed by a vapor barrier. Then you pour the slab and finish it level with the top of the foundation wall.

A variation on this theme is to pour the footings, but to build the shallow wall with concrete block. The top course of block is specially formed to receive the concrete pad or slab, which is poured atop a vapor barrier. In both three-part methods, an expansion joint is needed to separate the slab from the foundation wall; it is unnecessary with the monolithic slab method.

If the foundation will serve as a floor, you have to cure and finish it very carefully. After the surface is smoothed by floating or steel troweling, you can either leave it as is or apply a finish floor covering, either directly or with an underlayment interface. If you plan to install a built-up wood-frame floor, the concrete need not be as well-finished.

Before pouring any slab-on-grade foundation, be sure to carefully position all elements of the utility systems. Electrical conduit, water and waste pipes, ductwork, and such have to be set exactly in place first. Secure them in position and make sure they stay in place during the pouring and finishing processes. Moving them or making corrections is difficult later.

Perimeter Foundation

A perimeter foundation encompasses the outside edge of a structure to form an unbroken wall—except for vents or access hatches. The wall of modern versions is usually made of concrete blocks or poured concrete. It is based on a suitable concrete footing, set

about 36 inches below finished exterior grade level or down to local frost line depth, and extends at least 6 inches above exterior finished grade level. Crawl space depth can vary from three to five feet. In many cases, a series of piers or columns are located at strategic points within the crawl space to help support the structure's load.

Construction of a perimeter foundation begins with the footing. Normally, this footing is twice as wide as it is thick. The width of the wall will be determined by the thickness of the footing. The footing is made of poured concrete, and reinforcement is not necessary unless the soil is disturbed or soft. Residential block or poured

concrete basement walls should be at least 10 inches thick. Crawl-space walls can be 8 inches thick, or 10 inches thick if a brick ledge is necessary for a brick veneer.

The concrete footing can be poured into forms that are scratch-built or assembled from form sections made for the purpose. Sometimes the concrete is poured into carefully shaped trenches cut into the native soil, but this is not recommended in some areas, and may be prohibited by local codes. In the case of poured concrete foundation walls, a keyway should be recessed into the footing top. This is done by impressing lengths of 2 x 4's into the fresh concrete just after

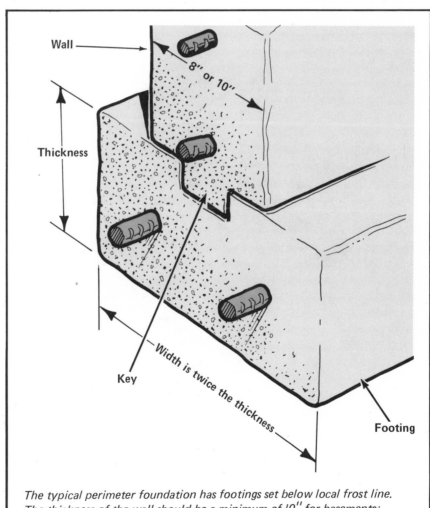

The typical perimeter foundation has footings set below local frost line. The thickness of the wall should be a minimum of 10" for basements; 8" or 10" for crawl spaces.

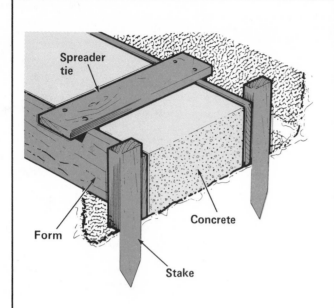

Footings: Concrete should be poured into forms that outline the width of the footing.

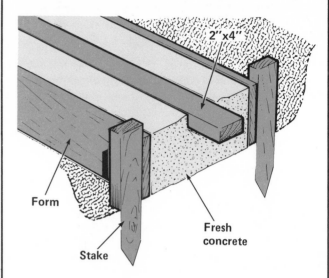

Making a keyway: A 2"x4" is pressed into fresh concrete footing, and removed just before concrete hardens.

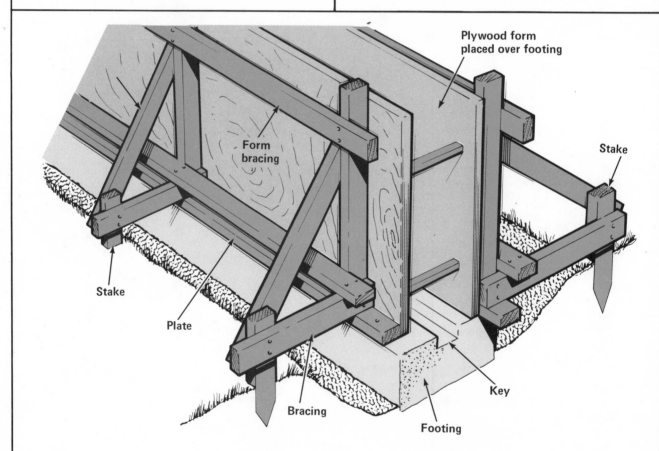

Forms are built to the height of the foundation wall. Concrete is poured from trucks. Concrete should be thoroughly cured before forms are removed.

pouring, and removing them just before the concrete sets up hard. Keep the footing moist for three or four days and protect it from the hot sun to cure properly. If forms are used, they're usually stripped away after the concrete has cured.

The next step is to either set up forms for pouring the concrete foundation wall, or to begin laying concrete block. For poured concrete, forms are built to the proper height, braced and supported, and ready-mixed concrete is poured from trucks. Anchor bolts to secure the sill plate are embedded in the fresh concrete every four feet. Most codes require ½-inch diameter bolts that are 10 inches long. Again, for about five days, keep the concrete moist and protected as you did the footing. You can damage the concrete if you strip the forms away before the concrete is sufficiently cured. So, don't begin bolting down sill plates and subsequent construction too early.

You can begin building a concrete block wall on the footing after the footing has cured for a few days. This construction involves mortaring the masonary units in place in a determined number of courses to bring the wall up to the proper level. For the last course, you can use cap blocks, or merely fill in the cores of the standard stretcher blocks with mortar to form a solid top surface. Anchor bolts to hold the sill plate are installed as the job goes along. Rough openings for ventilation louvers or access hatches are also blocked in. A concrete block wall should be left to cure for several days before construction continues.

If the building or addition is small, the perimeter foundation can be sufficient to bear the structure's entire weight. However, the structure's size and floor frame design may make it necessary to place additional supports at strategic points inside the foundation

walls. Unsupported girders, stretching from wall to wall, can bear the total load. But when further support is needed to transfer the load of the building to the ground, additional piers or columns, each with its own footing, can be built as needed.

Full-Basement Foundation

The full-basement foundation is a perimeter type, and it's constructed in essentially the same way as a foundation for a crawl space. Construction begins by pouring the footing around the perimeter, plus any small footings needed for interior supports for the floor frame. Then a concrete wall is poured or a concrete block wall built. There is, however, an additional consideration in full-height walls. You must take into account the

amount of lateral strain imposed on them as fill dirt pushes in. The walls have to be thick enough and sufficiently reinforced, if needed, to withstand these pressures and the downward thrust of the structure. Most codes specify minimum wall thicknesses and reinforcing, if required. The concrete floor is poured as the final step in completing the basement, and it does much to restrain the bottoms of the foundation wall from creeping inward.

Pier Foundation

A fairly common method of construction, the pier foundation can be used for small buildings as well as full-sized residences. It calls for setting a series of piers around the perimeter of the structure and at precalculated

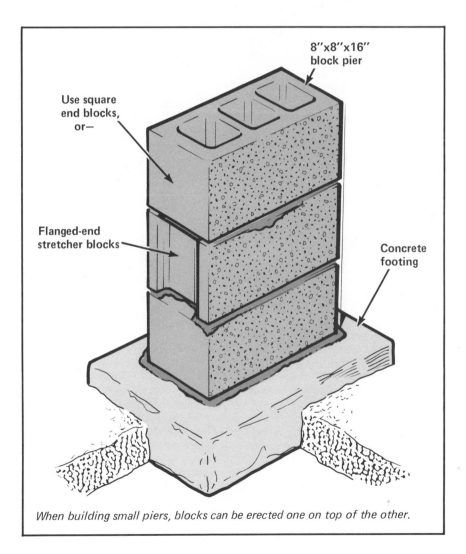

8"x8"x16" block pier

Use square end blocks, or—

Flanged-end stretcher blocks

Concrete footing

When building small piers, blocks can be erected one on top of the other.

midpoints to support the structure's load. Excavation is held to a minimum, and the piers can be adjusted easily to the topography. The foundation can be left entirely open, or you can build a compatible skirting from a light framework and finishing materials. Whether the piers are built of poured concrete or concrete blocks, they give you advantages of low cost and easy workability.

The process begins by determining the exact pier locations and digging a series of holes of suitable diameter and depth. Then footings are poured directly into the bottoms of the holes. Reinforcing bars are often set into the footings, or pads.

When the concrete has cured, special tubular cardboard forms can be set in place atop the footings to frame the pier. The forms are then filled with concrete; reinforcing rods or mesh are added if necessary. Anchor bolts are embedded after the forms have been topped up with concrete, and the piers are left to cure for at least a week before the construction continues. The cardboard forms are easily stripped away to just below grade level—the remainder will rot away.

For concrete block piers, construction begins with a poured concrete footing, or pad, of the appropriate size. Small piers are built by stacking

standard half or full blocks and mortaring them together. For larger piers, pier or stretcher blocks are stacked in pairs, with each pair set at right angles to the previous pair. For additional strength, one or more hollow block core series can be filled with mortar or concrete, and a No. 4 reinforcing rod bedded in each filled core. Once the piers have cured thoroughly, they can be backfilled, and construction of the floor can begin.

All-Weather Wood Foundation

The All-Weather Wood Foundation (AWWF) system has proven effective for a good many years. It's an excellent alternative to building a conventional foundation, especially where ready-mixed concrete is unavailable. This is a particularly good system for the do-it-yourselfer, because the foundation is made entirely of wood and is put together much like a standard wood frame stud wall. Ballast gravel is used instead of concrete footings. If a floor is required, as in a full basement, it can be made of poured concrete or specially treated wood components, using a certain set of techniques. The entire foundation can also be assembled in sections in a garage or workshop and assembled at the work site in a matter of hours.

All dimension stock and sheathing panels used in the AWWF foundation are pressure-treated with special preservative. Typically, a wall is made of 2 x 6-inch studs placed on 12- or 16-inch centers between a sole plate and top plate. A layer of plywood covers the outside of the framework, and the thickness of this sheathing depends upon stud spacing, wall height and lateral pressures expected. If necessary, stud spaces are filled with thermal insulation. You can cover the interior side of the wall frame with plywood or any other type of wall material.

Exterior faces of the plywood

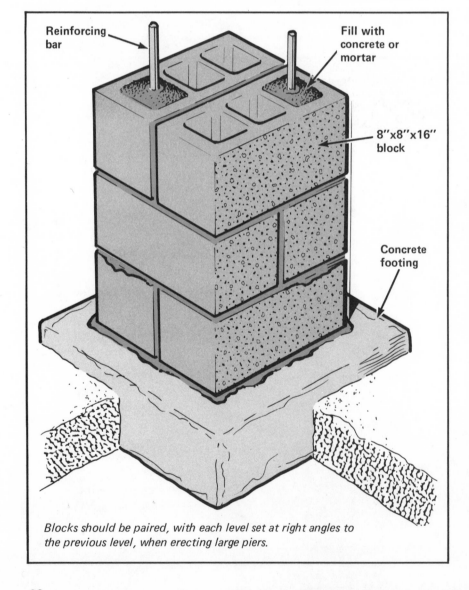

Reinforcing bar

Fill with concrete or mortar

8"x8"x16" block

Concrete footing

Blocks should be paired, with each level set at right angles to the previous level, when erecting large piers.

sheathing and interior portions below grade level are covered with polyethylene film glued with a special waterproofing compound. The foundation wall rests on a treated footing plate, which is usually a 2 x 12. This plate, in turn, rests on a carefully compacted and leveled layer of ballast gravel, placed below the frost line and on undisturbed native soil.

Although the system isn't widely known and isn't recognized by many building codes, it does have federal approval and has been accepted by many major code agencies. Ask your lumberyard or building supplies dealer about the system. If he is unfamiliar with it, you can get further information from the American Plywood Association, P.O. Box 11700, Tacoma, WA 98411.

Foundation Layout

Laying out the foundation on paper is the first and most important part of building the foundation. You must arrange, design, and dimension the foundation so it will suit the supported structure exactly and, if necessary, properly join an existing foundation. It's important to remember that one error during this phase will reap big trouble later on. You must plan carefully.

Once you have lined up all the technical details, you have to translate them into an on-site layout in preparation for excavation. The following are a couple of ways to do this.

The batter-board system is the most common method and is used primarily for rectilinear designs. You can set up batter-boards to accommodate all sorts of shapes and angles for both additions and freestanding buildings. They are arranged so that the actual foundation lines lie well within their positions—generally three feet. As the excavation proceeds, they stay in place, and the excavation outlines and true foundation outlines are determined by the use of reference taut lines correctly positioned across the batter boards. More guidelines are transferred from the taut lines to the bottom of the excavation. These serve as accurate locators for the foundation itself. Or, the taut lines can serve as reference lines for spotting posthole locations at ground level, and as reference lines in aligning the posts as they are set.

You can also line out a

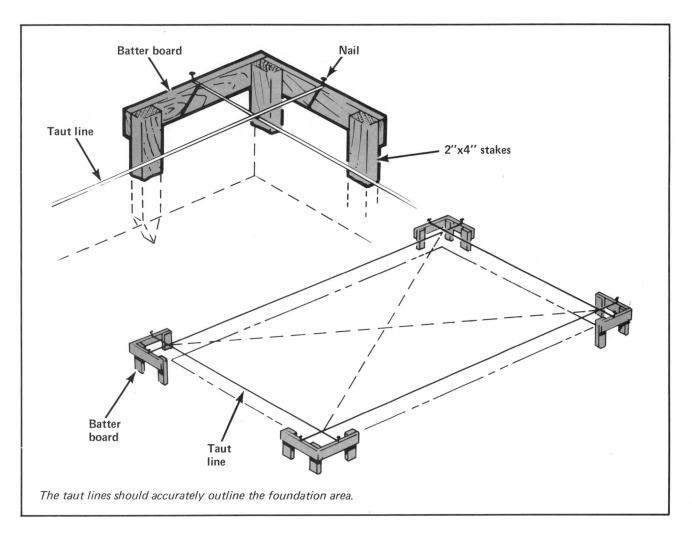

The taut lines should accurately outline the foundation area.

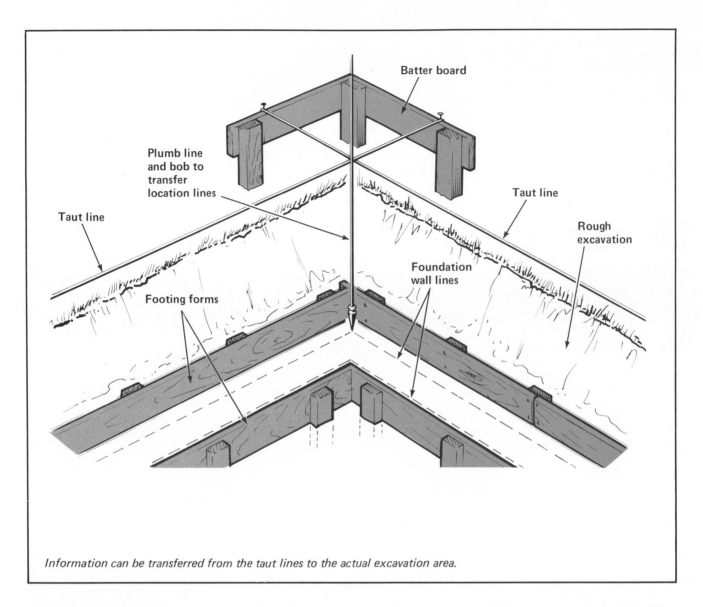

Batter board

Plumb line
and bob to
transfer
location lines

Taut line

Taut line

Rough
excavation

Footing forms

Foundation
wall lines

Information can be transferred from the taut lines to the actual excavation area.

foundation with stakes and string. First you set up a rough outline and slowly resolve it until the outline is perfectly accurate. Then the strings can serve as guidelines for excavating footing trenches, digging pier holes, or whatever needs to be done. The biggest difficulty is in making sure that all angles are accurate, all elevations are measured correctly, all lines are straight and true, and that the foundation top will be level and accurately dimensioned when finished. This means constant checking and cross-checking, preferably with a transit, but otherwise with levels and tape measure.

Foundation Excavations

Since building foundations are almost always buried in the earth to some degree, some sort of excavation must be made to accommodate them. In most cases, digging for foundations should be done by an excavating contractor who has the expertise and power equipment required for the job. Depending on the circumstances, it may be accomplished with a backhoe, crawler tractor, front-end loader, or some similar machine. Soil might be disposed of on the premises by filling or recontouring, or it can be dumped off site. The relatively small foundation holes needed

for posts, poles, or pilings can also be done by machine. There are several sizes of power posthole diggers. Small, portable one- and two-man power augers work nicely for shallow and small-diameter holes in easily workable soil. Deeper, large-diameter holes, especially in tight or rocky soils, are most easily dug with a heavy-duty auger mounted on a tractor, or a special truck-mounted unit.

Sometimes you can dig foundation holes by hand. This is true in the case of small slab foundations and when only small holes for posts are required. You can tackle the excavation for a slab foundation with a shovel, and a posthole shovel and posthole bar will take care of small holes needed for pier foundations. Even larger projects can be accomplished with pick and shovel, especially if you have some help to speed the job along.

Often, it's less trouble to do the work manually than to use heavy machinery, which needs sufficient access and must be scheduled in advance. And manual excavation costs less and creates less damage to the surrounding area.

Foundation Sizing

Obviously, you must be sure that the dimensions of the foundation match the structure that will rest on it. But how do you know that the foundation will be strong enough to support the building and withstand lateral pressures from surrounding earth fill? And how do you determine if the foundation is large enough to distribute the weight of the structure sufficiently to prevent movement?

The easiest way to determine the adequacy of your foundation design is to employ a licensed architect or engineer. And this is always the best course to follow in the case of exceptionally heavy additions, those of extraordinary design, or when unusual soil conditions are present. Also, professional help is advised when a foundation is built with posts, piers, or pilings. These professionals can prepare a complete set of calculations and plans that show what is best. Another way is to match the dimensions and materials of the new foundation to those of the existing one. If your house rests on a continuous-wall foundation of eight-inch-thick poured concrete on a 8 x 16-inch footing, you can assume that the same type of foundation will be adequate for a proposed small addition. Or you can consult with neighbors, local builders, and supply houses to find out what types of foundations have

been used successfully in your area. If your neighbor's two-car garage has stood atop a five-inch-thick monolithic slab-on-grade foundation for 10 years without problems, yours probably will too. However, before you make any final decisions, be sure to check with your local building department for its requirements.

Foundation Dampproofing

Codes may require continuous-wall foundations to be dampproofed, even if the construction area is relatively dry. The dampproofing is applied on the exterior of the foundation wall, from a point slightly above finished grade level down to the footing tops and across the top of the exterior of the footing.

There are several methods of dampproofing a foundation wall. One is to spray the entire exterior wall surface with two or more coats of hot liquid tar. This requires the services of a contractor with special equipment and expertise. If you want to do the dampproofing yourself, there is another method that's nearly as effective. You can merely apply one or two coats of cold liquid foundation dampproofing compound with a brush or roller. Block or brick foundations must be parged. This method of dampproofing is often used on masonry foundations, and involves coating the entire foundation wall with a thick layer of mortar, often applied in two separate coats like stucco or plaster. The two coatings also cover the footing top, and undergo separate curing stages. The final coat, which is steel-trowled to a high density, makes an excellent dampproofer.

Foundation Vapor Control

In addition to waterproofing the foundation wall, material should be installed to ensure adequate vapor control. For full-basement foundations, you can simply lay a vapor barrier over the entire floor area before the concrete is

poured. Frequently, this is deemed unnecessary, but when a vapor barrier is used it can be made of four- or six-mil polyethylene sheeting or a layer of 55-pound roofing material. Alternative methods are to apply three layers of 15-pound roofing felt with hot asphalt mopped on between each layer, or a layer of specially made asphalt-laminated vapor-barrier material. The same arrangements apply to slab-on-grade foundations.

Crawl spaces create a different situation. If the foundation is open, ventilation is more than adequate and nothing needs to be done. Although, the entire bottom of the building must be insulated. If the foundation is of the skirted pier or post variety, arrangements should be made to include ventilation louvers in the skirting to provide plenty of fresh-air flow.

There are two ways to handle fully enclosed, continuous-wall foundations. One is to install ventilation louvers in the wall which provide one square foot of venting area for every 150 square feet of crawl-space area. Alternately, the entire crawl space can be covered with a layer of sand or gravel about two inches deep. A vapor barrier of polyethylene film, strips of roofing felt, or similar material is then spread over the entire area and curled up the foundation walls, where it is pasted down with liquid tar. The barrier is then covered with another couple of inches of sand for mechanical protection.

Vents may not be required with this system if sufficient venting to the crawl space is obtained via interior basement area. If vents are necessary you only need one square foot of venting area for every 1,500 feet of crawl space area. In all cases, at least two vents should be installed, with the vents positioned so there is adequate cross-ventilation. They should also be covered with screens to keep small animals out.

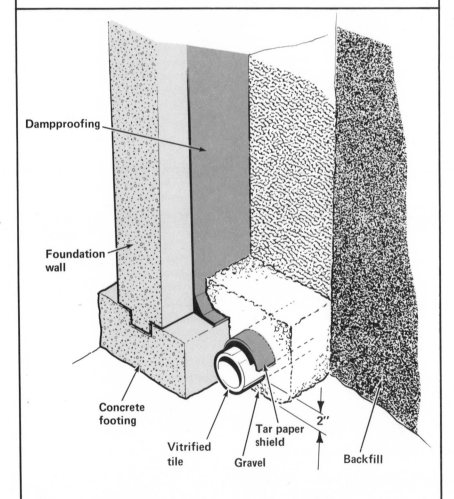

Foundation wall

Barrier lapped up and sealed.

2″ sand layer

Concrete footing

Vapor barrier

Dirt floor

When placing vapor barrier under crawl space, the ends should lap up on the sides, and be pasted down with a mastic asphalt compound.

Dampproofing

Foundation wall

Concrete footing

Vitrified tile

Tar paper shield

Gravel

2″

Backfill

Drains are often required by code, and should be installed next to footings early in the foundation process.

Foundation Drains

Foundation or footing drains are often required by code. And the installation is neither difficult nor expensive. The job begins with a layer of ¾-inch gravel about two inches thick and at least a foot wide, spread all along the outside of the footing. A run of clay drain tile or perforated plastic drainpipe is set on the gravel about two or three inches out from the side of the footing. More gravel is added to bury the drainpipe, and is banked up against the foundation wall to a depth of at least two inches over the footing top. At some convenient point, the drainpipes are extended beyond the foundation walls and into a sump pit, drywell, storm sewer, or other disposal system.

Foundation Insulation

In cold climates, foundation walls that enclose heated living spaces must be insulated. The type of insulation used is called rigid insulation and it is applied in sheets. With slab-on-grade foundations, the insulation is placed around the perimeter of the foundation where the slab meets the footings or foundation walls on the interior of the foundation. This insulation should extend down a minimum of 18 inches.

Continuous-wall foundations are often insulated on the interior by securing insulation directly to the masonry. They may also be insulated on the exterior by positioning the sheets before backfilling. The interior surfaces of unvented crawl-space walls are sometimes insulated, too. Either rigid or fibrous blanket insulation can be used. There is also a relatively new system that uses special concrete forms made of plastic insulating materials. The forms are locked together in whatever foundation configuration is required. Then the forms are poured full of concrete, and the whole affair is left to stand as is.

Joining Foundations

Sometimes when an addition is made to a house, only the structure sections are joined together, and the foundations remain separate. This is usually the case when the two foundations are dissimilar. For example, the foundations wouldn't be joined if one was a pier type and the other a crawl-space construction. But often the foundations must be linked together. This is common when both are made of either poured concrete or concrete block, or when one is concrete block and the other is poured concrete.

When new and old foundation walls are of unequal height, one of them could settle from lack of support, causing cracking and loss of structural integrity. In this case, some special steps must be taken. If the new wall extends to a shallower depth than the old, the ends that join the old wall rest on fill earth. And, unless the building is a good many years old, this earth will not have fully compacted. You, therefore, must build or pour extra-deep footings, based on undisturbed native soil through the extent of the filled area. The remaining footings can be placed below the frost line, and the new foundation built from there.

Often, the old wall is shallower than the new one, as when a full-basement addition is made to an existing crawl-space building. Under these circumstances, additional support must often be given to that portion of the crawl-space foundation from which the supporting earth fill is removed to make way for the new, full-foundation addition. This may require pouring or building a new foundation wall, full-height, directly alongside and joined to the existing wall.

You can join masonry to masonry in a number of ways. Tie strips can be used to anchor concrete blocks to a poured concrete wall. You secure the tie strips to the poured wall and

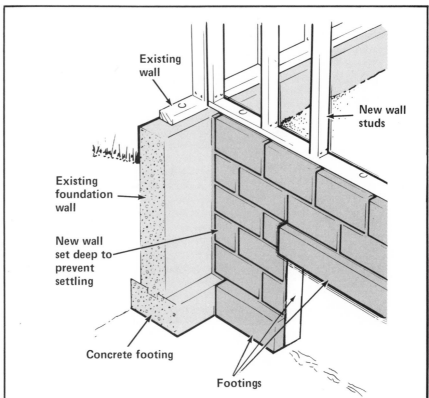

When a new wall is at shallower depth than the old wall, extra deep footings should be set where the new meets the old.

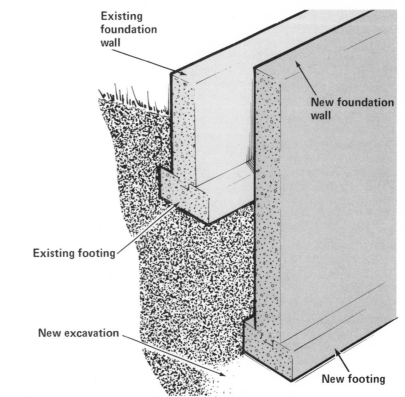

When the new foundation is deeper than the old, a new foundation wall may have to be built directly alongside and joined to an older, shallower wall.

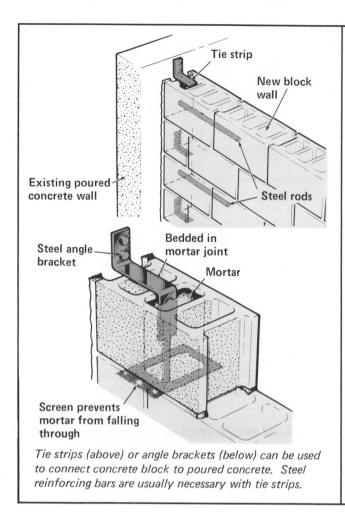

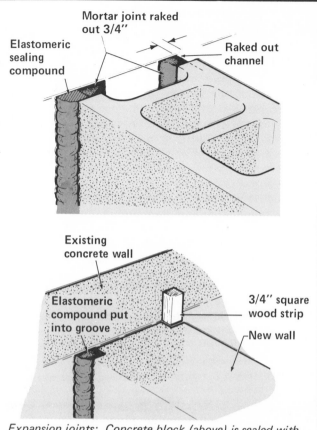

Tie strips (above) or angle brackets (below) can be used to connect concrete block to poured concrete. Steel reinforcing bars are usually necessary with tie strips.

Expansion joints: Concrete block (above) is sealed with 1/2 mortar, 1/2 elastomeric compound. Poured concrete (below) is sealed with compound poured in channels.

mortar the free ends of the strips into the joints between the blocks at every second or third course. Or, you can lag heavy steel angle brackets to the poured wall and mortar them into both the block joints and cores at every fourth course. This is a stronger arrangement, and it can also be used to join blocks to blocks. Joining poured concrete to poured concrete can be done by drilling steel re-bars into the existing wall and leaving long free ends protruding into the forms for the new walls. When the fresh concrete is poured, the walls will be bound together.

Where ground moisture leaking through the foundation walls is a problem, solid masonry joints like those just discussed may become leak points after a time. Despite careful waterproofing, minute

shifting and settling can open the joints a tiny bit. In such instances, the use of expansion joints is a better method. They are installed together with the metal ties. If concrete block is involved, the mortar joint between the old and new walls is raked out to a depth of ¾ inch on each side. With poured concrete, expansion-joint material is placed against the old wall before pouring the new, with a pair of removable ¾-inch wood strips positioned at the inside and outside of the joint between the new and old walls. After the concrete cures and the forms are stripped, the two wood pieces are pried out to leave two vertical channels at the joint. In both cases, the channels are then filled with a top-grade elastomeric sealing compound. Plus, the flexibility of the joint will allow each to expand and

contract without affecting the other.

Joining other types of foundations is most often a matter of tying one to the other in whatever way seems most practical. For instance, an All-Weather Wood Foundation can be joined to a concrete-block wall. This can be done by securing the wood wall ends to the masonry with lag screws and shields, with an elastomeric sealing compound squashed in-between, and heavy beads of caulk run down the joint seams on both sides.

In all cases, best results are obtained when the footings are properly sized and little or no settling is likely. If the soil conditions present problems, or if the situation doesn't look completely straightforward, you should definitely seek the help of an architect, builder, or engineer.

The Shell

The shell is composed of all the elements that make up the basic structure of a house or addition, plus items like unfinished interior stairways, fireplaces, chimneys, and porches. Utilities and finished interior items are not considered part of the shell.

Even though you may not want to do any carpentry work yourself, a knowledge of how a house shell is put together will be of considerable help as you draw up plans for an addition and inspect an expansion project as the work progresses.

Today, most residences and additions are constructed by a method called "platform-framing." Although it is not necessarily the best of all residential building methods, it is usually the easiest and most practical. With this method, most of the structure's framework sections are assembled on a platform and set into place as the job goes along. A platform-frame addition can be wedded successfully to existing structures built by other methods, like balloon-framing, post-and-beam, log, or masonry. And the fundamentals are easy to master, which makes this method ideal for the do-it-yourselfer or amateur carpenter.

Floor Framing

The first platform to be built is the first-level floor. You construct this piecemeal directly on the foundation walls or piers. Of course, if a slab foundation serves as the first floor, this platform isn't necessary. The following is the procedure for building a floor frame, which has become standardized throughout the country. Minor variations are possible, however, owing to local codes, available materials, and similar factors.

Sills

Step one is to set the sill plates—usually 2 x 6 planks, accurately aligned and secured to anchor bolts in the foundation walls. Heavier sills are sometimes installed on masonry piers or wood posts. Outside edges of the sills may be

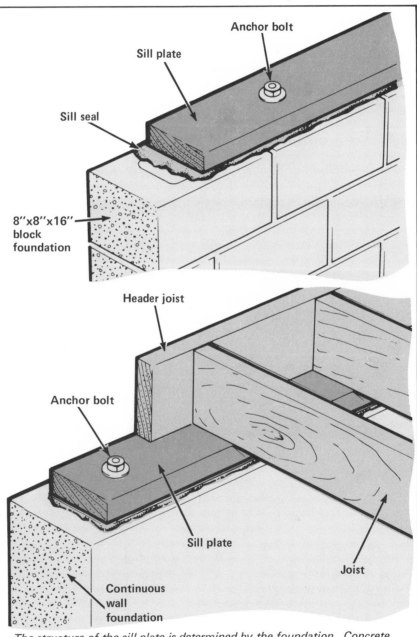

The structure of the sill plate is determined by the foundation. Concrete block (above) and poured concrete (below) continuous foundations usually require only one 2″x6″ sill plate and one header joist.

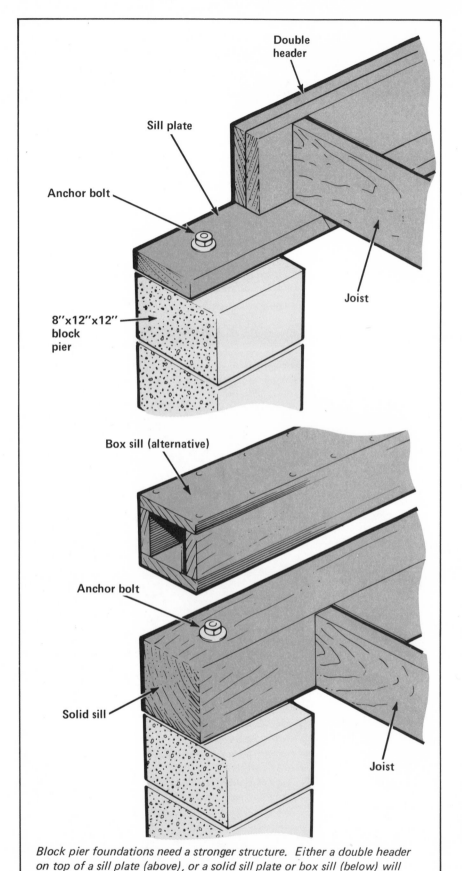

Double header

Sill plate

Anchor bolt

8"x12"x12" block pier

Joist

Box sill (alternative)

Anchor bolt

Solid sill

Joist

Block pier foundations need a stronger structure. Either a double header on top of a sill plate (above), or a solid sill plate or box sill (below) will suffice. There is no need for sealer when working with piers.

recessed to the depth of the sheathing or may be flush, according to code. They should also be accurately aligned to the overall dimensions of the structural framing to follow. Continuous-wall foundations call for sandwiching a sill seal—usually a thin strip of fiberglass insulation—between the sill plate and the tops of the foundation. But, if termites are a problem, a termite shield may be laid down first, directly on top of the foundation. You should be exceptionally careful when installing the sills, because they are the starting point from which all else follows.

Girders

Whenever the span or loading from wall to wall is so great that additional support is needed beneath the floor joists, girders are installed. In residences, these load-bearing structural members are usually made of wood or steel. Wood girders usually consist of two or more lengths of two-inch-thick planking, nailed together and stood on edge. The width of the planks depends on the amount of strength and stiffness needed.

The necessity for girders depends on several factors. There is an interrelationship between floor-joist size, spacing, length, and the average pounds-per-square-foot load that will be placed on the finished floor. Physical properties of the wood used for the joists also have a bearing. For example, assuming a plaster or drywall ceiling, 40-pound live load, and joists on 16-inch centers, spruce 2 x 12's might be used on a structure with a 20-foot span. But, 2 x 6's could also be used, provided they were supported along the foundation's longitudinal centerline by a suitable girder. You have to determine all these possibilities during the floor-frame design stages.

Girders are installed with each end bearing on at least four inches of foundation. Usually, they are inset into notches so that the top of the girder is level with the top of the sill plate, and there is a clearance of ½ inch between the girder ends and the foundation wall faces. Depending upon the girder's size, span, load-bearing requirements, and other factors, additional support columns may be needed. These columns are made of wood, steel, or masonry. They each have their own footing and are strategically positioned beneath the girder to help bear the load and increase the strength and stiffness of the floor.

Joists

The bulk of the floor frame is made up of structural members called "joists," which are used across the narrow dimensions of the structure. Typically, joists are 2 x 8 or 2 x 10 or 2 x 12 construction-grade dimension stock, although certain circumstances may dictate other widths and thicknesses. Conventional spacing between joists is 16 inches on centers (o.c.). That is, the longitudinal centerline of each joist is 16 inches away from the next.

Header joists, called box sill headers, are installed first. They are placed on edge and flush with the outside edge of the sill at right angles to the lie of the floor joists. Next, end joists are set on edge and flush with the outside edge of the sill along the foundation walls, which lie parallel with the floor joists. Nailing these members to the sill plate and to each other forms a shallow box-frame. When using two-inch-thick stock on pier or post foundations, you may need to double or triple the end joists and box sill headers for additional strength.

You install all the floor joists next, setting them 16 inches apart on centers and butting them tight against the box sill. Unless the joists are over 24 feet long—usually the longest length stock available—they should be made of single lengths of stock. If double-span joists are necessary, the two planks used

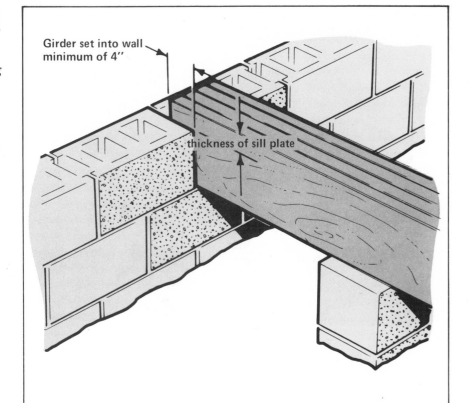

Girders are installed when the span or loading from wall to wall necessitates additional support.

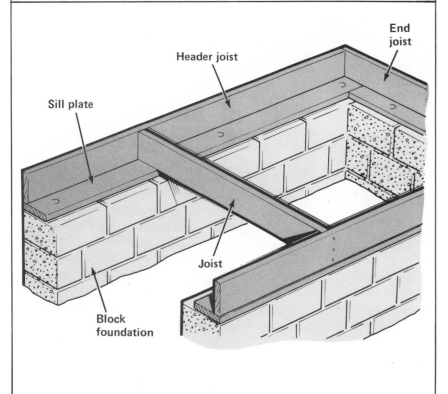

Header and end joists frame the area in which the joists sit. Joists are spaced 16 inches apart on center.

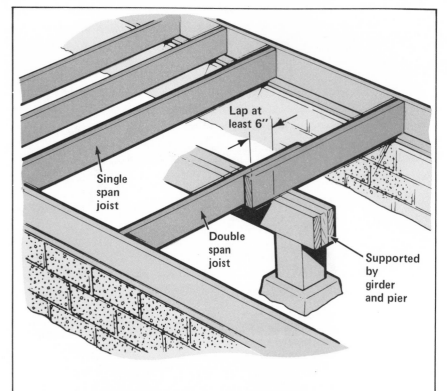

Double span joists are necessary when the distance spanned is over 24 feet—the longest joists available. Note the girder and pier underneath the lap of the double span joists.

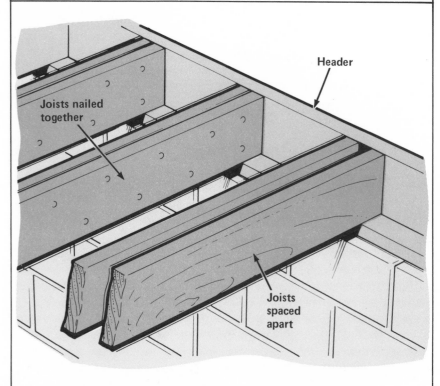

Double joists help support exceptionally heavy loads. When placed underneath partition walls, they can be spaced apart to contain wires and pipes.

to cross the span from one foundation wall to the other must overlap where they meet. This overlap should be six inches or more. Of course, this means that they won't line up evenly from side to side like single-span joists. Each set of joists will be offset from the other by 1½ inches, or whatever the joist thickness might be. The lap joint must be supported by a girder and pier. The joists are end-nailed to the box sill headers, and toenailed to the girders as necessary.

Doubled Joists

A doubled joist consists of a pair of floor joists set side by side and nailed together. They are often installed in floor locations which will bear exceptionally heavy loads, as well as around openings in the floor framework for chimneys and stairways. Doubled joists are always placed beneath interior partition walls that run parallel with the floor joists, for added strength and stiffness. In this case, the joists are sometimes spaced an inch or more apart, so that wires and piping can be easily run up into the partition wall cavity.

Floor Openings

It is rare floor framework that doesn't have one or more openings for stairs, ducts, or chimneys. In most cases, these openings require additional framing.

If the size of the opening is smaller than the space between a pair of joists, a light framework of headers is nailed between the joists to form the opening. These framework members are often the same size as the floor joists, but they can be smaller.

For floor openings larger than the space between the joists, a different procedure is required. In new construction, all common joists are installed, except for those that would run across the proposed opening. Then, a header joist is installed between the two common joists on each

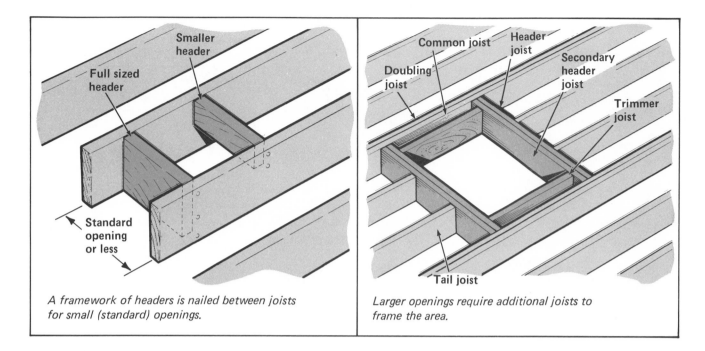

A framework of headers is nailed between joists for small (standard) openings.	Larger openings require additional joists to frame the area.

side of the opening to frame two of its sides; the ends of these headers are nailed to the common joists. Tail joists are run from the structure's sills on both sides of the opening and secured to the opening's header joists. Secondary header joists are then nailed to the first header joists. Next, trimmer joists are installed between the secondary header joists to frame the remaining two sides of the opening. Finally, to reinforce the opening's framework, a doubling joist is nailed to the common joist on each side of the opening.

Bridging

Bridging is a method of stiffening and strengthening the floor joist assembly. It also reduces vibration and deflection, and inhibits joist warping. Herringbone, or cross bridging, is one common technique. It consists of side-by-side 1 x 4's nailed diagonally top and bottom to opposite joists in a continuous line. The pieces of 1 x 4 are cut and nailed in place only at the top; the bottoms are nailed after the subfloor has been laid.

Metal bridging consists of preformed metal strips that are available in several different configurations. They are installed in much the same manner as wood cross bridging. Metal bridging is more effective and easier to work with, but it is more expensive.

Solid bridging, or blocking, is another alternative. This

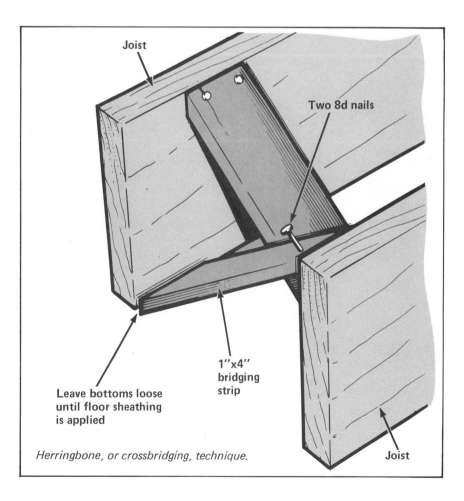

Herringbone, or crossbridging, technique.

91

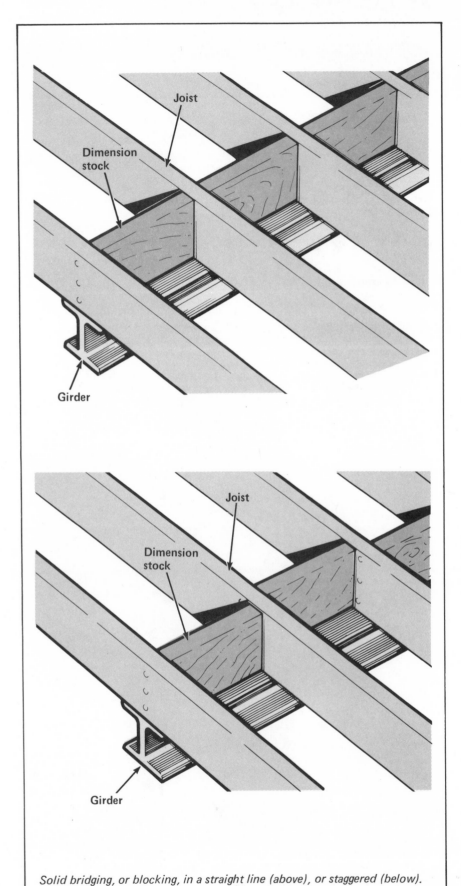

Solid bridging, or blocking, in a straight line (above), or staggered (below).

consists of short pieces of dimension stock that are the same size as the floor joists. The pieces are cut to fit snugly between the joists. They can be installed in staggered fashion for easy end-nailing, or successively in a straight line and end-nailed at one end and toenailed top and bottom at the other.

Subflooring

Laying the subflooring, or floor sheathing, is the last step in making the floor structure. There are several ways to do this.

The most popular material is plywood. The preferred type for conventional subfloor construction is interior-grade C-D with exterior glue; interior-glue C-D can also be used. Assuming the floor joists are on 16-inch centers, the thickness of the plywood can be ½ inch, ⅝ inch, or ¾ inch, depending on floor-loading factors, proposed additional flooring layers, and desired overall stiffness. The plywood sheets are laid with their long dimension at right angles to the joists, and with their better side, or face, up. A ⅛-inch gap should be left between the side edges of the panels, and a ¹⁄₁₆-inch gap should be left between the end edges. All end-joints should be staggered, and this is usually done on a ½-lap or ⅓-lap basis. Nail ½-inch plywood with 6d nails; thicker sheets with 8d nails. Nail spacing should be 6 inches around all edges and 10 inches along intermediate supports. An additional but worthwhile step is to run a bead of special construction adhesive on the top of each joist as the sheets of plywood are laid. This not only makes a much stiffer and stronger floor structure, but also virtually eliminates flooring squeaks.

The older method of using boards for subflooring is still acceptable. Either common boards, which have been planed on three or four sides, or tongue-and-groove boards can be used.

Either can be laid at right angles to the floor joists or diagonally. Laying the boards diagonally requires more labor, more complex cutting, and more waste than the right-angle arrangement. However, if the finish flooring will be of the strip or plank type, it can be laid either parallel with or at right angles to the lie of the floor joists. But if the subflooring is laid at right angles to the joists, the finish flooring must be laid at right angles to the subflooring. Diagonal subflooring also makes the floor assembly somewhat sturdier. Nailing at each end joist is generally done with two 8d nails for 6-inch-wide boards and three 8d nails for 8-inch boards. Construction adhesive can be used here, too, to virtually eliminate floor squeaks.

There are other possibilities that you might investigate. For example, 2 x 6 double-tongue-and-groove decking can be secured to floor joists spaced considerably farther apart than 16 inches—it makes an extremely strong floor. The decking itself can be treated with a finish application and left alone as a single-layer floor. Or, another type of material, called "five-quarter" (written 5/4), also makes excellent flooring. Several kinds of wood are available in various widths and lengths. The boards are 1¼ inches thick. When laid as a single-layer floor, they make a stronger and stiffer construction than a two-layer arrangement of identical thickness.

Other alternatives include laying plywood of the combined subfloor-underlayment type that is designed for direct application of nonstructural flooring such as tile, carpet, or 2·4·1 subfloor-underlayment construction. This is a quick, easy, and highly effective flooring system comprised of 1⅛-inch-thick sheets of plywood that can be laid on 2-inch-thick joists set on 32-inch centers or

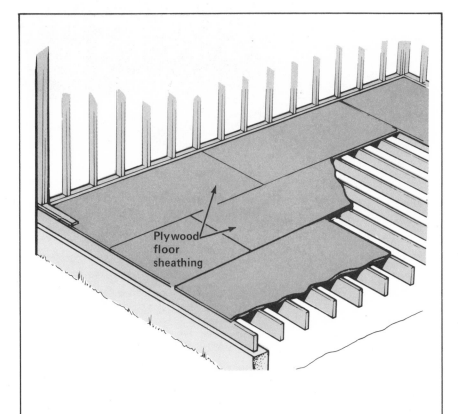

Laying a plywood subfloor.

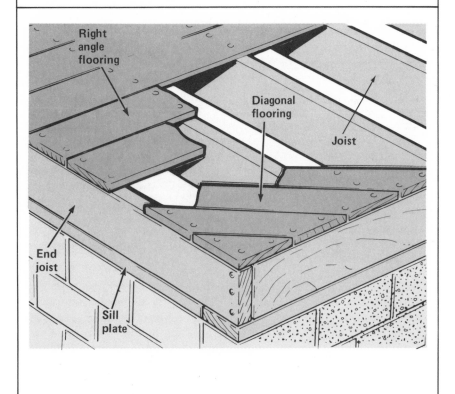

Using boards for the subfloor. Right angle method is easier and less wasteful, but diagonal method is stronger.

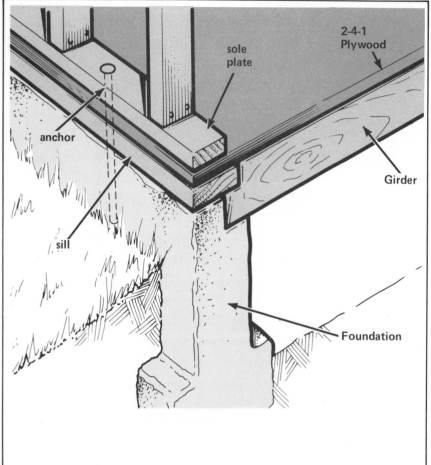

The 2-4-1 Plywood system combines the subflooring with the underlayment, making direct application of non-structural flooring (tile, carpet, etc.) possible.

on 4-inch-thick joists set on 48-inch centers. It is made for direct application of either nonstructural flooring (sheet vinyl, carpet) or structural flooring (hardwood plank).

Joining New to Old

Most often, joining a new floor frame to an existing one is relatively easy. Existing siding must be removed, but you can leave the sheathing on if practical. The abutting end or header joist of the new floor frame is spiked, or bolted, directly to the sill or an end or header joist of the existing floor frame. This is done either directly or through the sheathing. Foundation support is seldom needed under this side of the new floor frame, because the existing building and its

foundation carries the load.

Of course, if the difference between the levels of the new and old subfloors amounts to six inches or more, you don't have to worry about joining the two floors. You just put in a step or two. But if the two floors are to be level, you must carefully choose the proper thickness of floor sheathing or underlayment material.

The height of the new foundation and the alignment of the new floor frame with the existing one, especially the new abutting header joist, must be calculated precisely. As little as $\frac{1}{8}$-inch difference in floor levels is difficult to cover. And a $\frac{1}{4}$-inch or more difference can be dangerous. If the levels are less than an inch apart, you can fit the joint with a wedge-shaped

molding or special transition threshold for appearance and safety. But if construction difficulties make the difference an inch or more, it can be better to change the level of the entire new floor to provide a full step of six inches or more.

Wall Framing

Work can begin on wall sections when the first-level floor platform is finished. But, before you start, be sure to tack plywood temporarily over all floor platform holes to prevent accidents.

Wall sections are built one at a time on the floor platform. They're laid out, assembled, and sheathed in the horizontal position. When each is finished, it is raised, set in position, and nailed in place. Temporary props—boards nailed to the wall tops and the subflooring—hold everything in place until the structure is self-supporting.

Most often, all major wall frame structural elements are construction-grade 2 x 4's. However, in some areas 2 x 6's are preferred (or mandated) to allow for a greater thickness of thermal insulation in the wall cavities.

Plates

The sole plate is the horizontal member that runs along the bottom of a wall section. When the wall section is being built, the sole plate is a continuous piece, which even runs across the bottoms of door openings. But it is cut away from these openings after the wall has been erected.

The top plate is the sole plate's opposite member. It's placed horizontally across the tops of the wall studs. This continuous piece runs around the perimeter of the exterior walls and caps the interior partition walls as well. Usually, this member is doubled.

The longest walls are usually built first, and the first step is to lay out the sole plate and a single top plate. Cut them to the overall length of the wall. Then stand them on edge on the floor platform, about as far apart as the wall is high. In the case of a very long wall section, two or more pieces of stock may have to be joined end to end. This is done by splicing as the wall construction proceeds.

Studs

Studs are the wall's vertical members, and they're made of the same material as the top and sole plates. Normally, studs are placed 16 inches apart on centers. But sometimes the spacing is 24 inches on centers when 2 x 4's are used in light construction, or when standard-duty construction incorporates 2 x 6's. Local building codes may specify these dimensions. In any case, accurate spacing is important, because it allows the installation of standard sizes of sheathing and wall covering panels without unnecessary cutting.

In a simple wall without openings or structural members other than studs and plates, you begin construction by marking the stud locations on the plates. Then, beginning at either end, subsequent studs are nailed in place. The first of these should be placed so that its center is located 16 inches from the outside edge of the wall frame. Successive studs are placed every 16 inches on center.

Unless the wall frame length is a multiple of 16, the spacing obviously won't come out even. If it doesn't, an extra stud is placed at some convenient point. The spacing of this stud can be anything less than 16 inches, but should not be more.

All studs are nailed in place by driving a pair of 16d nails *down* through the top plate and *up* through the sole plate. You have to be careful that all members are correctly aligned and well-fitted, even though the work is done on a presumably flat floor. It's also important to keep the framework in square as much as possible.

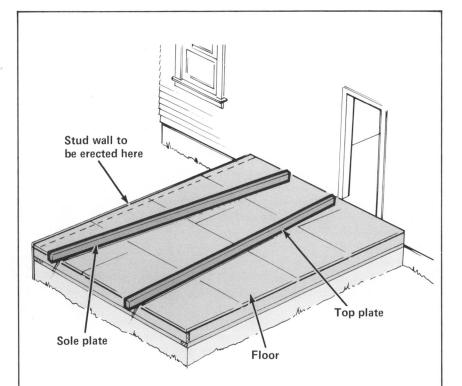

The plates are the top and bottom of the wall. Walls are most easily erected on a horizontal surface and then raised and secured in final vertical position.

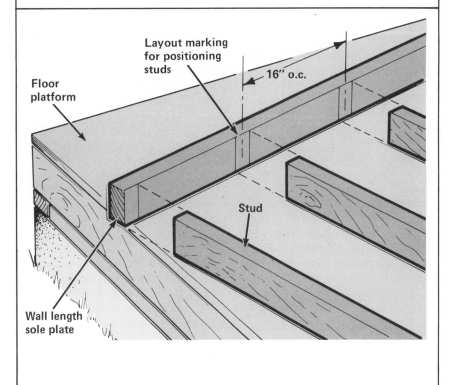

Studs are usually set 16 inches apart, from center to center. They are nailed into premarked positions on sole and top plates.

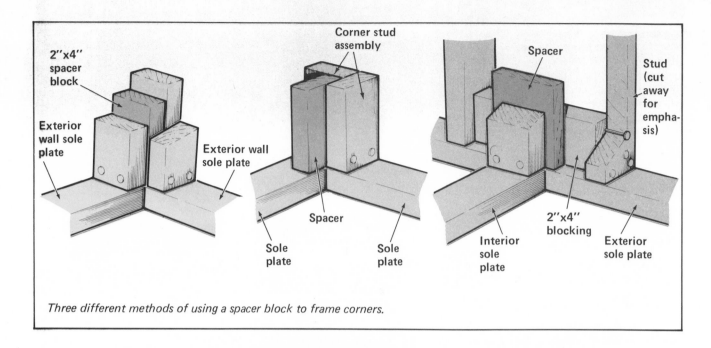

Three different methods of using a spacer block to frame corners.

Corners

Wherever one wall intersects another—at a corner or a midspan—some additional framing is needed for both strength and nailing surface. Of the many ways to do this, the most common is to use three studs, along with a series of spacer blocks made from scrap, for each intersection. For each intersection, allowances must be made dimensionally and built into the wall sections.

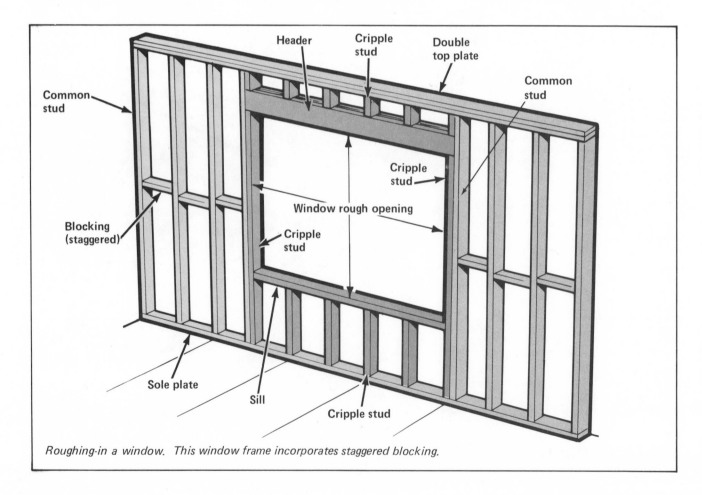

Roughing-in a window. This window frame incorporates staggered blocking.

Openings

The process for making rough openings (RO's) for doors and windows is called "roughing-in." These openings are always made larger than the actual size of the units to be installed. Just how much larger varies. So, for easiest installation, it's best to first obtain the specific recommendations from the manufacturers of the doors and windows to be used.

Whenever window openings are made in a wall frame, full-length studs are placed at the extreme outsides of the opening, and a sill is placed horizontally between them at an appropriate height above the sole plate. The sill may be a single member, but it is often doubled for strength. Then a header is installed above the opening. This is composed of two pieces of dimension stock stood on edge and spaced with a scrap piece of plywood or other material. The spacer material must be thick enough to make the overall thickness of the header equal to the width of the studs and to make all faces flush on both sides. These pieces are nailed together in a "sandwich" and installed between the two common studs on either side of the opening. Trimmer, or jack studs, are nailed to the inner sides of the common studs. Cripple studs are then installed between the sole plate and sill, and between the header and the top plate. Door openings are framed in much the same way, except there is no sill member. In both cases, end-nailing is done with 16d nails, and flat nailing (two members nailed face to face) with 10d nails.

Blocking

Blocking is not required in all areas of wall assemblies, but it is recommended throughout for several reasons. The procedure makes a wall section stronger and stiffer, and the blocks help prevent studs from bowing or warping. It also helps to retard the spread of fire by minimizing the flue effect in wall cavities.

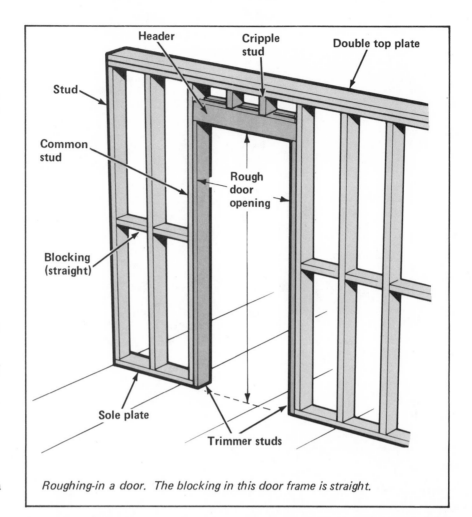

Roughing-in a door. The blocking in this door frame is straight.

You can either place a single run of blocks at the midpoint of the wall, or you can divide the wall into thirds horizontally with two runs. And the blocks can be either staggered from bay to bay or they can run in a straight line. If you stagger them, both ends of each block can be end-nailed through the studs. When blocks are placed in a straight line, you start at one end and end-nail the first block at both ends. Subsequent blocks are first end-nailed at the free end and then toenailed through the stud and into the block on both faces.

Bracing

You can forget about wall bracing if the exterior corners of the walls will be sheathed with plywood panels that are at least ½-inch thick. Where bracing is required, the usual method is to "let in" a strip of 1 x 4 stock

diagonally at each corner. The stock is recessed into notches cut for the purpose along the outside faces of the studs—starting at the top plate and

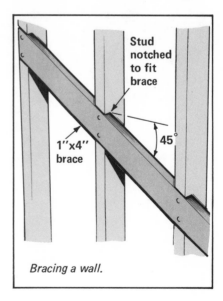

Bracing a wall.

97

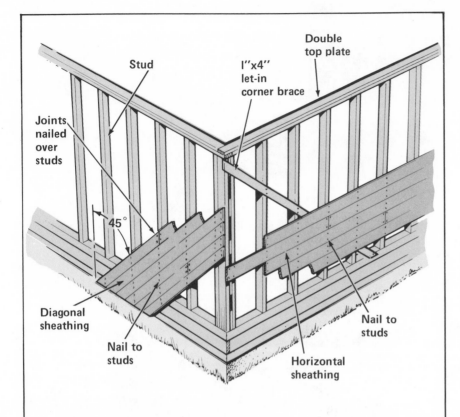

Sheathing with boards. Diagonal method is the stronger; horizontal method is easier and less wasteful.

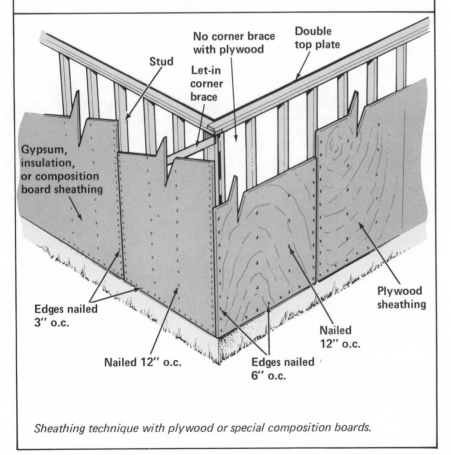

Sheathing technique with plywood or special composition boards.

descending to the sole plate at a 45-degree angle.

Sheathing

In most cases, an exterior wall section can be sheathed while it still lies on the platform floor before erection. This is the quickest and easiest way to do it. There are three types of materials in general use for exterior wall sheathing.

Ordinary boards—planed on three or four sides or tongue-and-grooved—can be applied horizontally, at right angles to the studs. However, it's better to set them diagonally. This involves more labor, material, and waste, but makes a much stronger structure.

Or, plywood panels can be used. The advantage here is in the plywood's ample nail-holding power, which eliminates the need for nailer strips or nailing only at stud locations when installing some kinds of finish siding. Panel thickness can range from ½ to ¾ inch, depending upon local code requirements and structure design. And, sheets may be applied with the face grain either parallel to or at right angles to the studs. A $\frac{1}{16}$-inch space should be left at all panel end joints, and a ⅛-inch gap should be left at all panel edge joints. The panels are usually nailed with 8d common, ring-shank, or galvanized box nails. These are spaced 6 inches apart along the panel edges and 12 inches apart on intermediate studs.

Panels of special composition board is a third alternative. Often, this material is asphalt-impregnated or otherwise treated for moisture resistance. The application procedure is similar to that for plywood panels, except nailing is done with roofing barbs and the sheets are usually positioned vertically. The material thickness is generally ½ or ¾ inch, and it should only be applied to wall sections having corner bracing.

Applying any kind of

sheathing is simple. The panels are laid out on the wall frame, accurately positioned and nailed down. Small window openings are usually covered over and cut out later. Larger window openings and door openings are cut to fit or "pieced-in" as the sheathing is applied.

At the base of the wall, you must make overlap allowances so the sheathing will lap down over the floor joists and sills. Similar allowances must be made at mating corners where the sheathing must overlap the end stud of the adjoining wall. Before applying the sheathing, the wall frame section should be checked for squareness. Nailing sheathing to an out-of-square frame assembly can result in a frustrating job of realignment.

Joining New to Old

New abutting exterior walls and interior load-bearing walls must be solidly anchored to existing wall framing wherever they meet. At the least, the end studs of the new walls must be nailed to the old structure through their full length. If the new and old walls are of matching height and a metal tie-strap can be run from the new top plate to the old, so much the better. Existing exterior siding must be stripped off, and usually the sheathing as well. In most cases, a new wall-intersection stud assembly, made the same way as for new construction, must be built and installed in the old wall. This provides an anchoring point for the new wall end stud, the exterior wall sheathing, and the interior wall covering. The new wall frame is butted, aligned, plumbed, and secured in the usual fashion. Nonload-bearing interior partition walls should be secured so that they are not loose or wobbly; this can usually be accomplished by driving a few nails into any solid material or surface.

Wall Erection

The usual procedure for building walls is to construct and sheath

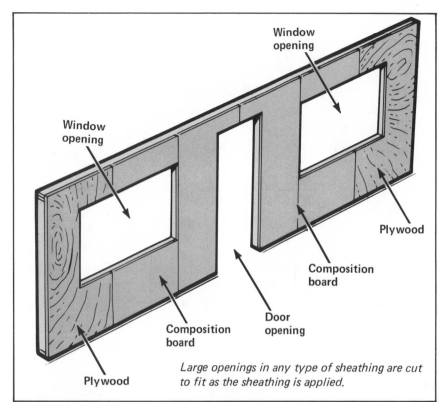

Large openings in any type of sheathing are cut to fit as the sheathing is applied.

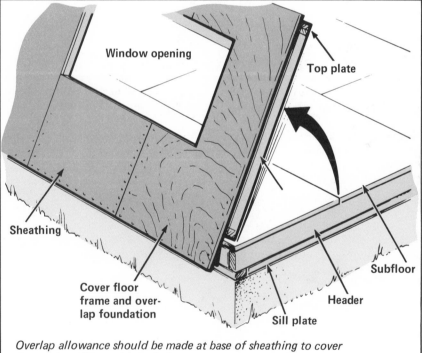

Overlap allowance should be made at base of sheathing to cover floor joists, sills, and foundation.

the first one, stand it in place, brace it, and then go to the next wall. All exterior walls are done first, starting with the longest ones. Interior partition walls, which are not covered with sheathing at this stage, are usually built after all exterior walls are up and correctly aligned. Again, the longest ones are built first.

On finishing a wall assembly,

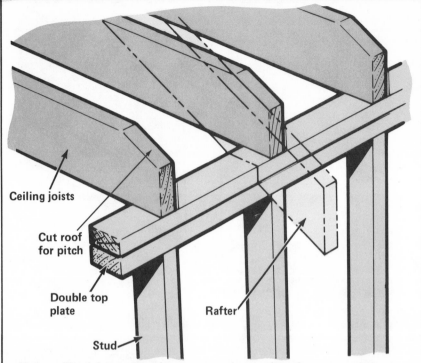

Ceiling joists

Cut roof
for pitch

Double top
plate

Rafter

Stud

If the ceiling joists rest on the same top plate as the rafters, an angled cut may be necessary to allow for the roof's pitch. Rafters and joists are usually nailed together.

you move it along the platform and bring it into alignment with its final position. Raising a wall section is usually a two-man job. Both men raise the wall and wiggle it into position. Then one person holds it in place (unless there's too much wind), while the other checks alignment and drives a few nails through the sole plate into the floor joists. Then you install a suitable number of temporary props and secure the section further by

driving more nails through the sole plate. As the walls continue to go up, they are aligned with one another and nailed together at the intersections. Plenty of bracing should be installed until nearly all walls are up and solidly interlocked and anchored. A partial installation may look sturdy until an unexpected gust of wind topples it.

Ceiling Joists

Not all additions or houses have ceiling joists. For example, small structures of open or cathedral ceiling design need none. The underside of the roof becomes the finished ceiling, and no additional structural members are required to cross from wall-top to wall-top. In larger structures of this design, additional support is often needed. Sometimes tie-beams of heavy stock, widely spaced and finished to match the interior decor, span the structure crosswise. Where more strength is needed, or tie-beams are undesirable, various kinds of open-truss designs, laminated roof beams, or other special roof construction can be employed.

In conventional construction, however, the ceiling is a separate substructure, generally placed between 7½ and 8 feet above the finished floor. In a house with a useable attic, the ceiling joists also serve as floor joists for the attic. Design and construction of a second-level floor and floor frame is identical to that of a first floor. Instead of end and header joists being set on a sill plate, they are secured to the top plates of the first-level wall.

If there is no second floor, the joists are simply set on the wall top plates and toenailed into position. The outboard ends of the joists may have to be cut on a taper to accommodate the roof rafter pitch. The rafters and joists are nailed together where they meet. Because the direct load involved is only ceiling drywall, plaster, or tile, these joists are often of smaller dimension-stock than would be

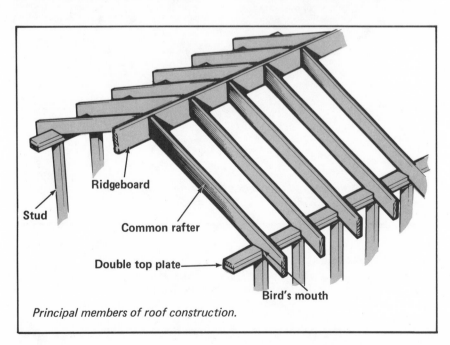

Ridgeboard

Stud

Common rafter

Double top plate

Bird's mouth

Principal members of roof construction.

needed to support second-floor live and dead loads. These joists might also be set on 24-inch centers instead of standard 16-inch centers. For the strongest construction, ceiling joists should lie directly above wall studs, and also be aligned with the roof rafters. Ceiling joists can, however, fall between studs if a double top plate is used.

Joining New to Old

How you join ceiling joists depends upon whether the addition's joists run at an angle, or parallel to those of the existing structure. If the new joists run at right—or other—angles to the old building wall, their ends are secured to a ledger plate attached to that wall. You set them atop the plate and either nail them down, or anchor them to the plate with metal joist hangers. When joists run parallel to the old building wall, the adjoining end joist is set in the usual fashion—nailed to the new wall top plates. It can also be attached to the old wall's framework by driving a few nails into the studs. In some types of ceiling construction, the end joist can even be eliminated entirely.

Roof Framing

This is the most complicated part of framing a house. Although flat and shed styles are relatively simple to put together, mansard and gambrel roofs are not. The familiar gable roof is about average in degree of construction difficulty.

The principal members of a simple roof construction are called "common rafters." Their bottom ends rest on a plate—usually the top plate of the exterior wall. At the top, the rafters may or may not be attached to a ridgeboard. Not all double-pitched roofs have a ridgeboard, and flat or shed roofs never have one. The roof frame is extended beyond the ends of the structure by means of assemblies called "lookouts," or "lookout ladders."

More complex roof frames have additional structural members. Chief among these are the "valley" and "hip" rafters. Both are installed where the roof surface changes direction. A valley rafter extends diagonally from top plate to ridgeboard in an inside corner; the hip rafter travels the same way, but in an outside corner. The shorter, secondary members that extend from one principal member to another are called "jack rafters." A "valley jack" is a member that runs between a valley rafter

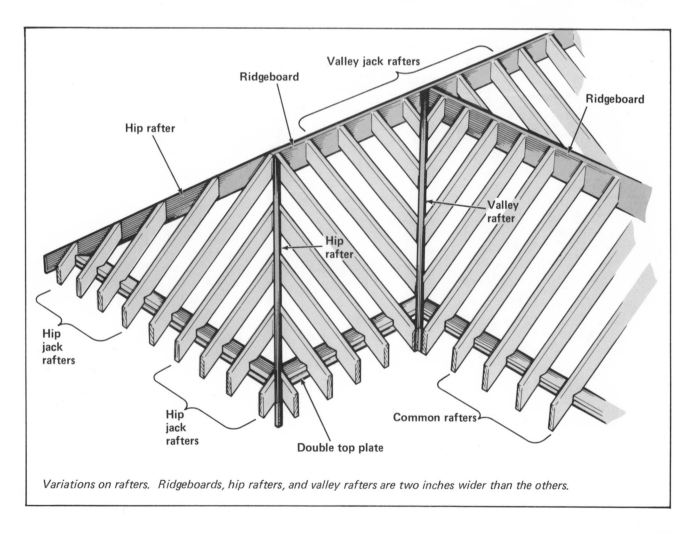

Variations on rafters. Ridgeboards, hip rafters, and valley rafters are two inches wider than the others.

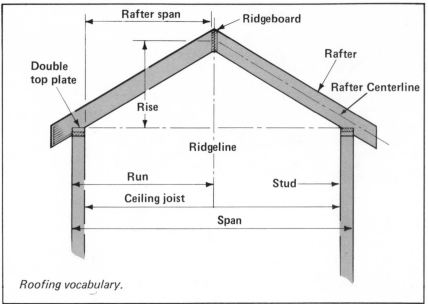

Roofing vocabulary.

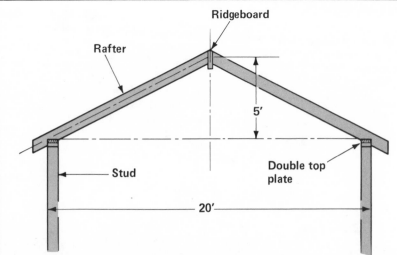

To calculate a roof's pitch in terms of fraction, divide the rise by the span. The pitch of this roof is 1/4: 5' (rise) ÷ 20' (span) = 1/4 (pitch).

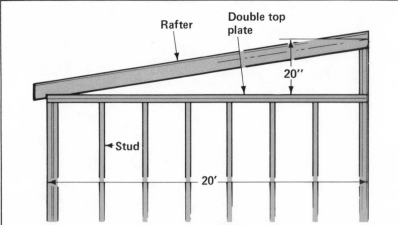

A second way to express pitch is to calculate the inches of rise per foot of run. This roof rises one inch per foot (20" rise, 20' run). It could be called a 1-in-1 pitch, 1-in-12, or better yet, a 1-pitch.

and the ridgeboard, while a "hip jack" extends from a top plate to a hip rafter. "Cripple jacks" run between valley jacks and hip jacks.

There are some other terms worth knowing, too. For instance, the "span" of the roof is the distance that it covers from wall to wall in the direction of the rafter lie, measured from the outsides of the wall top plates. The "run" is measured from the outsides of the wall top plates. The run is measured in one of several ways, depending upon the type of roof. In the case of a common, double-pitched roof, the run is the distance from the outside of one wall top plate to the ridgeline. Gabled roofs with equal sides have a run that is half of the structure's span. The run of flat roofs is the distance between the outside faces of opposite top plates, and it is equal to the roof's span. Shed roofs have a single run, from lower top plate to higher, opposite top plate. Saltbox roof styles have two runs of unequal length, one from each top plate outside face to the ridgeline.

The "rise" of the roof is the height of the ridgeline above the top of the plate, measured from plate top to ridgeboard centerboard. You use the rise measurement to figure out "pitch"—the amount of slope a roof section has. Pitch is expressed in a few different ways. One is as a fraction, determined by dividing the roof's rise by its span. If a roof has a five-foot rise over a 20-foot span, it is a ¼-pitch (5÷20=¼). Or, pitch can be expressed in terms of inches of rise per foot of run. For example, if a roof section rises 20 inches over a 20-foot run, the rate of rise is one inch for every foot. This might be called a 1-in-1 pitch, a 1-in-12 pitch, or simply a 1-pitch. If the rise were 20 inches in 10 feet, this would be a 2-pitch, or a 2-in-12 roof.

Note that roof measurements are taken from the end of the

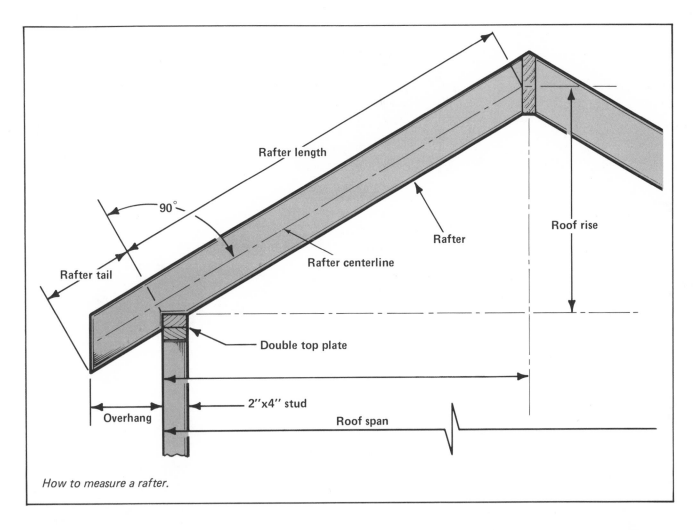

How to measure a rafter.

rafter to the ridgeline. The "length" of a rafter is measured between the outside edge of the top plate and the horizontal centerline of the ridgeboard. The part of the rafter that projects out beyond the top plate is not included in the measurement. This overhang is called the "tail" of the rafter. It is measured from the outermost end point of the rafter to the exterior face of the wall that it overhangs.

These are only some of the many fundamentals of roof-framing. There's a great deal more to learn if you plan to tackle the project yourself. Many roofs have been owner-built, but even constructing the simplest type of roof, the 4-to-6 pitch shed style, is a substantial chore. If you contemplate building your own roof, be sure to investigate further into roof

construction and the myriad of details involved—especially with respect to framing tables and the framing (or rafter) square, an important tool. However, the basic information contained in this section can be a good guide for overseeing or inspecting the work of a contractor.

Building a Shed Roof

In a shed-roof design, the common rafters extend from the highest wall's top plate to the top plate on the lower, opposite wall. If the ceiling of the structure is the underside of the roof, end walls are framed to rise in a slope that matches the roof pitch and aligns with the roof rafters. When ceiling joists are installed, however, the end walls of the first-floor level are framed in the usual fashion, the ceiling joists installed, and slanted stub walls framed and erected to

enclose the ends of the attic area and align with the roof pitch. Or, individual studs can be notch-fitted to the outboard rafters after the roof has been framed. In the case of an addition made with the rafter lie at right angles to an existing building wall, the common rafters extend from the top plate of the low addition wall upward to a ledger plate attached to the wall of the existing structure. There is no need for another wall frame at that location, because the wall of the existing structure serves this purpose.

Rafters are generally made of at least 2 x 6 construction grade hemlock, Douglas fir, or spruce stock. Although, 2 x 8's and 2 x 10's are commonly used. Sometimes 24-inch spacing is used for light construction or steeply pitched roofs, but the norm is 16 inches on centers.

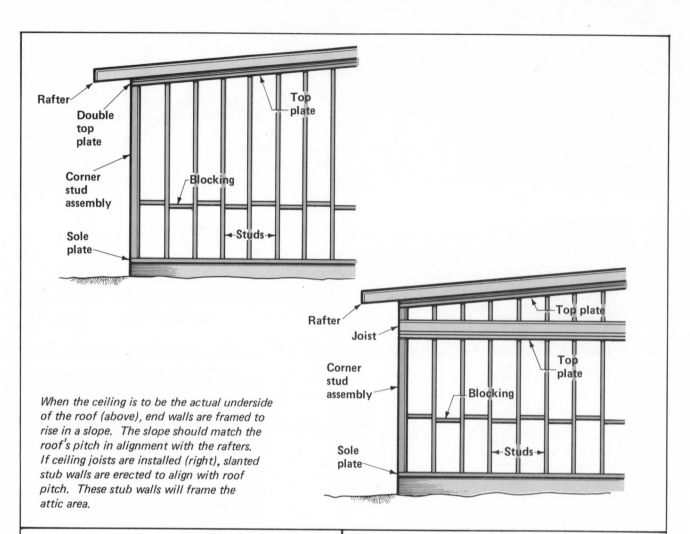

When the ceiling is to be the actual underside of the roof (above), end walls are framed to rise in a slope. The slope should match the roof's pitch in alignment with the rafters. If ceiling joists are installed (right), slanted stub walls are erected to align with roof pitch. These stub walls will frame the attic area.

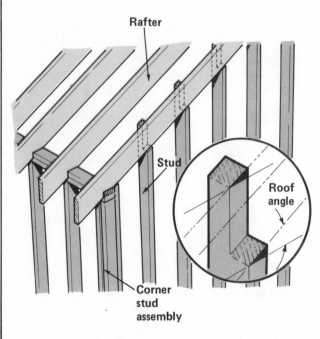

Notched studs could be erected along the outboard rafters to align with roof pitch.

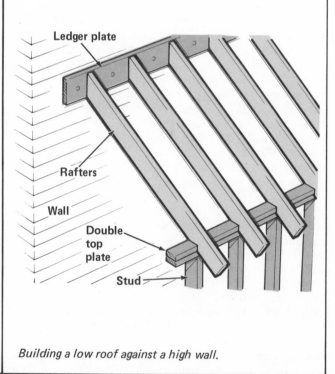

Building a low roof against a high wall.

Spacing wider than 24 inches is rare, but occurs in some exceptional circumstances.

Determining rafter length and the length of the tail is the first step in roof framing. Free-standing structures and end-to additions have some overhang at both front and rear—a few inches to two or three feet. Side-to additions have an overhang on only one side of the roof. The roof pitch will have already been determined, and perhaps the end walls built to suit, too. With this pitch angle in mind, the next step is to cut notches at appropriate points in the rafters so they'll seat flat on the top plates. This is the "bird's-mouth" cut.

If the structure is an addition and the rafters will snug up against an existing sidewall, you have to make a plumb cut. This is an angle cut made across the end of the rafter so that the cut face will lie vertical and parallel with the wall or plate that it butts up against. The heel cut is used to make a rafter fit a top plate without any overhang. Rafter tails that overhang the walls can be cut or bobbed in several different ways. One is to make plumb cuts so the rafter ends are perpendicular. Another is to make a flat cut so the end of the rafter is parallel with the top of the top plate. Or, the ends can be squared. They also can be cut plumb, and then recut across the heel parallel with level; this is the ell, or angled, cut. You can make various scrolled or artistic cuts too, if the ends are to be left exposed to view.

The usual practice is to work out the details and dimensions, cut one rafter, and try it on for size. Once a proper fit is achieved, that rafter can serve as a template, or pattern, for the others. However, only this one should be used for the pattern. Cutting each successive rafter from the one just cut can compound minor dimension errors to the point where the tenth or fifteenth rafter does not fit.

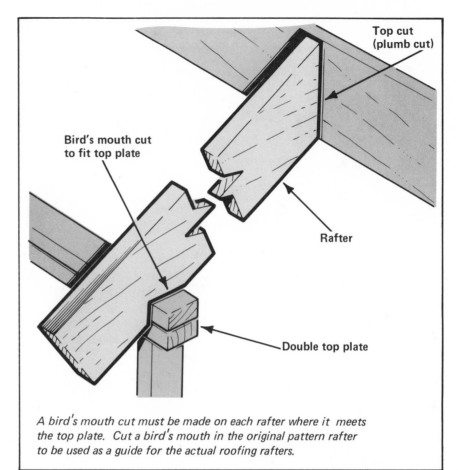

A bird's mouth cut must be made on each rafter where it meets the top plate. Cut a bird's mouth in the original pattern rafter to be used as a guide for the actual roofing rafters.

After the rafters are prepared, their locations can be marked on the top plates. The rafters are then boosted onto the wall top, stood on edge and fitted to the top plates, and toenailed down. Often, solid blocking is added between the rafters and directly above the top plate. These are called "frieze blocks." They are cut and fitted so that their bottoms lie flat on the top plate, and their tops are beveled to match the roof pitch and lie flush with the rafter tops. This serves to totally enclose the structure's interior.

If there is to be no roof overhang above the end walls, the outboard rafters are installed with their faces flush with the outside of the end-wall top plates. Where an overhang is part of the design, a "lookout ladder" must be built to gain proper support. There are a number of minor variations in lookout construction. For example, you can eliminate the end rafter and attach the "rungs" of the ladder by end-nailing through an inboard rafter and toenailing to the end-wall top plates. The outermost rafter is then nailed to the ends of the ladder rungs and it becomes a fascia backer or the fascia itself.

Building a Gable Roof

Basically, a gable roof and a shed roof are built the same way. The gable roof consists of two opposing shed roofs that meet at a ridgeboard and partially support one another. Installing the first few rafters and the ridgeboard is the hardest part of the job. After that, the job is much easier.

The first step is to prop the ridgeboard into place. This ridgeboard is *normally* a piece of two-inch stock that's two inches wider than the rafter width. If length limitations prevent using a single, full-length piece of

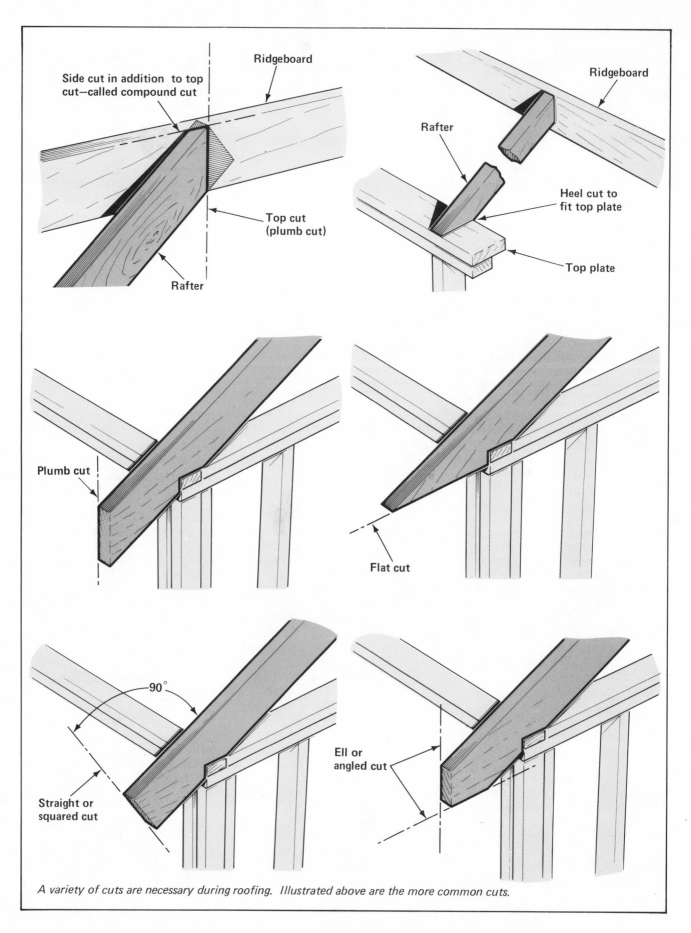

Side cut in addition to top cut—called compound cut

Ridgeboard

Top cut (plumb cut)

Rafter

Ridgeboard

Rafter

Heel cut to fit top plate

Top plate

Plumb cut

Flat cut

90°

Straight or squared cut

Ell or angled cut

A variety of cuts are necessary during roofing. Illustrated above are the more common cuts.

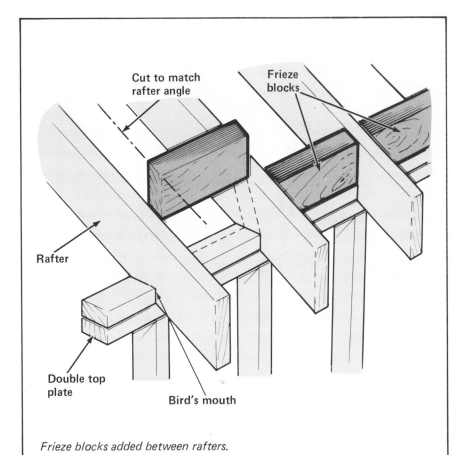

Cut to match rafter angle

Frieze blocks

Rafter

Double top plate

Bird's mouth

Frieze blocks added between rafters.

Lookouts

Plate

Rafter

Lookout ladders are necessary when an overhang is part of the roof's design. A rafter nailed to the lookouts adds support and can serve as a fascia backer—or the fascia itself.

stock, pieces are spliced together with pieces of plywood or board—splice locations are calculated to lie between rafter locations. The ridgeboard is set in place, leveled, aligned, and propped with temporary braces. Then a template rafter is prepared.

Now you must "crown" the rafters. This is done by sighting down the members to see if they have a natural bow, or crown. This crown should always be placed up.

A plumb cut must be made at one end of each rafter so it fits flush against the side of the ridgeboard, and properly angled bird's-mouths are made where the rafters will lie on the top plate. The rafter tails can be bobbed as desired.

After crowning and cutting, rafter locations are marked on the ridgeboard and the top plates, if necessary (the spacing can also be calculated so that rafters lie alongside ceiling joists) and the first pair of rafters can be raised. Work usually begins with an end set. The first rafter is fitted to the top plate, and the rafter is toenailed in place with a pair of 16d nails. The nails are driven slightly downward, through the ridgeboard and into the rafter end. The matching rafter on the opposite side is set next. It is nailed to the top plate, and then secured to the ridgeboard and the opposite rafter by toenailing with three 16d nails. As you position the rafters, you must check them for proper alignment and trueness. And they have to be double-checked after they are nailed up. If everything is okay, the job can continue with the rafters set at the opposite end of the structure, or the next pair in line.

Gable end walls can be built either before or after constructing the roof frame. If built before, typical wall, platform-framing techniques are used, with the exception that the top plates are slanted to match the roof pitch. The wall is erected and secured to the top

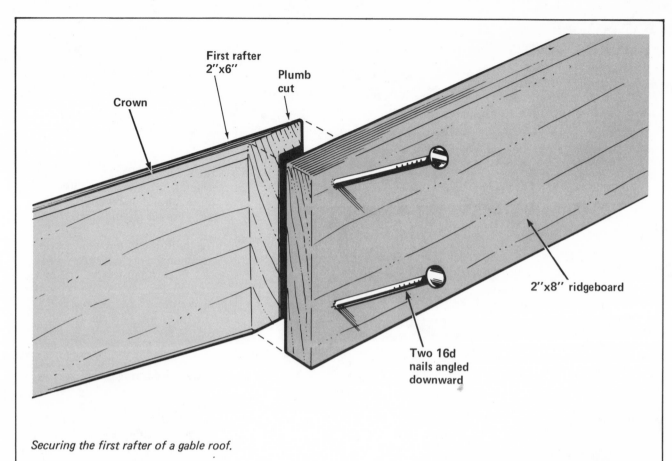

Crown

First rafter 2"x6"

Plumb cut

2"x8" ridgeboard

Two 16d nails angled downward

Securing the first rafter of a gable roof.

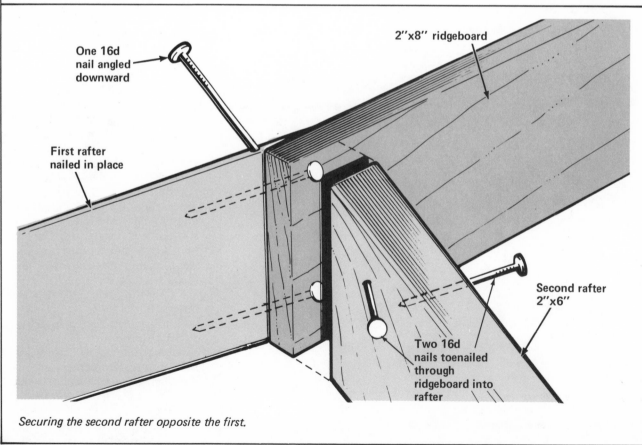

One 16d nail angled downward

First rafter nailed in place

2"x8" ridgeboard

Second rafter 2"x6"

Two 16d nails toenailed through ridgeboard into rafter

Securing the second rafter opposite the first.

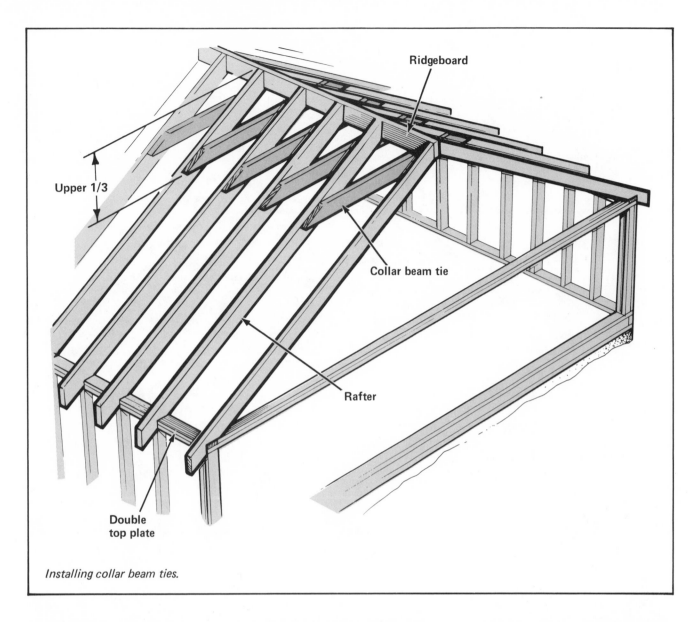

Upper 1/3

Ridgeboard

Collar beam tie

Rafter

Double
top plate

Installing collar beam ties.

plate of the end wall below or to the lower-level joists. If built after, you simply enclose the open end by securing studs to the top plate at the bottom, and notching them against a properly aligned roof rafter at the top.

Installing "collar-beam ties" can give a gable roof extra strength, and they may be required in some form by code. These structural members tie rafter pairs together in the form of an "A," adding considerable strength and stiffness to the roof assembly. The ties are usually made of 1 x 6 boards, run from rafter to opposite rafter in the upper third of the

triangle created by the pair of rafters. They are face-nailed to the rafters with three 8d nails. Usually, one tie on every third rafter set is ample for most applications.

Roof Openings

Like floors, roof frames often require openings for chimneys, skylights, roof windows, or dormers. Each major opening must be reinforced with additional framing members called headers. Small openings, as for vent pipes are not framed, but simply bored through the roof sheathing. Somewhat larger openings that fit between rafters

can be boxed in with structural members the same size as the rafter stock. This work can be done after the roof frame has been completed. Large openings are treated the same as floor-frame openings, and are framed up as construction proceeds.

Dormers

The same procedures used for walls and roofs are used for dormers, just on a smaller scale. A suitable opening is framed into the roof structure. Then the dormer wall sections are built up and secured to the roof frame, followed by a roof frame for the dormer unit.

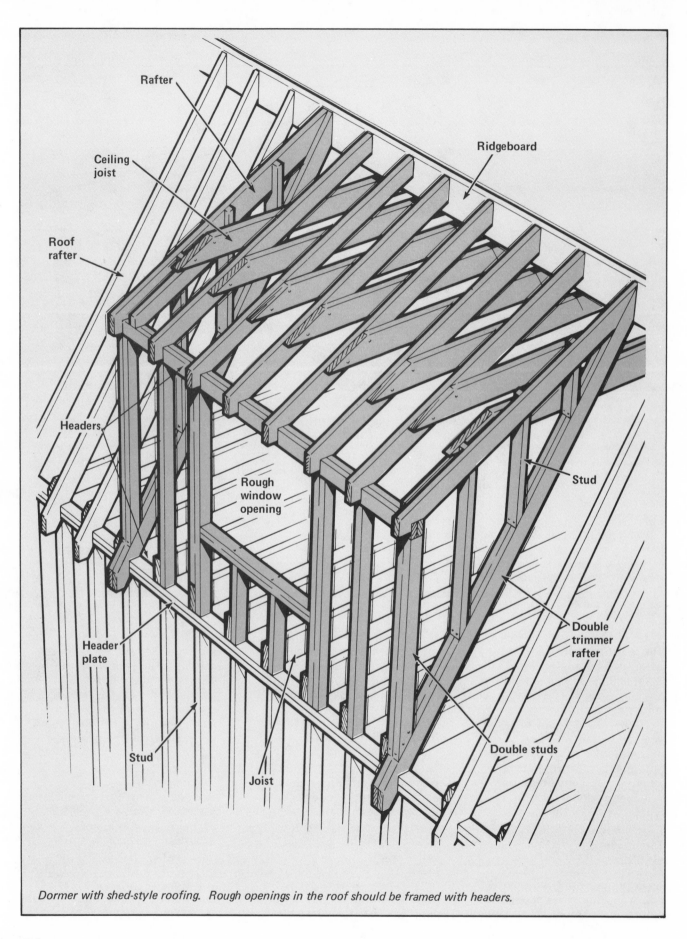

Rafter

Ceiling joist

Ridgeboard

Roof rafter

Headers

Rough window opening

Stud

Header plate

Double trimmer rafter

Stud

Joist

Double studs

Dormer with shed-style roofing. Rough openings in the roof should be framed with headers.

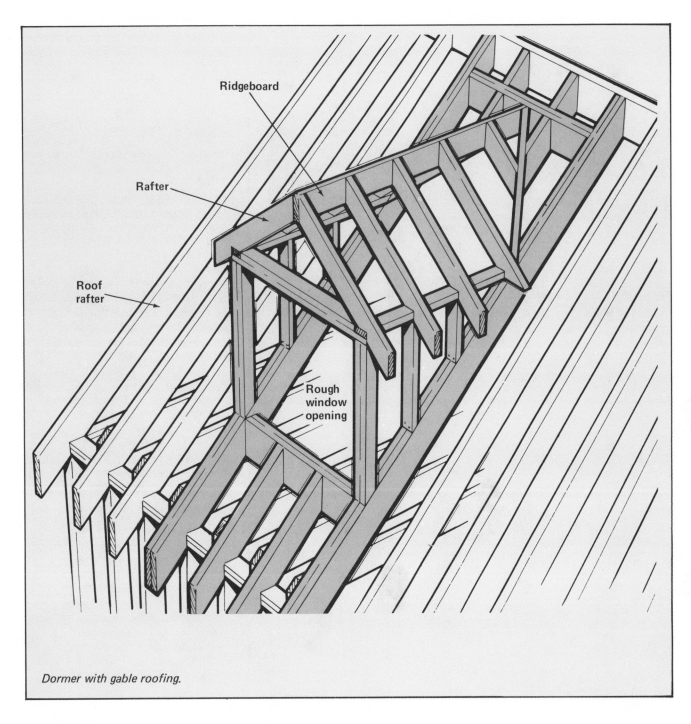

Ridgeboard

Rafter

Roof
rafter

Rough
window
opening

Dormer with gable roofing.

Roof Sheathing

As soon as the framing is complete, roof sheathing should be applied to protect the framework and structure interior from the weather. There are three principal choices for sheathing material: boards, plywood, and decking.

Roofing boards, sometimes called "roofers," are applied at right angles to the rafters. They are usually 1 x 6's or 1 x 8's, but 1 x 6's are more desirable. The stock may be planed on three or four sides, or it may be tongue-and-grooved. Generally, as when asphalt shingles are used, the boards are applied in the closed technique. Each board is snugged up against the next, presenting an unbroken surface.

The open technique is only used for wood shakes and shingles and clay tile. In this method, three or four boards starting from the eave are 1 x 4's or 1 x 6's, tightly fitted together. But subsequent boards are actually nailing strips for the finish roofing. These are usually 1 x 4's, applied with spaces left between them. The relative positions of the nailing strips are lined up according to the nailing requirements and exposed weather surface of the specific size finish roofing material.

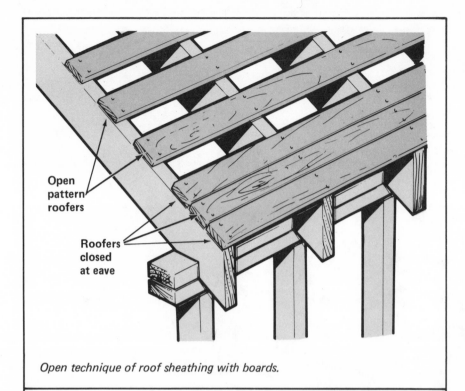

Open technique of roof sheathing with boards.

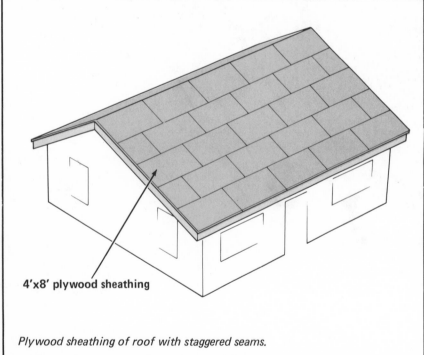

Plywood sheathing of roof with staggered seams.

The panels are laid with their face grain at right angles to the roof rafters, with a $\frac{1}{16}$-inch gap at panel ends and $\frac{1}{8}$-inch gap at panel sides. Nailing is done with 8d size nails. They should be spaced 6 inches apart all around the edges, and 12 inches apart at intermediate supports. All panel joints should be staggered, with $\frac{1}{2}$-lap being common practice because it causes less waste.

Various kinds of decking can also be used for roof sheathing. Wood decking, for instance, is available in 3 x 6 double-tongue-and-groove planks; it is sometimes used on roof frames with wide-spaced rafters or with beam construction. There are also certain insulating deckings made of various materials. Some of these are made with one finished face. This kind of decking is used where there will be no ceiling and the underside of the roof decking is left open to view. In any case, be sure to follow the manufacturer's directions for installation, because specifications for decking materials vary widely.

Exterior Finish

Although some of the finish work, especially in regard to the roof, is carried on as the framework and sheathing is being done, the major part begins when the shell is completed. This exterior finish work is comprised of four principal elements: roofing, siding, doors and windows, and trimwork.

Roofing

There are several different ways to make a roof weathertight and attractive, with further variations for flat roofs, cold roofs, and built-up insulated roofs. The method described here is a common system used with conventional pitched roofs on residential buildings.

Underlayment. The first step is to apply a roofing underlayment that forms a protective interface between the roof sheathing and the weather

The most effective and most commonly used roof sheathing material today is plywood. Thickness depends upon rafter spacing, expected wind and snow loads, type of roofing, and local codes. Sheathing thicknesses range between $\frac{5}{16}$ and $\frac{3}{4}$

inches. Thicker panels are sometimes used under special circumstances. The panels should be of exterior-grade glue. Specify "CDX" for value. This type has one side "C," one side "D" and is made with exterior glue.

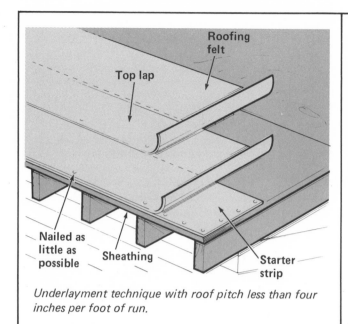

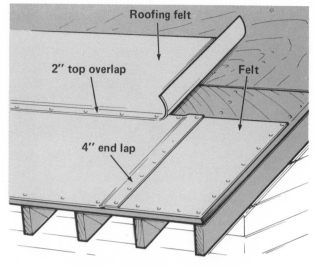

Underlayment technique with roof pitch less than four inches per foot of run.

Underlayment technique for roof pitch more than four inches per foot of run.

surface. It also temporarily protects against moisture before and during the weather surface application.

The material used is asphalt-impregnated felt that comes in standard rolls of various weights. Roofing felt is designated in terms of its weight per 100 square feet. The higher the weight, the thicker the felt and the shorter the roll in running feet. Roof sections with a rise of less than four inches per foot of run are covered with #15 or #30 roofing felt. The #15 variety is preferred for asphalt shingles, due to wrinkles. It is applied to the entire roof deck, starting at the eaves. The process begins by applying a continuous horizontal strip, aligned with the eave. This is nailed down with roofing barbs of suitable length, but nailing is done as little as possible, because when you nail the shingles, you also nail the felt. The second strip—full width—is laid with a full top-lap over the first. Successive strips are laid top-lapped until the roof is covered. Where pieces must be joined end to end to make one run, they should be end-lapped by more than four inches.

If the roof pitch is more than four-in-one, #15 roofing felt is adequate. However, the top-lap need be only two inches at each horizontal seam. Vertical seams should be end-lapped by at least four inches. Nailing is the same as for the lower pitch.

Edging. A metal drip edge should be installed next, although it is not always used. This is a specially formed strip of metal that lies flat on the roof along the edge. It is bent downward and then slightly outward in a lip to divert moisture away from the sheathing edges. Drip edging should be applied all along the eave edges of the roof, and can be placed along the rake (sloping) edges as well.

Flashing. An additional layer

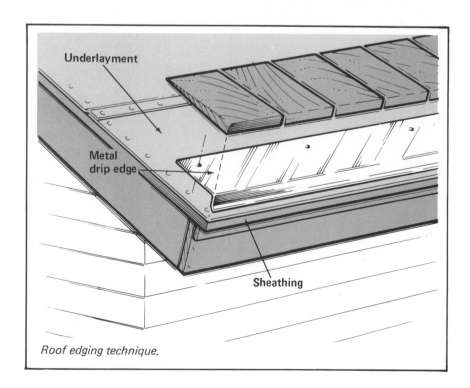

Roof edging technique.

of material, called flashing, is applied at all roof joints and angles, and often along eaves as well, to give extra moisture protection. Flashing is *always* installed around chimneys, stacks, vents, skylights (unless self-flashed), dormers, and along roof valleys, as well as other jointures. Aluminum and galvanized steel flashing is widely used. Copper is sometimes chosen, and lead flashing is only used for plumbing stacks. Some plastic materials are now coming into use. Asphalt roll roofing is also effective in valleys.

Excellent additional ice-dam protection along roof eaves can be gained by adding a single strip of 90-pound, smooth-surface mineral roll roofing. Since the strip is 36 inches wide, a single run is generally sufficient. However, if the roof overhang is exceptionally large, two strips or more ½-toplapped may be necessary, so the uppermost edge of the top strip lies at least a foot beyond the exterior wall lying beneath the roof assembly.

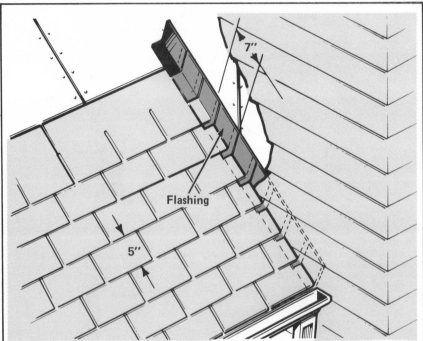

Flashing is always applied where new roofing meets existing structure. The above "closed method" hides the flashing underneath the roofing.

The complicated task of installing chimney flashing is usually left to the mason. He installs it as the chimney is built, and mates it with the finish roof covering as that is applied. Prefabricated steel chimneys, plumbing vent stacks, and such are often fitted with special collars called roof jacks or flashing sleeves. They are installed as the roof weather surface is applied. In most cases, the upper two-thirds of the flashing plate lies beneath the roof weather surface and the lower third above, with the whole plate sealed liberally with roofing cement or other sealing compound.

You can apply valley flashings using 90-pound, mineral-surfaced roll roofing. This is run up the length of the valley in a single, double-layer strip (first layer down with rough side), so the flashing extends 18 inches outward on each side from the valley centerline. Or, strips of metal flashing can be laid in similar fashion. The metal flashing may extend as much as two feet to either side of the valley centerline. The roof weather surface is applied over the flashing.

Weather Surface. A wide selection of roofing weather

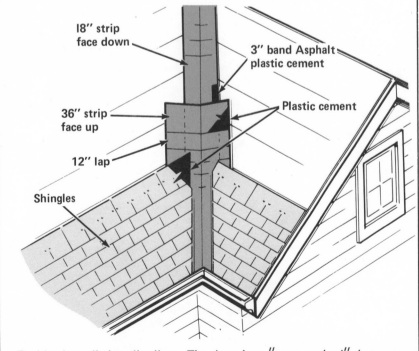

Flashing is applied at all valleys. The above is an "open method" that leaves the flashing exposed to view.

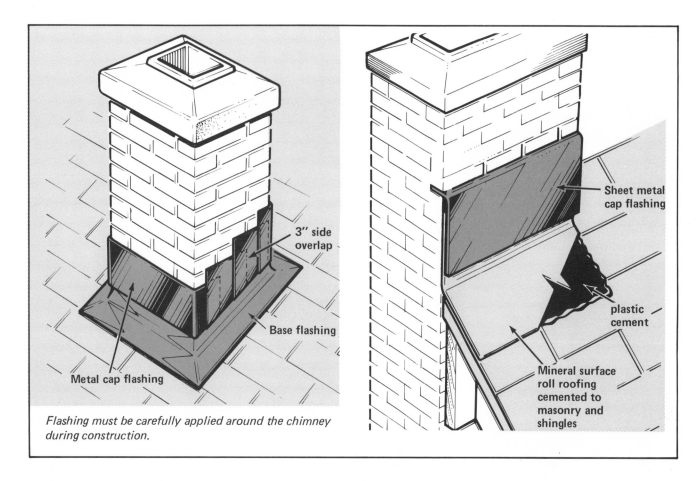

Flashing must be carefully applied around the chimney during construction.

3″ side overlap

Base flashing

Metal cap flashing

Sheet metal cap flashing

plastic cement

Mineral surface roll roofing cemented to masonry and shingles

surfaces is available to the homeowner. Mineral-surface roll roofing, an old standby, can be applied in either single or double coverage. Asphalt three-tab shingles are available in several styles and many colors. Cedar shakes or shingles are very popular and may be laid as individual pieces or in panels or strips; however, they cannot be used under some local building codes unless fire treated. The new varieties of aluminum, fiberglass, or vinyl materials, molded to simulate wood shingles and in various other patterns, are now coming into widespread use. Slate and tile roofing is still laid in some areas. Even metal roofing, usually aluminum or galvanized iron, is sometimes employed in residential applications.

Some of these roofing weather surface materials can only be used if the roof deck is sloped above a certain minimum pitch. For example, a roof with low or zero pitch would be covered with multiple cross-lapped layers of heavy roofing felt sealed with mopped hot tar. This would be topped with a layer of roofing stone bedded in more hot tar. Asphalt or wood shingles are generally only used on pitches of four-in-one and up. Double-coverage roll roofing is suitable

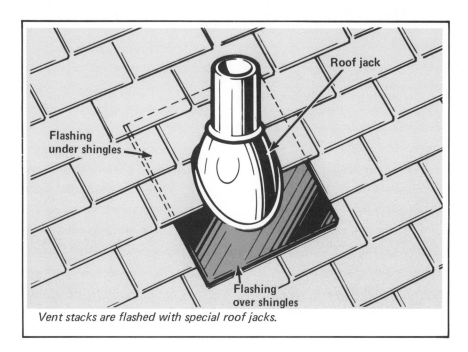

Roof jack

Flashing under shingles

Flashing over shingles

Vent stacks are flashed with special roof jacks.

on a roof with a two-in-one pitch and up, but sheet aluminum should not be used below a six-in-one pitch. Specific application details of weather surface materials vary widely; manufacturer's instructions and recommendations should be followed explicitly. Material weight, longevity, fire resistance and other characteristics, as well as warranties, are also quite variable. Check and compare them.

Joining New to Old. When a new roof is to be a direct, level continuation of the old, the two roof sections must be matched so the joint isn't obvious. Sometimes you can butt the old and new sections together successfully, edge to edge, with underlayment, sheathing, and weather surface of the same type or thickness. The two sheathings can be butted, too, but the new underlayment should overlap the joint and extend onto the old roof for about a foot. This means removal of the old weather surface back to about a foot from the edge. Sealing with hot or cold roofing tar is a good idea, especially on a shallow-pitch roof. Then you can lay the new weather surface, overlapping the joint and weaving in the new with the old. Exactly how you do this depends upon the material you're using. In some cases it may be advantageous to remove the old sheathing back for the space of one or two rafters, perhaps in staggered fashion. This reduces the chances of the joint becoming obvious due to weathering and expansion and contraction of the two building sections.

Where a new roof butts up against an existing building wall, the joint must be completely sealed and flashed. Existing exterior siding must be removed, and you must then wrap the new roof underlayment up the wall against the sheathing for a foot or so. After sealing it with roofing tar, the metal flashing can be applied.

How this is done depends upon the type of weather surface material and exterior siding. The simplest method is to install a continuous run of sheet metal, crimped to an appropriate angle, on the roof and against the wall. The metal should extend a couple of feet in each direction, and be secured with a few nails at the outer edges. Again, sealing with tar gives extra protection. The exterior siding and the roof weather surface is then applied over the flashing.

Doors and Windows

When the roof is weathertight, you can install the exterior doors and windows. Specific installation details vary widely from unit to unit, and manufacturers usually provide directions for installation. Window units should have been selected during planning, and wall openings later roughed-in to accept them. To install the units, you set them in the openings, level, square and plumb them, and nail them in place through the jambs or casings into the wall-framing members. Vinyl-clad units frequently have wide plastic flanges with pre-punched nail holes, making installation simple.

Stock exterior doors are made in certain standard sizes, and the rough openings should have been sized to accommodate them. Standard door height is six feet, eight inches, but seven-foot exterior doors are sometimes chosen. There are several standard widths, with two feet, eight inches being common. But a three-foot width is much more practical for an exterior door. Door thickness is usually 1¾ inches. However, custom or specialty doors may be thicker.

The door frame consists of side and head jambs, door stop, exterior casing, and trimwork. It may be built up on the job site and the door itself fitted and hung as a separate unit. Or you can buy a prehung door assembly, which is complete and

ready to install in the rough opening. Choosing a prehung assembly is more expensive and limits style selection, but it saves a lot of work.

Door and window installation is a tricky business. It must be done accurately for best appearance and minimal operational difficulties later on. This requires careful alignment and fitting, wedging and shimming where necessary, and secure fastening.

Siding

Exterior siding is applied over the sheathing on all exposed wall surfaces. A few types of siding allow you to eliminate the sheathing and apply them directly to the wall framing. In many instances, however, this procedure is neither recommended nor allowed.

A wide variety of finished and unfinished wall siding is available. Some types can be applied in more than one way. Frequently, you can combine one or more kinds to good effect, or one type can be applied in several directional orientations.

Plywood and composition board sheathing needs no further treatment before siding is applied. Board sheathing requires stapling on a layer of tar paper or waterproof building paper (but not an impervious membrane) first. This reduces air infiltration through the sheathing cracks and gives extra moisture protection. The siding is then installed according to the manufacturer's or supplier's directions.

Vertical Siding. Vertical siding is especially popular in many areas. It is often used on single-story houses, on gable end walls, and in combination with horizontal siding for architectural emphasis and effect. Vertical siding, generally made of ¾-inch boards, often rough-cut or resawn, can be applied in a number of ways. You can simply stand them straight up and tightly snugged together, with no further

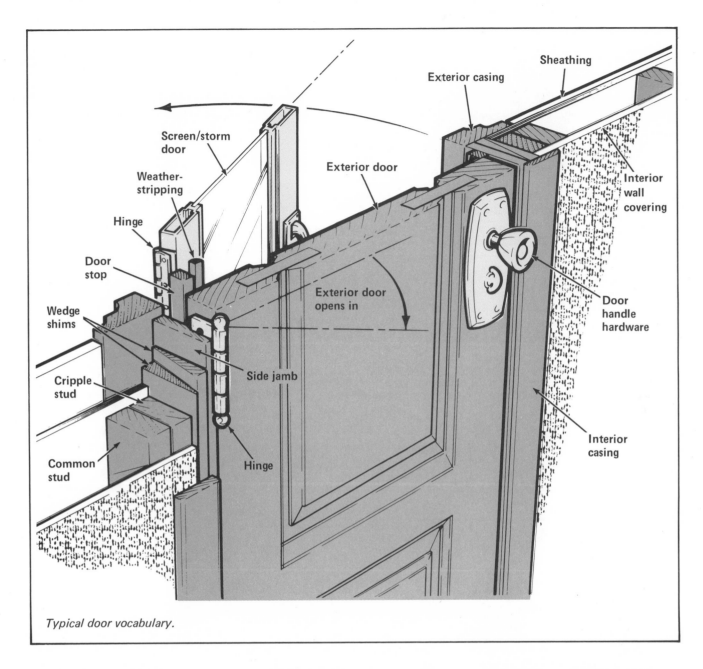

Labels on illustration:

Screen/storm door

Weather-stripping

Hinge

Door stop

Wedge shims

Cripple stud

Common stud

Hinge

Side jamb

Exterior door

Exterior door opens in

Exterior casing

Sheathing

Interior wall covering

Door handle hardware

Interior casing

Typical door vocabulary.

treatment. Or, they can be spaced with a slight gap between each board and narrow strips of wood applied over the cracks. This is the familiar board-and-batten siding. The converse, called "reverse batten," is made by applying the narrow vertical strips directly to the sheathing; the boards are nailed over the battens. A variation is the board-on-board system where wide gaps are left between the boards nailed to the sheathing, and additional boards of the same width are nailed over the gaps.

Horizontal Siding. Beveled siding, or clapboard, is probably the most popular type of horizontal siding. This material is available in several widths and different woods, and is easily applied. Other popular kinds of siding are available in ¾-inch thickness and various designs and pattern names, such as channel-lap, novelty siding, and drop siding. Clapboards overlap one another to a small degree, leaving most of the surface exposed to the weather. But, many other kinds of siding lie flat against the sheathing and

lock together top and bottom with shiplap or tongue-and-groove joints. Several varieties of prefinished hardboard strip siding are available, too.

Shingles. Shingles, or hewn shakes, have long been a favorite exterior siding material. They come by the bundle, are the same as those used on roofs, and are applied individually in either straight or staggered patterns. Although wood shakes and shingles can be purchased in several lengths, widths are most often random. So, applying them is time consuming—but it's not

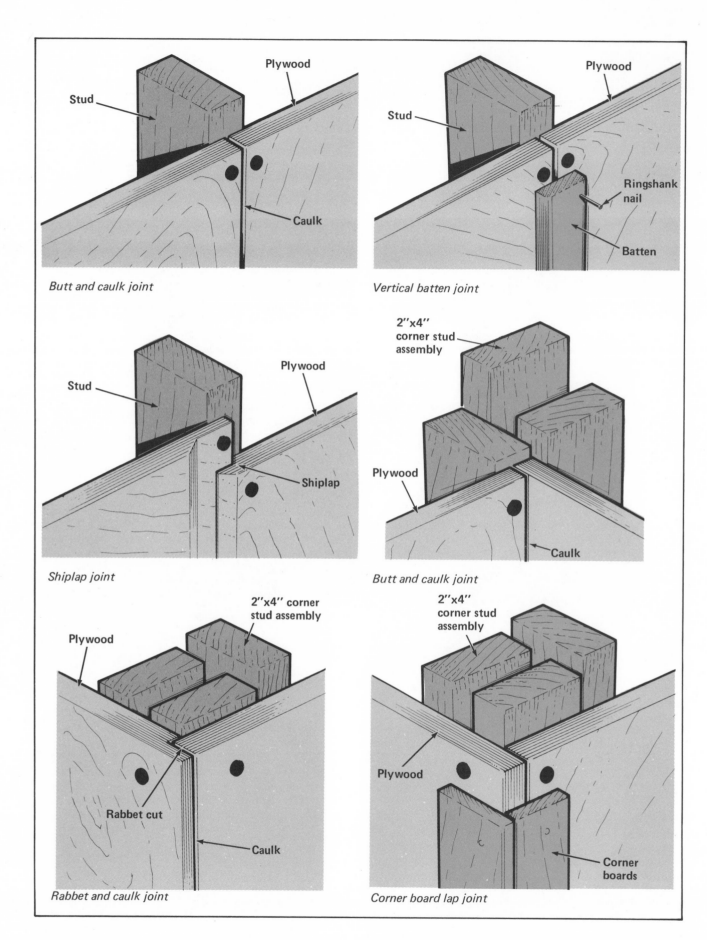

Butt and caulk joint

Vertical batten joint

Shiplap joint

Butt and caulk joint

Rabbet and caulk joint

Corner board lap joint

hard work. Shingles can be applied in single- or double-coverage, the latter affording additional weather protection as well as enhanced shadow lines and a more emphatic siding design. Some manufacturers produce shingles premounted on long backing strips, which facilitates application.

Plywood. Plywood is widely popular because it's tough, strong, and a cinch to apply. A number of exterior-grade patterns are available in both sheets (for vertical or horizontal application) and lap-siding strips. Among the most commonly used is 303 Siding, Texture 1-11 pattern in panels, but there are many others from which to choose. Thickness range is from $\frac{5}{16}$ to $\frac{3}{4}$ inch. You can apply them over plywood or other sheathing—sometimes even directly to wall studs in certain types of construction. Local building codes and the design of the structure dictates the specific application technique to be used.

Panel joints require a special waterproofing treatment. The treatment depends upon the type of joint you're dealing with. Vertical wall joints are butted

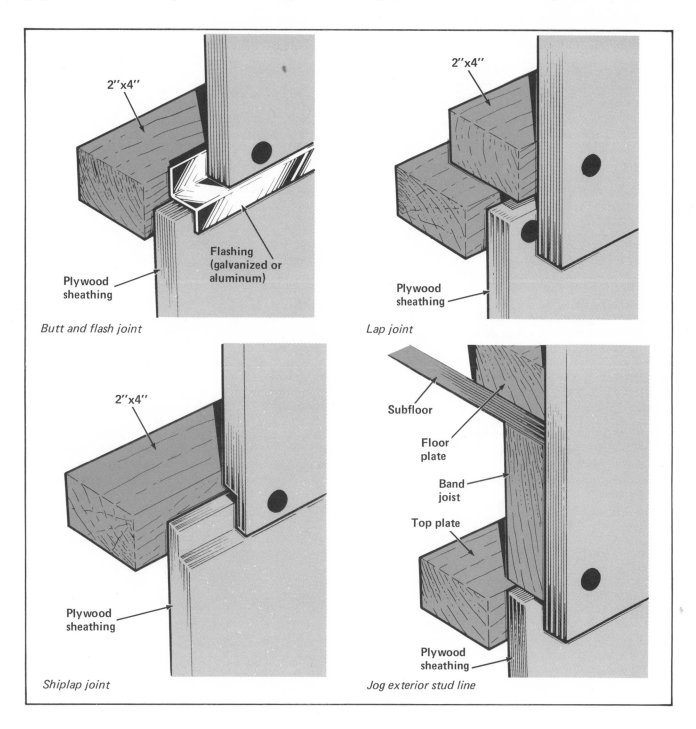

Butt and flash joint

Lap joint

Shiplap joint

Jog exterior stud line

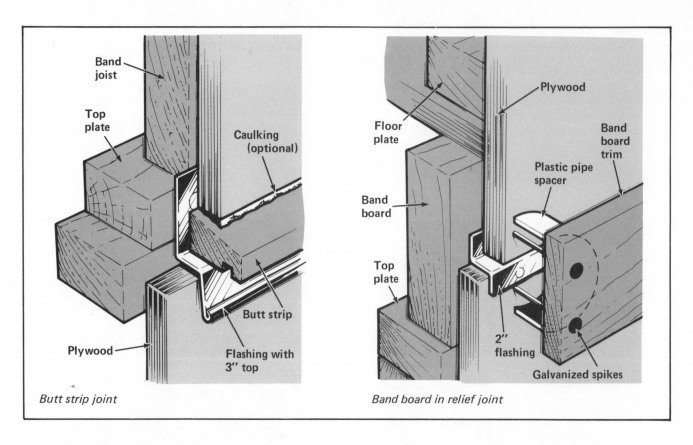

Butt strip joint

Band board in relief joint

and caulked, made with a shiplap joint, or covered by a vertical batten. Vertical corner joints are butted and caulked, rabbeted and caulked, or covered with corner boards. Horizontal joints can be butted and flashed, lapped, or joined with a shiplap joint. Where panels meet in a beltline joint, as in multiple stories or in end-walls, the joint can be jogged, lapped, fitted with a butt strip and flashing, or Z-flashed and covered with a band board. Vertical lap-siding joints should be caulked and backed with a shingle wedge.

Aluminum and Vinyl. Aluminum siding is available in many patterns and colors, and has many advantages. It provides long life with low maintenance, and some types even have a certain amount of insulation value. Embossed vinyl siding is relatively new, but has the potential to become even more popular than aluminum. It can be obtained in numerous colors, textures, and surface patterns for applying either

horizontally or vertically. Manufacturers of this type of siding claim the products offer exceptional weather resistance, colorfastness, resistance to mechanical damage, and low maintenance.

Masonry. Masonry siding, usually called "masonry veneer," enjoys some popularity, despite its high initial cost. Brick veneer is probably the most common, although stone is used, too. A stucco finish, which can be applied in many colors and patterns, is similar to plaster in both appearance and application. All masonry coverings usually require professional application.

Exterior Trim

There's no hard and fast rule concerning exactly when trim should be applied. For example, some trimwork must be installed before particular sidings are applied. In other cases, you can put trim on after everything else is done, or add it as other exterior jobs go on.

Much of the exterior trimwork

concerns the treatment of cornices and roof projections, or overhangs, at eave edges. If there is an overhang along the roof ends, called a "rake projection," trim is also required here. In the simplest construction, the rakes and cornices are left open and the rafter tails and lookout ladder rungs are exposed. This is the "open method," but instead of being left open, a trim board called a "finish fascia" is often nailed across the exposed ends of the rafter tails; the outboard rafter face of the lookout ladder serves the same purpose. One or more trim molding strips may be applied to the fascia. In such open construction, the gaps between the rafters are filled with frieze blocks, and the finish siding fitted around the rafter tails and extended to meet the underside of the roof sheathing. All seams and cracks should be caulked.

The alternative to the open cornice is the "box cornice." This requires the addition of a soffit, which encloses the open

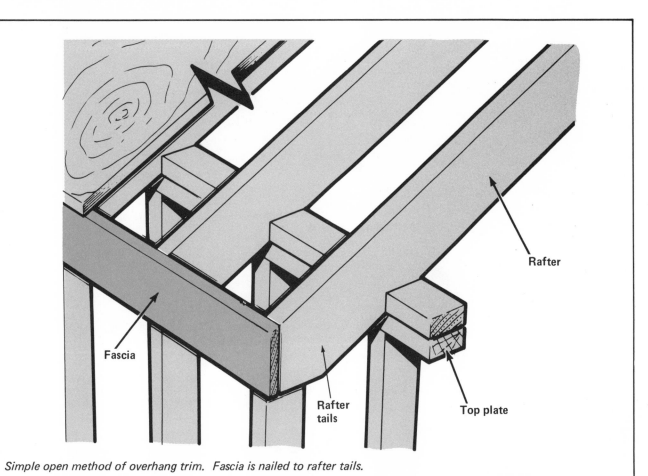

Simple open method of overhang trim. Fascia is nailed to rafter tails.

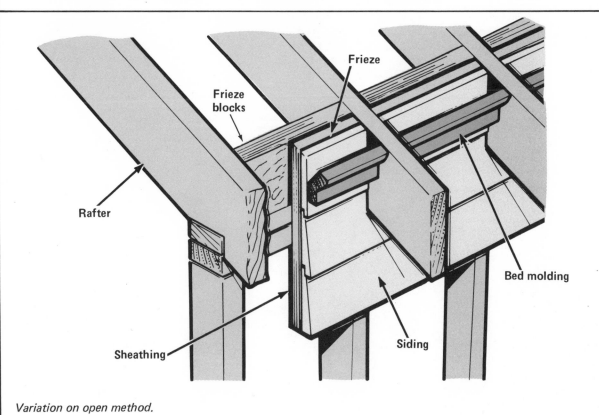

Variation on open method.

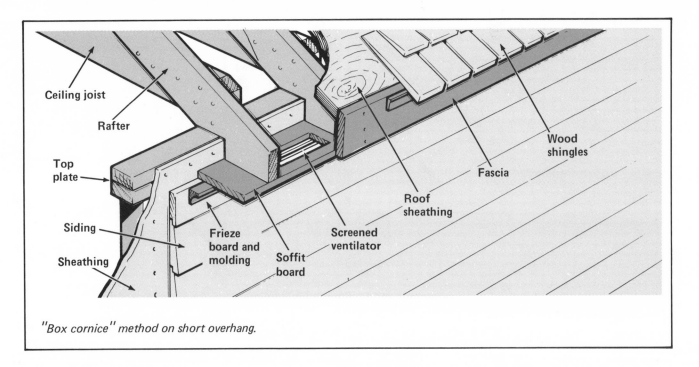

"Box cornice" method on short overhang.

area beneath the eaves or the rake projection. There are a number of ways to accomplish this. One method used where the overhang is very short is to trim the rafter tails on a horizontal line from the wall to the tail tip. A continuous soffit board is attached directly to the faces of these cuts, and a fascia is nailed across the exposed rafter ends.

The fascia usually extends slightly below the soffit-board edge, and a shingle or roofing molding is frequently applied along the upper part of the fascia, with the roof weather surface extending slightly beyond the molding. The finish siding can be butted directly against the soffit board, or a frieze board might be installed

along the joint between the soffit board and the wall sheathing. A frieze molding is sometimes also installed along the top of the frieze board to seal the joints between the frieze board and the soffit board.

When the roof overhang is considerable, you can install either a flat or sloping soffit. The sloping soffit is fastened

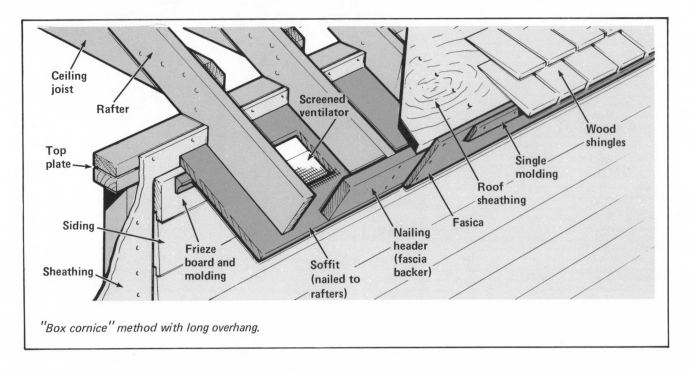

"Box cornice" method with long overhang.

directly to the underside of the
rafter tails, so it pitches upward
at the same angle as the roof. As
with the narrow box cornice, a
fascia is nailed across the
exposed rafter ends. If you wish,
a frieze board or molding can be
installed at the soffit/wall
sheathing joint. The flat soffit
requires building a lookout. The
lookout rungs are attached to a
lookout ledger plate that is
nailed to the wall, and the free
ends are secured to the rafter
tails. This forms a horizontal
framework to which a soffit can
be applied. Again, fascia and
frieze boards, along with
assorted trim moldings, can be
installed or not, as desired.

Although plywood is perhaps
the most commonly used soffit
material, there are other suitable
choices. Ordinary boards of
appropriate width can be
attached parallel to the walls, or
short pieces can be secured
perpendicular to them on a
framework. Strips of hardboard
will also work; the perforated
type is often used where eave
ventilation is desired. Particle
board is useable, too, but it is
the hardest material to work
with. A water-resistant gypsum
wallboard is adequate if well-
sealed. Special metal soffit
panels, usually prefinished
aluminum and available either
blank or perforated, can also be
installed; in this case the soffit
should be dimensioned and
constructed to suit the
particular kind of panel, rather
than trying to fit the panels to
an off-sized frame.

If there is no rake projection
at the roof ends, the
construction is called a "close
rake." This is trimmed out by
first installing a fascia block—a
strip of wood nailed to the gable
end sheathing and flush with the
surface of the roof sheathing.
The exterior finish siding is
butted up against the bottom
edge of the fascia block. The
fascia itself is a bit wider than
the fascia block, and is attached
to the fascia block with the top
edge flush and the bottom edge

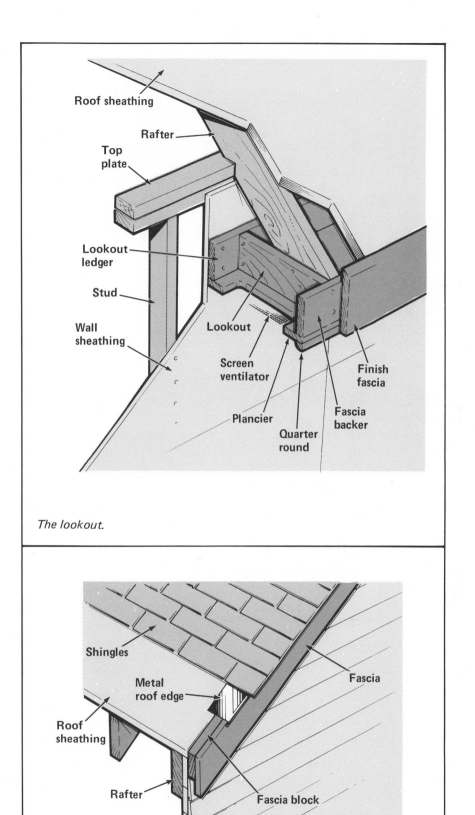

The lookout.

"Close rake" method with no overhang.

123

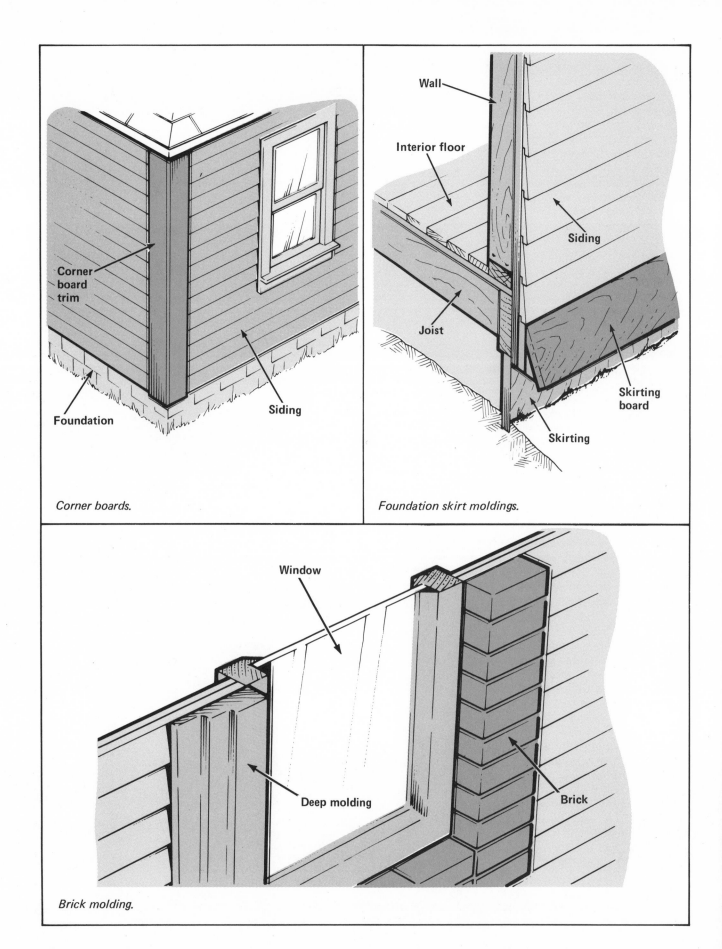

Corner boards.

Foundation skirt moldings.

Brick molding.

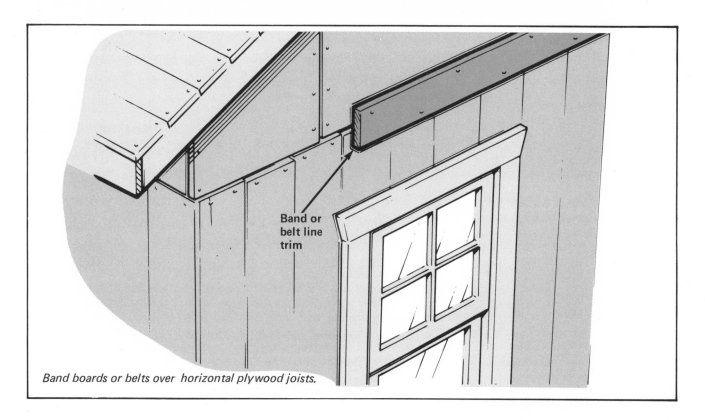

Band boards or belts over horizontal plywood joists.

over-hanging slightly. The roof drip edge and weather surface is applied to overhang the fascia by a small amount.

Some designs call for other assorted bits of trim. For instance, corner boards are sometimes used with certain kinds of exterior finish siding. These are two-to-eight-inch wide strips of wood, that are applied vertically at all inside and outside corners, with the siding butted up to their edges. Or, foundation skirt moldings, or skirt boards, may be called for. This molding or board stock is applied just above the foundation and at a 45-degree angle to the siding to divert moisture away from the skirting below. Extra trim, such as brick molding, may be applied around windows or doors to enhance shadow lines and provide architectural emphasis. Wide exterior casings are sometimes put up for much the same reason. Band boards or belts may be installed over horizontal joints in plywood exterior siding, or outside vertical battens may be applied

over inside corners or other types of exterior joints. Moldings may be scribed to fit alongside masonry sections to help seal them from the weather.

Victorian, Swiss, or Bavarian styles may require the attachment of a certain amount of carvings, gingerbread, or other fancy woodwork.

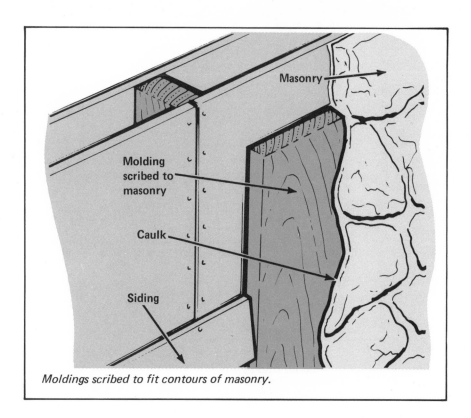

Moldings scribed to fit contours of masonry.

The Interior

Some aspects of finishing the interior, such as roughing in plumbing, can be done as soon as the shell is weathertight and in the final stages of completion. Most of the interior finishing, however, is usually left until the shell is totally constructed. When to begin a particular project is often only a matter of convenience.

Electrical Wiring

When the structure's framework is completed, you can begin roughing in the new electrical circuits. But before doing anything, *always* check your local electrical code and the latest National Electrical Code to make sure the installation will be proper and safe.

You can start the roughing-in with either the electrical wires or the device boxes. The boxes are the best choice, because once they're set, it's easier to select routes for the cables. Wall boxes for duplex receptacles are usually installed at about 12 inches above floors, or 9 inches above countertops. Switch wall boxes are usually placed uniformly at about four feet above the floor. The boxes can be attached with either nails or screws. If the wall covering is noncombustible, the boxes should be adjusted to protrude beyond the framing members so they will set back no more than ¼ inch from the finished wall surface. Boxes set in combustible material must be set flush with the finished surface. In any case, the boxes should be accurately aligned and plumb. You can use either metal or plastic boxes with nonmetallic cable, but metal boxes must be used with conduit or other metallic raceway. Fixture boxes can also be installed at all lighting fixture locations, and junction boxes mounted wherever necessary.

After installing the device boxes, it's time to run the cables. This requires boring holes and driving staples. Holes

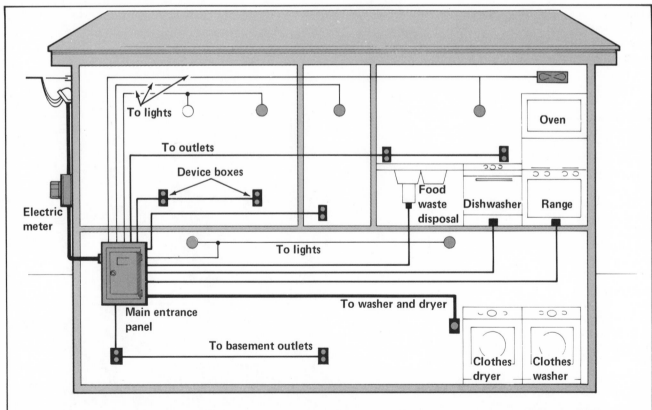

The typical house wiring system is illustrated above. Before "roughing in" the electrical system for your addition, make sure to consult the local electrical code, as well as the National Electrical Code.

126

for cables should be drilled as closely as possible to the center of the member involved. This is done so the drywall installer won't penetrate cables with nails or screws. If you can't drill the holes at the center of a member, the hole should be at least two inches from the nearest edge of the member—at least 1½ inches from an edge in the case of 2 x 4 studs. Holes should be bored as straight as possible, splinters should be removed, and successive holes should be fairly well aligned. Otherwise, cables may hang up or be damaged when pulled through. Where cables are not run through holes, they must be stapled with specially made staples of the proper size—never with fence staples or bent nails. Cable should be secured every 4½ feet at a minimum, with one staple placed no more than 12 inches ' from a metal device box, and 8 inches from a plastic device box.

You can run nonmetallic cables free in framing cavities—like spaces between wall studs or floor joists—in any way that's handy, as long as you close the cavities later to protect the cables. Or, you can fish them through existing cavities. Cables may be stapled to framing members in unfinished or relatively inaccessible locations, or stapled to runner boards. They should not be stapled along the bottom edges of floor joists or rafters, but rather up on the sides. Where a cable turns a corner, the bend should not be more than a radius less than five times the diameter of the cable—about 2½ inches for #12 two-conductor cable, for instance. In all cases, route the cables so they won't interfere with something else, or compress thermal insulation so much that its effectiveness is reduced. Leave a bit of slack in the cables, and be careful not to damage them when stapling or pulling through holes. Also, leave at least six inches of free cable inside each device box for making connections later.

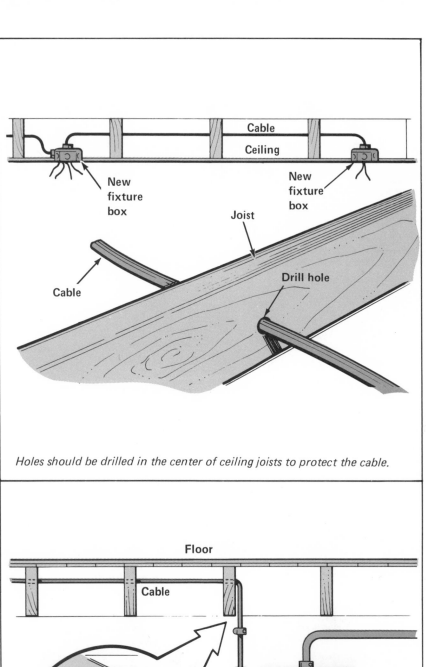

Holes should be drilled in the center of ceiling joists to protect the cable.

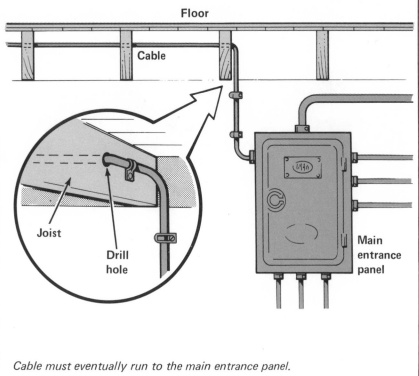

Cable must eventually run to the main entrance panel.

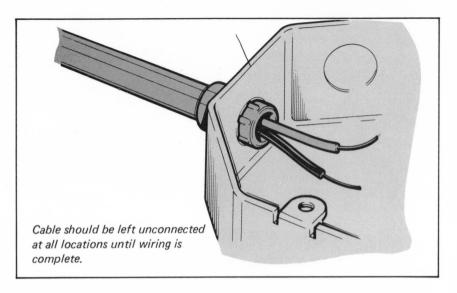

Cable should be left unconnected at all locations until wiring is complete.

Device, switch, and convenience-outlet circuit loops should be installed according to earlier plans, and cables routed as directly as possible. In the case of circuit extension, one or more cables will run back to existing circuits. Otherwise, one or more "home runs"—that part of a circuit between the main service entrance panel and the first outlet—must be taken back to the main entrance panel, or the nearest load center, for later connection.

Branch circuits to serve appliances, heating units, water heaters, and such can run directly to outlet boxes. But in some cases, a stub of cable is left hanging loose at the proper location for future direct connection.

The remainder of the electrical work is done after all interior finish work is completed. Then the lighting fixtures can be mounted and connected; duplex outlets and lighting switches

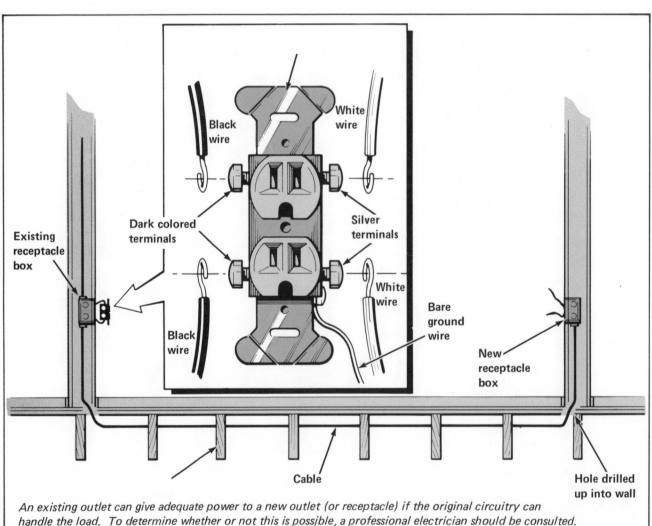

An existing outlet can give adequate power to a new outlet (or receptacle) if the original circuitry can handle the load. To determine whether or not this is possible, a professional electrician should be consulted.

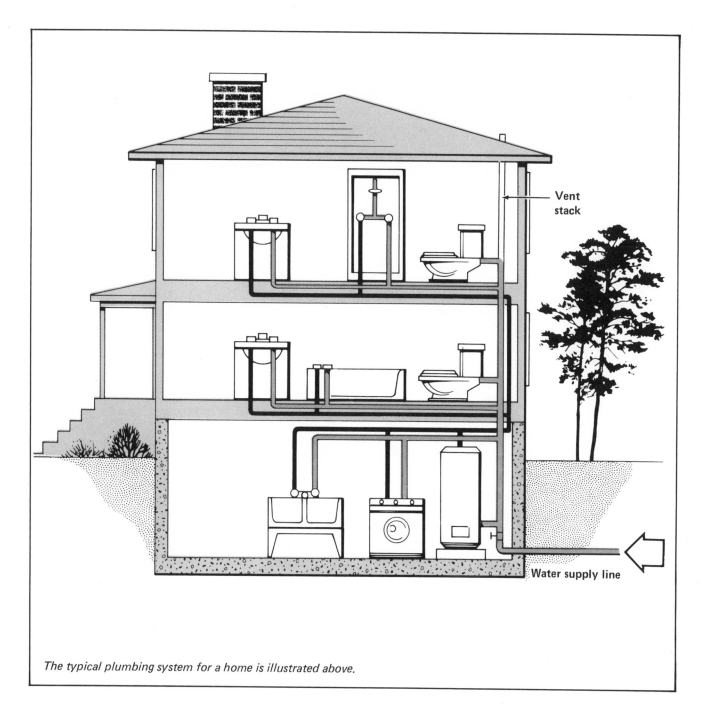

Water supply line

The typical plumbing system for a home is illustrated above.

connected, placed into their boxes, and the finish plates attached; and appliances installed, connected, and tested.

If the existing electrical system needs upgrading, it can be done at any time before, during, or after the expansion program. New circuits serving the expansion project are left unconnected until the new, upgraded electrical system is put into operation to avoid additional work and overload.

Plumbing

Fixture and appliance locations, and general pipeline routing should have been determined during planning stages, and checked for code compliance. Plumbing needs can be roughed-in as soon as the shell is far enough along to accept them, however it's best to rough-in stacks prior to roofing. All pipes and fittings are installed first. Fixtures are put in and

connected when most of the interior finish work has been completed.

Water Pipes

Roughing-in water pipes is usually the easiest part of the job. Copper pipe or tubing, CPVC (chlorinated polyvinyl chloride) plastic pipe or PB (polybutylene) plastic tubing (where allowed), or galvanized steel pipe can be used for both hot and cold water supply lines.

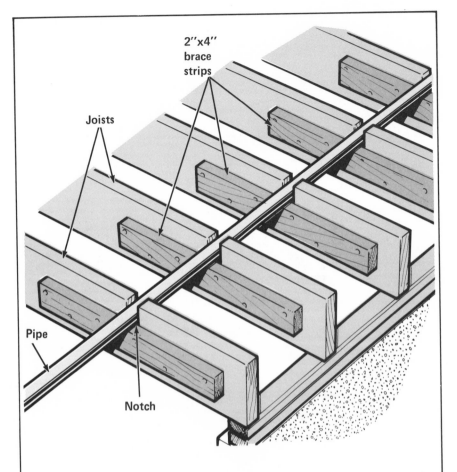

Notches can be cut for pipes to run through joists. Braces must be attached to compensate for the lost strength of the joists.

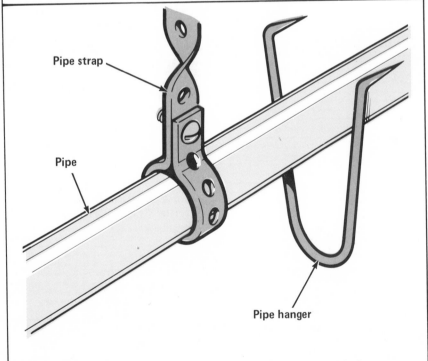

Pipes can be run through free cavities when hung with a special pipe strap.

Flexible PB tubing is the simplest to use, because you can run it through bored holes like electrical cable. Plastic pipe is also simple to install, especially for the do-it-yourselfer, and copper pipe or tube is not much harder. However, many local codes still prohibit or limit the use of plastic pipe. Threaded, galvanized steel pipe is the most difficult to work with.

In any case, installing plumbing is a matter of choosing the most direct and convenient routes from fixture locations to the nearest existing pipelines that can be tapped. If one or two normal-volume fixtures are involved, they can be connected with ⅜-inch pipe. But if one is a high-volume fixture, like a shower, or if several fixtures need to be connected, ½-inch pipe is best. You run the pipe piece by piece and fitting by fitting through walls, ceilings, and floors, as necessary. Lines should always run on the inside of any thermal insulation, and be kept away from cold areas as much as possible. It's best to choose locations where the air surrounding the pipe will be the same, or just slightly lower than room temperature. Pipes should be stubbed out of the floors or walls at fixture locations, and left unconnected at the existing supply line. And you should install shutoff, or stop, valves wherever necessary. Lines should also be pitched, so they can be drained easily.

Drain, Waste, and Vent (DWV) Lines

These are roughed-in much like the water supply lines. However, minimum pipe size is 1¼ inches for drain lines and three inches for waste lines. The diameter for toilet vent stacks must be at least three inches, but individual vent stacks for sinks or washbasins should be 1¼ or 1½ inches in diameter. Today, copper or plastic pipe is used for these installations.

The horizontal drain line for nonhuman liquid wastes should

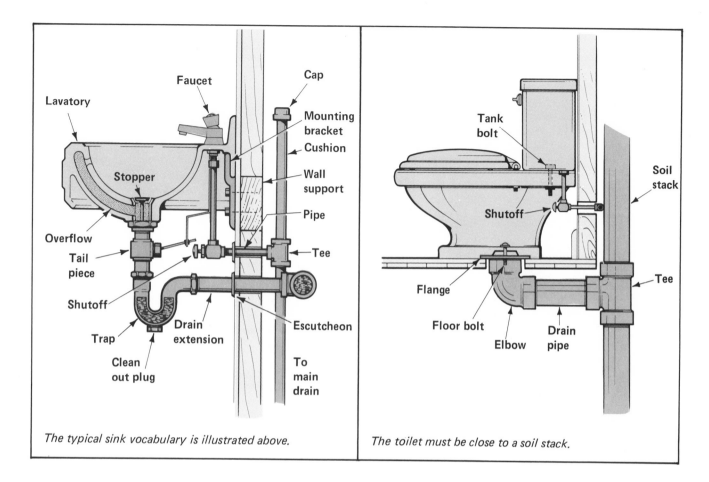

The typical sink vocabulary is illustrated above.

The toilet must be close to a soil stack.

run from a fixture location to a point where it can be tapped into an existing main drain. With appropriate pipe sections and fittings, you can connect two or more fixtures to the same lateral. For example, a darkroom sink, washbasin, bar sink, and shower stall might share the same lateral, provided they're relatively close together. These drainpipes can be almost any practical length, although there are code and physical limitations. But they should be pitched downward toward the main drain connection at a rate of ¼ inch per running foot. If the fixture location and main drain are too close together to do this over the entire span of the pipe, the line should run at the ¼-inch pitch and then change to an angled drop into the main drain.

There's a different procedure for connecting a toilet. This fixture requires a three-inch waste line feeding directly into a

vertical soil stack, which also serves as a toilet vent stack. This is done by first installing a special closet flange in the floor and connecting the toilet to the flange. Then you attach a closet bend to the bottom of the flange, and run an appropriate length of soil pipe into the stack. Since the drainpipe shouldn't be more than five feet long, a new soil stack has to be installed unless the toilet is close to an existing one. The soil stack makes a bend below floor level and is continued as a lateral, pitched ¼ inch to the running foot, to its connection point with the main house drain.

When fixtures are tightly grouped in a complete bath installation, often the new or existing soil stack may also serve as a vent for the fixtures. Dimensional specifics vary with local plumbing codes. Further venting is required when fixtures are widely separated, or when you can't make

connections to a nearby soil stack. You can provide a new vent stack for an individual or small group of fixtures, or revent to a principal soil or vent stack, either existing or newly installed. Individual vent stacks are installed by continuing the drainpipe up past the fixture and out through the roof. Reventing is done by extending the drainpipe up past the fixture and across through a ceiling or other cavity to join with a soil or vent stack at a level higher than the fixture drain.

Each fixture drain also requires a trap. A trap lets waste flow in one direction, but retains a plug of water to prevent air and sewer gases from entering the house. Traps are absolutely essential, and should *never* be modified or omitted. Traps must be installed in floor drains, and drains for tubs, showers, washbasins, washing machines, and such. The only exception is the toilet, which has

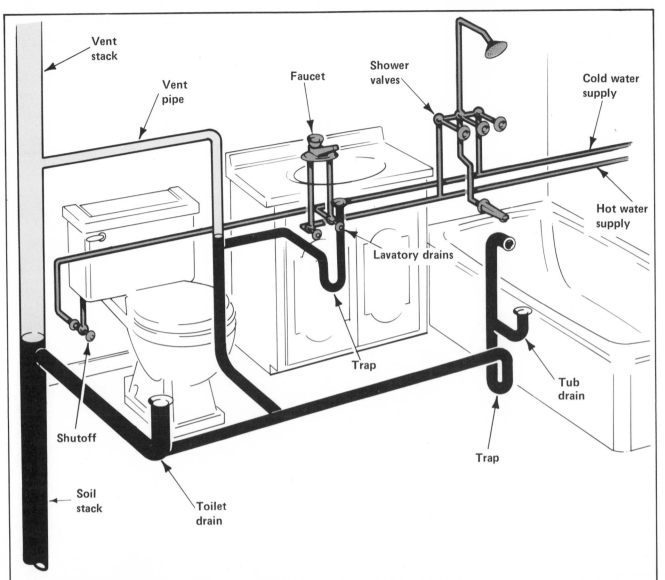

Vent stack

Vent pipe

Faucet

Shower valves

Cold water supply

Hot water supply

Lavatory drains

Trap

Tub drain

Trap

Shutoff

Soil stack

Toilet drain

The soil stack can serve as a vent when bathroom fixtures are grouped tightly together.

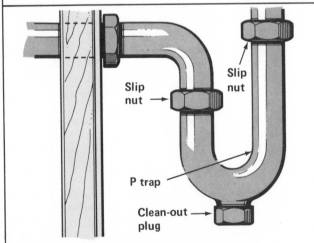

Slip nut

Slip nut

P trap

Clean-out plug

The typical sink (P) trap is illustrated above. Diameter is 1-1/4" for bathroom sinks; 1-1/2" for kitchen sinks.

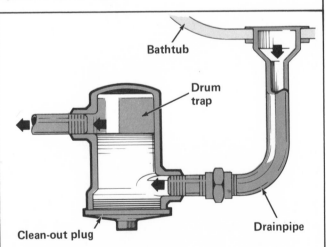

Bathtub

Drum trap

Drainpipe

Clean-out plug

Tubs frequently utilize a drum trap. These not only protect against sewer gas, but also collect hair and dirt that otherwise clogs drains.

132

a built-in trap. These traps take several forms, and the one to use depends on the fixture and its installation method. A trap is connected to the drain outlet of the fixture, with the other end connected to the drainpipe.

Fixture Installation

Most plumbing fixtures are installed after everything else in the immediate area has been completed. This is because some fixtures are intended to rest on finish coverings. With others, later installation is simply easier and reduces risk of fixture damage. This is the case with sinks and washbasins that mount on finished counter or vanity tops, and toilets that rest on finished floor coverings. Built-in items, like bathtubs and shower stalls, are the exception. They are usually installed at early stages of the construction. Plumbing connections don't always have to be made at that point, although they often are.

The specifics of fixture installations are quite variable. But the fixtures usually come with detailed instructions for easy installation. In general, making the connections involves installing traps as necessary between the fixture drain outlets and the fixture drainpipes, and attaching the water supply lines to faucet assemblies. Shutoff

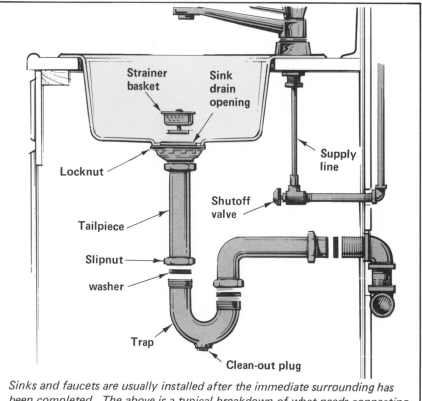

Sinks and faucets are usually installed after the immediate surrounding has been completed. The above is a typical breakdown of what needs connecting.

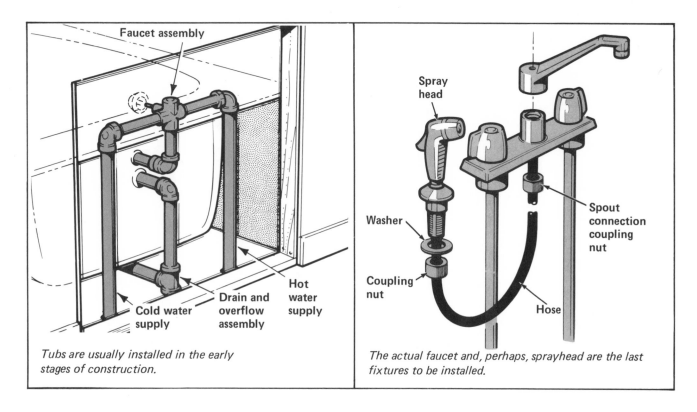

Tubs are usually installed in the early stages of construction.

The actual faucet and, perhaps, sprayhead are the last fixtures to be installed.

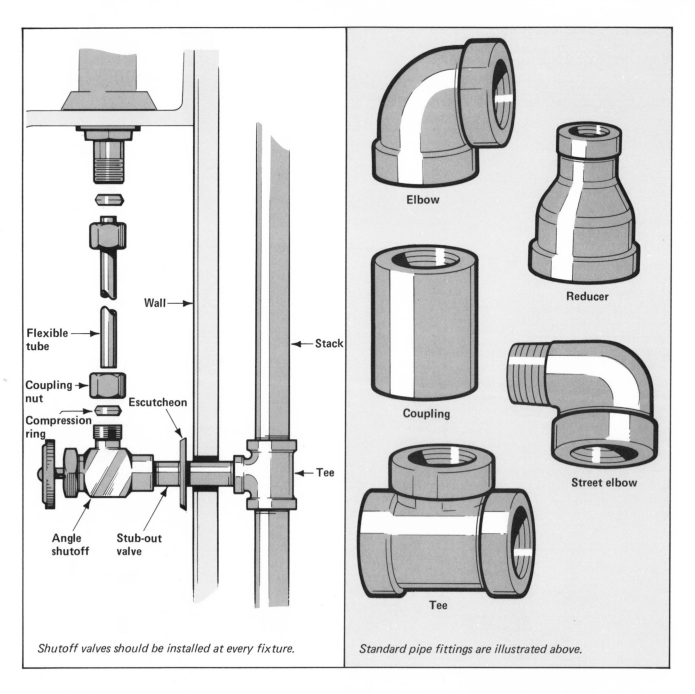

Flexible tube

Coupling nut

Compression ring

Wall

Stack

Escutcheon

Tee

Angle shutoff

Stub-out valve

Shutoff valves should be installed at every fixture.

Elbow

Reducer

Coupling

Street elbow

Tee

Standard pipe fittings are illustrated above.

valves should be installed in water supply lines at all fixtures. And all connections must be checked thoroughly under pressure for leaks.

Plumbing Connections

Connecting new water supply and DWV lines to an existing plumbing system is best done after everything else is hooked up and ready to go. The procedure for doing this is different for almost every project. And describing the

hundreds of possibilities is beyond the scope of this book. However, there are dozens of different adaptors and standard and transition fittings available for all types of pipe. So, coming up with the right combination for a good connection is largely a matter of finding the right parts and putting them together properly.

For example, you can use a special fitting called a "saddle tee" to make a connection to an existing copper or galvanized

steel pipe. You needn't cut the existing pipe. You just clamp the saddle tee to the existing pipe, drill a hole, and attach the new line to the fitting. Connections to some kinds of drain lines can be made with special couplings and clamps. And, plastic pipe or tubing can be connected to iron pipe with special transition fittings. You must, however, be careful not to let dissimilar metals come in contact with one another, because electrolysis will occur.

Heating and Cooling

If the house's heating system has adequate capacity, extensions can be made to serve an addition. This is largely a matter of tapping into the existing system at convenient locations, and running new hot-air ducts and cold-air returns, or new hot-water supply and return pipes to the addition. And, in some cases, it might be desirable to establish a new heating zone with additional controls. When the addition is sufficiently complete, hot-air registers or hot-water baseboard radiation units are installed as necessary. Naturally, ducts, registers and radiation units should be properly sized and located for even, efficient heating.

Some additions, particularly detached ones, are more easily heated with individual electric comfort heating units. Initial cost is low, and installation is simple and flexible, although electric heating may be expensive in the long run. Baseboard units are most common, but radiant ceiling panels or wall-mounted, fan-equipped units are equally useful. If heat is needed in early construction stages, the units can be installed at that time, or you can wait until the final finishing stages. Gas-fired comfort heating units, available in many sizes, are equally effective, and usually cheaper.

If the existing heating system is also used for cooling, both heating and cooling the addition will be taken care of by extending the ducts to the new living space. Where this isn't possible, you can install either fixed or portable cooling units in the addition. Fixed units are wired directly into the electrical system, while portable units are usually window-mounted and plugged in. In any case, the electrical system must be of sufficient capacity to handle these high-load machines.

Fireplaces, and particularly stoves, can be installed in an addition to provide a primary or auxiliary source of heat. In auxiliary use, they supplement the conventional heating system. When used as a primary source, another backup source may or may not be installed.

Masonry fireplaces and large masonry or tile stoves are usually built by professional masons, often while the house

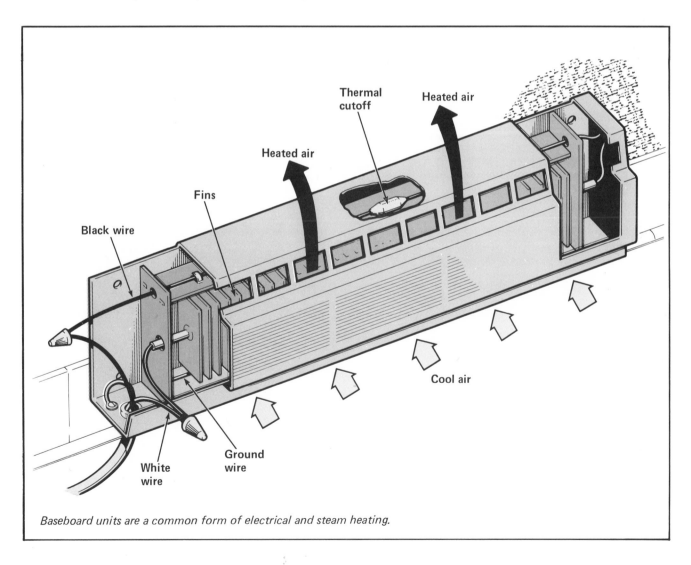

Baseboard units are a common form of electrical and steam heating.

135

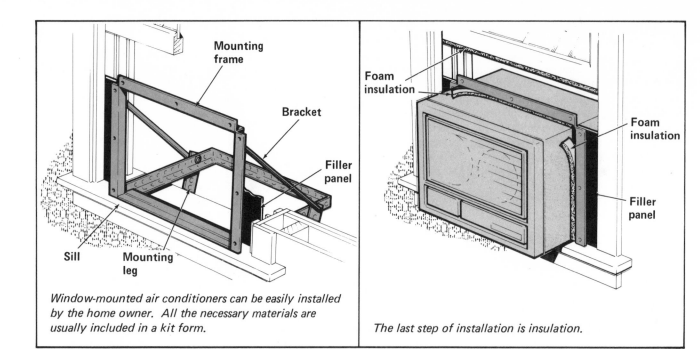

Mounting frame

Bracket

Filler panel

Sill

Mounting leg

Window-mounted air conditioners can be easily installed by the home owner. All the necessary materials are usually included in a kit form.

Foam insulation

Foam insulation

Filler panel

The last step of installation is insulation.

shell is being constructed. Freestanding fireplaces and wood-burning stoves, however, are popular do-it-yourself projects. You can place these units practically anywhere, and setup merely involves following the manufacturer's directions for proper clearances from combustible surfaces and placing the unit on a satisfactory hearth or mat. The appliance chimney is complete with installation instructions. It can be put in just before you apply the roof's weather surface, or you can delay installation until much of the finish work is underway. Unless there's an immediate need for heat, the heating unit itself is usually one of the last things to be installed.

Active or passive solar heating is also a consideration. An active system requires certain equipment, such as storage tanks or vaults, plumbing or ductwork, and heat collectors. Passive systems don't use mechanical equipment. They encourage the admittance of solar heat into the addition by virtue of the structure's design. But heat storage devices, like a Trombe wall, can be made part of the design to add to heating effectiveness. There are dozens

of ways to introduce solar-assist heating into a building, and all details must be sorted out in the planning stages. Generally speaking, the installation starts at the very beginning of construction, and runs from

foundation to final finishing stages. Some kinds of solar-heating equipment can be retrofitted as an afterthought, but you get the best results by starting with a solar design in the first place.

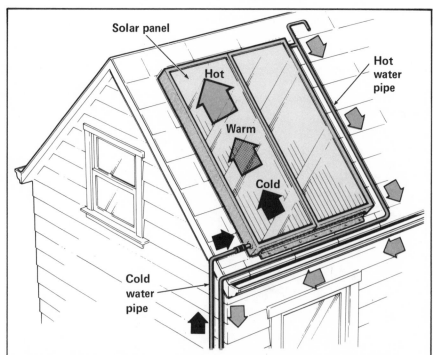

Solar panel

Hot

Warm

Cold

Hot water pipe

Cold water pipe

The flat plate unit is the most popular active solar system. If solar panels are part of your addition plans, the roof should be angled precisely in the original design.

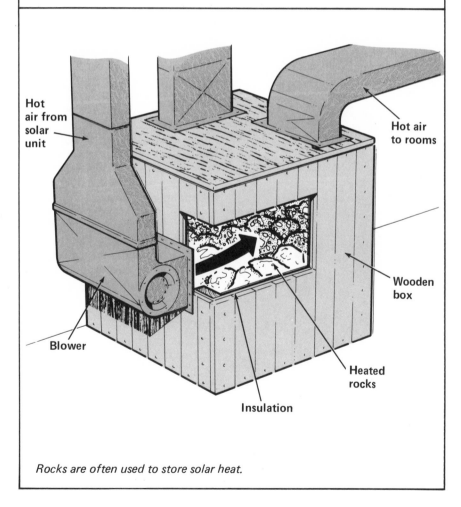

Flat plate collector

Hot water

Transfer valve

Hot water supply

Thermal pump collector

Cold water supply

Cold water

Pump Supply tank Thermal sensor Solar tank Supply valve Supplemental hot water heater

In a solar hot water system, a circulator pump is generally used to carry water through the collector.

Hot air from solar unit

Hot air to rooms

Wooden box

Blower

Heated rocks

Insulation

Rocks are often used to store solar heat.

Insulation

After roughing-in all utilities, and completing all work in the structural cavities, insulation can be installed. However, building departments usually want to inspect the "rough" prior to insulation work. Rolls or batts of mineral wool or spun fiberglass are most commonly used. Other possibilities include blown-in mineral wool or chopped cellulose; pour-type insulation, such as vermiculite; and rigid sheets of polystyrene or similar plastics. Reflective insulation may be used in areas where the climate is benign year-round. Some insulation is installed during the earlier construction stages. This is the case when rigid insulation is sandwiched between exterior siding and wall sheathing, or when the hollow cores of concrete block walls are filled with pour-type, granular insulation. However, most insulation, especially that prone to moisture damage, is applied after the shell is weathertight, and the interior finish work is about to begin.

Insulation thickness required depends upon many factors, including the material's R-value per inch of thickness, local weather conditions, local building code requirements, and the degree of thermal efficiency desired. All details must be worked out in the planning stage. Blown-in insulations are machine installed by contractors, usually after interior walls and ceilings have been covered, but before final finish work begins. Pour-type insulation can be emplaced at any convenient time. It's usually installed by hand above the covered ceiling joists in an open attic, either before or after final finishing. If affixed to a kraft paper or foil backing, roll or batt fiberglass or mineral wool is stapled in place. Unbacked batts or strips are simply stuffed into structure cavities, where they cling by friction.

In general, whenever there's a

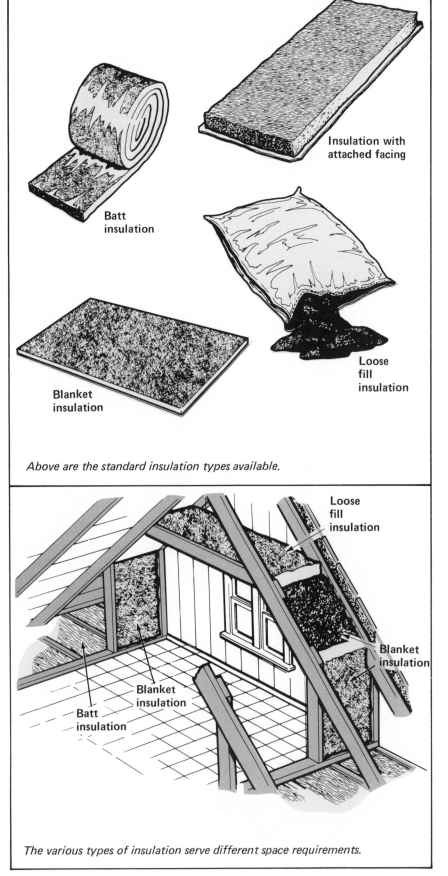

Above are the standard insulation types available.

The various types of insulation serve different space requirements.

Insulation with attached facing

Batt insulation

Loose fill insulation

Blanket insulation

Loose fill insulation

Blanket insulation

Blanket insulation

Batt insulation

relatively consistent temperature differential of more than 15° or 20°F between one surface and another, insulation should be installed. This includes all exterior walls, roof, floors over an unheated basement or crawl space, walls between a partially or unheated garage, and so on.

For an effective installation, all areas must be fully covered to uniform depth or thickness, and seams must be tightly butted or overlapped to eliminate cracks. Blanket insulation should retain its full loft, and not be unduly compressed or squashed flat by pipes, wires, ducts, or framing members. For any kind or brand of insulation, follow the manufacturer's instructions carefully.

Sealing the structure to prevent excessive air infiltration or exfiltration is important, too. Mechanical barriers must be used wherever cold or warm air might enter or exit the structure. For instance, all cracks and spaces appearing between a window or door unit and rough opening framing members should be stuffed with blanket insulation. All exterior joints should be heavily caulked. Doors and windows require weatherstripping, and all other openings to the exterior need insulation and caulking. Framing, sheathing, and exterior siding materials must be applied carefully and sealed with caulk wherever necessary. Even tiny cracks can admit surprising amounts of air under some conditions, so it pays to take extra care with this process.

Vapor Barriers

Besides insulation, a vapor barrier is essential for heating a structure effectively during cold weather. A properly installed vapor barrier forms a virtually impermeable membrane that encloses the entire interior of the heated portions of the structure within an envelope. The object is to prevent the escape of water vapor from within the structure.

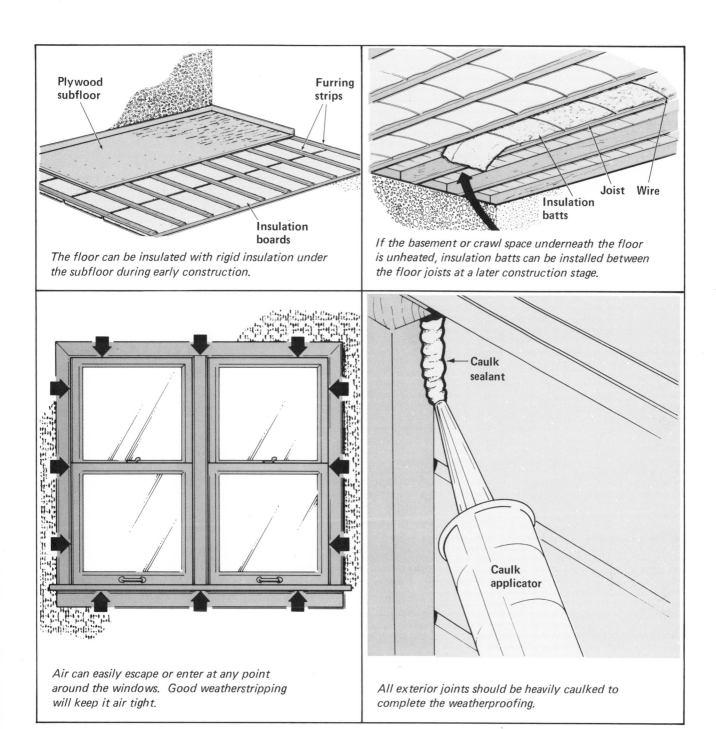

Plywood subfloor

Furring strips

Insulation boards

The floor can be insulated with rigid insulation under the subfloor during early construction.

Insulation batts

Joist   Wire

If the basement or crawl space underneath the floor is unheated, insulation batts can be installed between the floor joists at a later construction stage.

Air can easily escape or enter at any point around the windows. Good weatherstripping will keep it air tight.

Caulk sealant

Caulk applicator

All exterior joints should be heavily caulked to complete the weatherproofing.

If it escapes, the vapor can condense within the thermal insulation or on the insides of exterior surfaces, reducing the insulation's effectiveness. A vapor barrier also eliminates or reduces problems like paint lifting and blistering on exterior siding, dry rot resulting from excessive condensation within the framework, and growth of hidden mildew and mold.

Random air infiltration is reduced, too.

Some types of insulation, notably blanket forms, are attached to a backing that serves as a vapor barrier. Other kinds, like rigid polystyrene sheets, are inherently waterproof. But when no built-in vapor barrier is present in the insulation, a separate barrier must be installed.

Separate barriers are commonly made of polyethylene plastic sheet. A two-mil thickness is adequate and inexpensive, but the four-mil thickness is tougher, easier to work with, and more readily available. The barrier is always installed to the inside of the heated section. It should be laid beneath concrete slab floors and between floor sheathing and

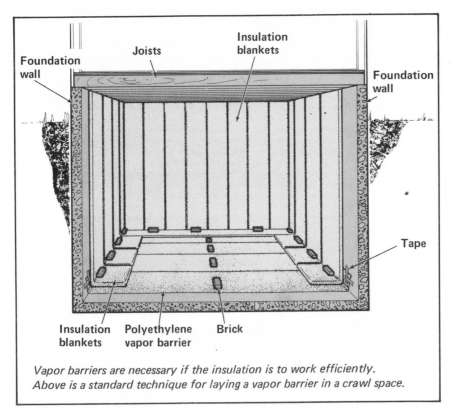

Foundation wall

Joists

Insulation blankets

Foundation wall

Tape

Insulation blankets

Polyethylene vapor barrier

Brick

Vapor barriers are necessary if the insulation is to work efficiently. Above is a standard technique for laying a vapor barrier in a crawl space.

underlayment or finish floor covering. On exterior walls, the sheet is stapled to the interior edges of the studs; on ceilings it's stapled to the interior edges of the roof rafters. The vapor barrier is laid directly on the smoothed dirt floor of enclosed crawl spaces, then covered with a few inches of sand or gravel for protection.

Finish Materials

Final aspects of finishing the interior can begin after roughing-in all utility and auxiliary systems, and installing insulation and vapor barriers. We'll discuss various projects separately as a matter of convenience. But, in practice, the jobs are interrelated and are frequently carried on concurrently rather than in any strict sequence. Various areas of the structure may be in different stages of finish at any given time.

Walls

Interior work generally begins with the walls. There's a wide

selection of wall coverings, and the choice depends mainly on cost, personal preference, and compatibility with the decor. No one type is necessarily better than another.

Drywall has largely supplanted the once-common plastered walls. It's available in several standard sheet sizes and thicknesses, but the ½-inch-thick, 4 x 8-foot sheet is the popular choice for residential applications. You cut this material by scoring it with a sharp utility knife and breaking the pieces apart. Both vertical and horizontal installation is possible; smaller pieces can be cut and fitted easily as required.

The material is secured to the inner edges of the structural members with glue and special wallboard nails, spaced about six inches apart. The glue will prevent the nails from popping out, due to wood shrinkage. However, glue cannot be used if a poly moisture shield is installed under the drywall. Cracks between pieces are covered with a special drywall

joint tape and drywall plaster compound, which is sanded smooth and flush with the drywall surfaces after curing.

Some special drywalls have prefinished decorative surfaces, but most are plain and require further finishing. You can prime and paint drywall with interior house paint, or treat it with exterior solid-body stain. It can also be primed or sized, and then covered with wallpaper, vinyl wall covering, fabric wall covering, or similar finish materials. You usually apply such materials last, to avoid damaging them.

Prefinished paneling is a popular alternative to drywall. It comes in dozens of styles in standard 4 x 8-foot, ¼-inch-thick sheets. Other sizes and thicknesses are available, though. The paneling is either made of plywood with a prefinished face veneer, or hardboard with a prefinished face, such as simulated wood grain or leather. Plastic laminates in various designs are also offered.

For best results, and to comply with some codes, thin paneling should be applied over a solid, fire-retardant backing of drywall. Without a drywall backing the finished wall will be ripply, wavy and susceptible to puncture. It will also transmit noise like a drum. The underlying drywall may be required to be taped by code. But it needn't be filled or even fitted very carefully, except for making sure it's secured tightly and free of bumps. The paneling is cut with ordinary shop tools and fitted with care. Then it's secured with panel adhesive, special nails, or both.

Solid wood also makes a fine wall covering. Nominal one-inch-thick planks can be laid vertically, horizontally, or diagonally, and thin planking strips can be laid in any direction—including patterns and designs. If the material is ¾-inch-thick or more, the planks can be applied directly to framing members by blind-nailing or face-nailing (the nail heads must be set and the holes plugged). Thin wood strips are generally glued to drywall or plywood. Knotty pine paneling is perhaps the most familiar example of solid wood wall covering. But many types of wood can be used—either smooth-planed or rough-cut with either straight or interlocking edges. Sometimes no further finish treatment is desired. In other cases, paint, stain, varnish, or wax is applied for surface protection or decorative effect.

You can also use tile. Sizes range from tiny ceramic mosaic tiles through standard 4¼-inch wall tiles of ceramic, plastic, or metal, up to 12-inch square tiles of various materials. Glass mirror tiles are popular for accenting areas, as are Mexican, Dutch, Spanish, Delft, and other decorative ceramic tiles. Thin marble tiles are sometimes used for accent on walls, as are laminated-wood parquet flooring tiles. The latter are available in many patterns, either finished or unfinished.

You must apply wall tiles to a solid, firm, and smooth backing, such as drywall, plywood, or wallboard. You install them by a method known as "thin set," which uses a special mastic adhesive—the type varies with the tile used. If you use a type of tile that butts together tightly, the job is done after gluing them in place. But some kinds of tile, notably ceramic ones, leave open joints that must be filled with grout. Which of the several types of grout to use depends upon conditions and the type of tile. Some grouts consist of a very fine cementitious material that is mixed with water and applied with a squeegee. Some types are furan resin or epoxy-based, and are generally tougher and more resistant to staining and corrosion by household chemicals. Particular kinds of tile are grouted with an elastomeric compound.

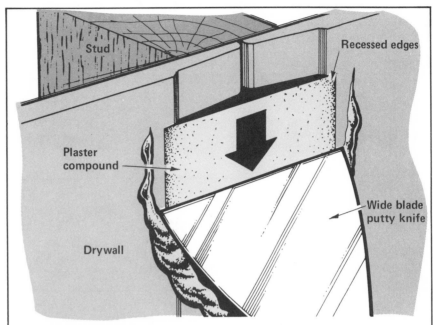

Special drywall compound is used to seal recessed edges between wallboards. A drywall tape is applied over the compound, then plaster compound over the tape.

Then there are simulated and real masonry materials. These are used as finish wall coverings, especially as accent sections, wainscoting or refractory barriers around or behind wood stoves and fireplaces. Natural brick and stone are possibilities, as are their simulated counterparts in various styles

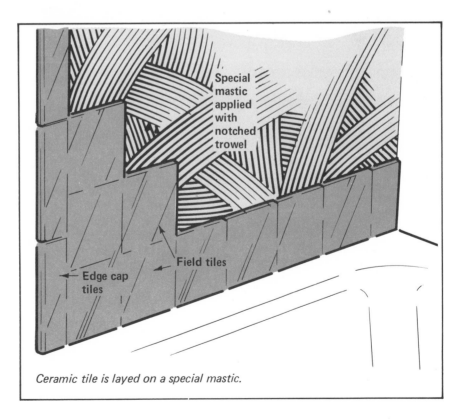

Ceramic tile is layed on a special mastic.

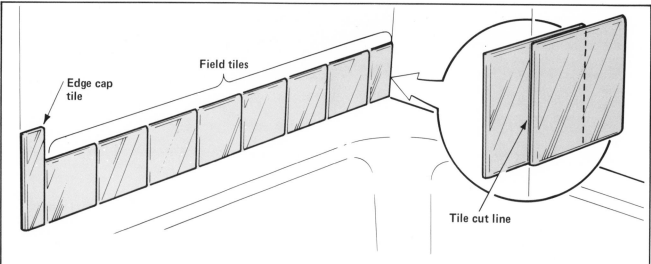

Special edge cap tiles make good trim pieces. Regular field tiles can also trim an area when cut with a glass cutter.

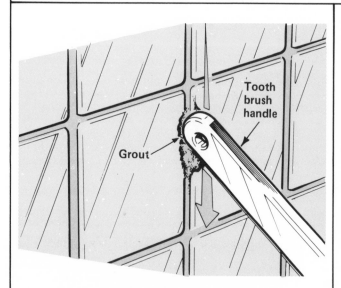

Grout can be rubbed between tiles with a toothbrush handle.

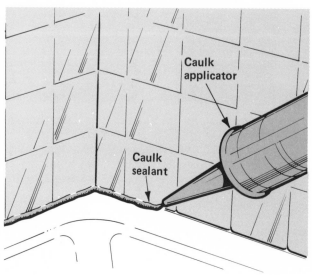

The gap between the tile and floor or tub line should be caulked.

and colors. Some simulated materials are refractory, and others are not. The sections are thin, easy to work with, and usually applied with adhesive mastic. When put behind heat-producing units, however, they should be installed with cement mortar.

Exterior siding materials can often be applied indoors to good effect, too. These include numerous exterior hardboards and plywoods, cedar shingles, cedar or redwood clapboards, and hand-cut cedar shakes.

Ceilings

Drywall and tile are the two most common ceiling coverings. The same unfinished type of drywall used for walls is used for ceilings. Joints are covered with tape and compound and application of final finish is left for later. This final finish might be paint, a plaster-like texture coating, or perhaps even wallpaper.

Some ceiling tiles are applied by stapling or gluing them directly to a solid backing, such

as drywall. Or, they can be stapled to a gridwork of wood strips nailed across the ceiling joists. Grid or suspended ceilings consist of a metal gridwork hung in place at any desirable distance below the ceiling joists. Special tiles are set into this gridwork. Such ceiling systems usually also have provisions for installation of integral or recessed lighting fixtures.

A ceiling doesn't need to be a broad, blank expanse of banality. By using your imagination to apply common materials in an unusual way, you can turn the ceiling into a focal point. For instance, rough-cut wood planking makes a handsome ceiling, especially when set in herringbone or some other geometric pattern.

Moldings, bas-relief carvings, or natural or artificial beams can also be used. A ceiling needn't be on one level, either. Edge valances, raised centers, reversed stair-steps, dome, or other configurations can add emphasis. Arches or vaults

covered with simulated brick set between beams makes for an interesting effect, too. These are only a few examples. Any material that looks attractive and can be secured firmly in place can be used for finished ceilings.

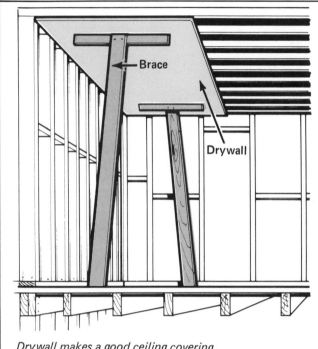

Drywall makes a good ceiling covering.

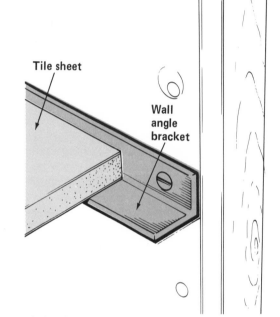

Suspended ceilings are attached to the walls with wall angle brackets.

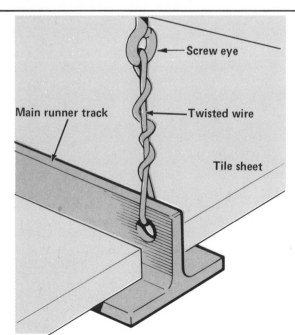

The tile sheets are supported throughout the ceiling by main runner tracks. These are attached to ceiling joists with wire and screw eyes.

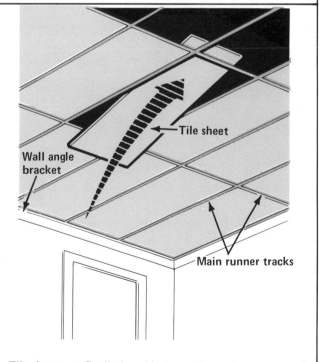

Tile sheets are finally layed between the main runner tracks.

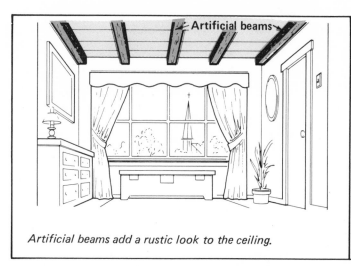

Artificial beams add a rustic look to the ceiling.

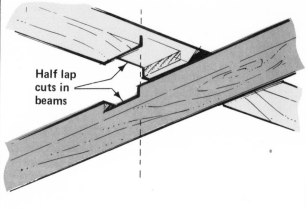

Half lap cuts in beams

Foam beams can be cut and crosslapped across the ceiling.

Cabinets and Built-ins

Cabinets are usually installed before final finishing of the floors and walls and laying of finish floor material. Base and wall cabinets are either constructed from scratch on the job site, or purchased as prefabricated, finished, or unfinished units. In any case, they are permanently installed by securing them to the structural framework. Built-in cabinet work, such as bookshelves, storage walls, mantelpieces, and permanent room divider screens are built right on the work site to conform to particular space requirements.

To avoid extra work later, construction and installation of such furnishings must be

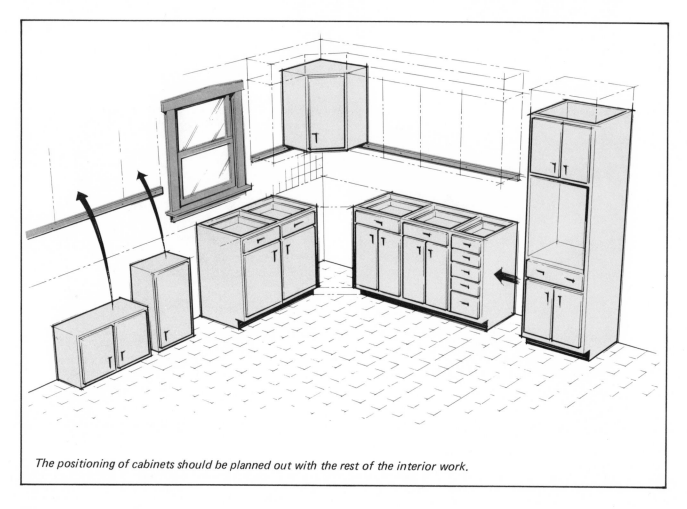

The positioning of cabinets should be planned out with the rest of the interior work.

carefully coordinated with the rest of the interior finishing job. Also, coordinating the projects allows application of final finishes without fear of damage from further construction work going on in the vicinity. Prefinished, prefabricated cabinetry should be installed near the end of the interior finishing work. Built-ins are often covered with prefinished materials, such as paneling, so the framework is built early, and the finishing material is put on toward the end of the job.

Floors

Final finish floor covering is usually the last major part of an interior finishing job to be completed. However, if the covering requires an underlayment, this can be applied early in the project, or whenever it's most convenient— as long as other work in progress is not disturbed. If a combination sheathing-underlayment is used, no further work is needed. But, if the sheathing consists of boards or plywood, an underlayment of particle board or hardboard is often laid atop the sheathing to form a suitable base for the finish floor covering.

Due to easy maintenance and good appearance, wall-to-wall carpeting has become one of the most popular finish floor coverings. It's almost always professionally laid on a special padding over an underlayment. This job is usually left until everything else has been completed.

If wood flooring is ¾-inch thick or more, you can apply it directly over the floor sheathing. Thin wood strips or tiles, however, do require an underlayment. Strip flooring is available in various hardwoods, such as oak, birch, and mahogany. And there are tiles in straight, geometric, and parquet styles, made of oak, teak, walnut, pecan, and other woods. Thick strip flooring is applied by blind-nailing, while thin stock

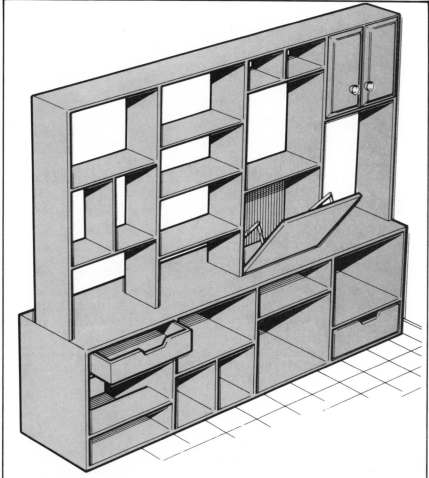

Storage shelves are usually built on the work site to meet space requirements.

can be either nailed or glued. Wood floor tiles are generally glued down with a special mastic, although some have a self-stick adhesive backing.

A reasonable selection of vinyl-asbestos, asphalt, and similar 12-inch-square floor tiles are still available, but they have lost favor to vinyl sheet floor covering for residential applications. Vinyl sheet offers a wide selection of colors and styles, and comes in large rolls, like linoleum did years ago. Staples are sometimes used to apply this material, although it's more common to use a special adhesive mastic. In most cases, a clean, smooth underlayment is necessary for best results. It's possible for an ambitious do-it-yourselfer to lay this flooring, but it's likely that a professional

can do a better job. Vinyl tile, however, can be laid successfully by the home handyman.

Several kinds of ceramic and masonry materials work well, too. Ceramic and mosaic tiles are available in an incredible profusion of colors and patterns; terrazzo is another possibility. Certain types of building brick can be used, as can brick and precast concrete pavers. Flagstones have been popular for years, and may be made of colored slate, sandstone, or precast colored concrete. Marble tiles are also making a comeback.

All these flooring materials are heavy. So, if any great expanse is to be covered, the floor frame must be sturdy enough to accept the weight. For sections only a few feet square, no extra support

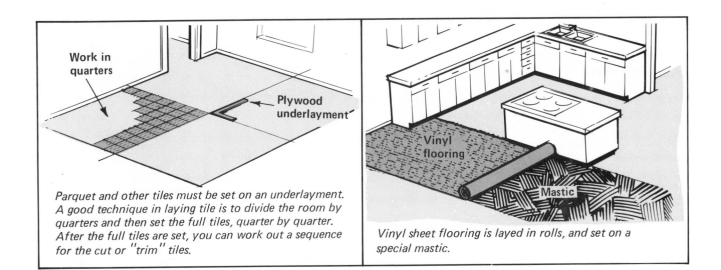

Parquet and other tiles must be set on an underlayment. A good technique in laying tile is to divide the room by quarters and then set the full tiles, quarter by quarter. After the full tiles are set, you can work out a sequence for the cut or "trim" tiles.

Vinyl sheet flooring is layed in rolls, and set on a special mastic.

is generally needed. In any case, the subflooring must be smooth, level, and stiff enough to be vibration-free.

Two basic methods are used to apply ceramic or masonry floor materials. One is called "full-mortar-bed" or "mud-set," and consists of a thick layer of standard mortar laid on a waterproof membrane atop the floor sheathing. The flooring units are bedded in the mortar, and the joints between the units mortared in. The second system is called "thin-set installation," and makes use of a thin coating of a dryset mortar or an organic adhesive to bond the units to the backing. New types of adhesives and grouts have made the latter system practical for residential application. Whatever type of flooring unit is installed, it's best to follow the manufacturer's or supplier's installation instructions explicitly.

Trimming-Out

This is the very last phase of interior finishing. Trimming-out includes all the finishing touches that go into the makeup of the final decor, and some relatively major jobs as well.

Door Frames

Although exterior door frames are usually installed during the framing and sheathing stages, the interior frames are most

often put in after laying the finish flooring. A prehung interior door assembly comes with the door already mounted

in a prefabricated frame, with the trimwork bundled up separately. And, the entire door and frame unit is installed at

Door frames can be installed piece by piece, or bought prehung and installed at once.

146

once. However, interior door frames frequently are built in place.

The door frame consists of four parts: the right and left side jambs, head jamb, and door stop. The jambs are assembled first. They're stood in place, shimmed at sides and top, leveled, squared and plumbed, and nailed down tight. You have to nail carefully to prevent the jambs from bowing or going out of plumb or square. Jamb sets are available in various widths to match the wall thickness, and the jamb edges should be aligned flush with the finish wall surfaces. Side-jamb lengths are cut to match the door height, plus one inch for clearance. The head jamb is matched to the door width, plus $\frac{3}{16}$-inch clearance.

The door stop is a special molding that runs up both side jambs and across the head jamb. It is nailed in place, spaced in from the hinge-side edge of the jamb-set by the thickness of the door being installed.

Prehung door units are generally installed by shimming the entire unit in the rough opening, leveling and plumbing, and securing with nails; instructions are usually included.

Casings

Trim pieces used to finish off doors and windows are called casings. They cover the rough-opening gap between the wall and window or door frame. You install casings by nailing them to the jambs at one side and through the wall covering and into the wall studs or headers on the other. There are many special moldings available for this purpose—some with curved or hollowed-out backs to aid in making a true fit. However, practically any kind of flat stock can be used as well.

The simplest door casing consists of lengths of thin and narrow "clamshell moldings" that attach to the jambs like a picture frame. They are simply fitted with miter joints at the

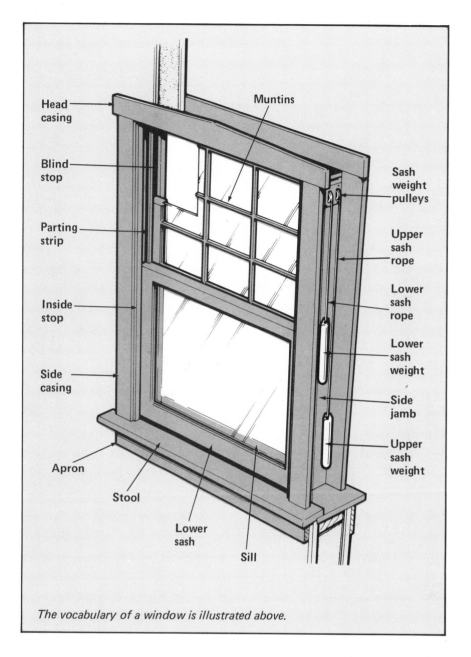

The vocabulary of a window is illustrated above.

upper corners and nailed tight with finish nails. If desired, door casings can also be very ornate by applying moldings to flat stock, using carved or routed stock, or carved inserts.

Window casings are installed in the interior just like a door casing. The side and head casings may be made of special molding or of flat stock in any style or shape desired. Another piece, variously called a "sill cap," "stool," or "interior window sill" is applied horizontally atop the window-sill piece; this is usually the first

piece to be installed, followed by the side casing. The "apron" lies directly beneath the stool, covering the gaps between the bottom of the window and the rough-opening sill. Window stops are installed the same way as door stops, but serve to retain the window sash. These may or may not be required, depending upon the type of window. As with door casings, installation is merely a matter of sizing, cutting, and fitting the parts in their proper locations, and securing them with finish or casing nails.

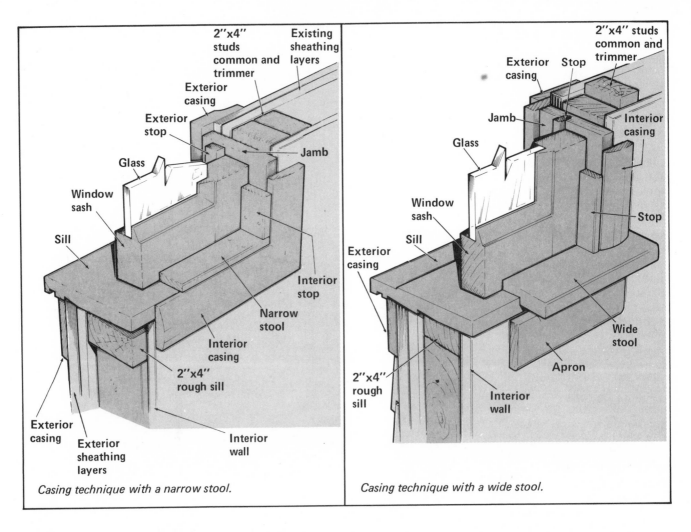

Casing technique with a narrow stool.

Casing technique with a wide stool.

Moldings

Among the many kinds of moldings, baseboard, also called "mopboard" or "base," is perhaps the most common. Although it comes in various forms, one popular style is a run of clamshell molding, applied continuously along the wall just above the finish flooring to hide the floor-wall joint. Often, the finish flooring runs under the baseboard, though not always. Baseboards can also be much more complex. For instance, they can be comprised of a wide baseboard stock with a base cap molding on the top edge and a base shoe molding on the bottom edge, against the floor. Outside baseboard corners are usually made with miter joints. Inside corners may be either miter or butt joints if the stock is flat and rectangular in cross

section. Cap or shoe moldings are made with miter or coped joints, depending on the molding's shape.

Sometimes ceiling moldings are installed to hide the gap between wall and ceiling. In particular, they're used with wall paneling to cover irregularities or gaps and provide a more finished appearance. They range from tiny quarter-round, or stop moldings, to ornate and broad crown and cove moldings. You cut and fit ceiling moldings with miter and coped joints as necessary, and secure them to the framing members with finish nails.

Other types of ceiling moldings or trim stock may be applied directly to the ceiling surface to create a pattern or motif. Some, like screen molding, are quite small. But they can

also be substantial, as in the case of simulated beams or half-beams. Shallow or full box beams may also be applied; these are often fitted with side moldings as well.

As a general rule, it's much easier to sand, prime and paint, or stain full lengths of these moldings before they are cut and fitted in place. You must cut the finish stock very carefully with a fine-toothed miter saw or similar tool. The molding pieces are installed in the usual fashion, nail heads set, and the holes plugged with a filler that needs little or no sanding after drying. The filler can be applied with an artist's palette knife and smoothed out with a fingertip. The last step is to carefully paint over the plugged holes, and the molding joints if necessary, with a small artist's brush.

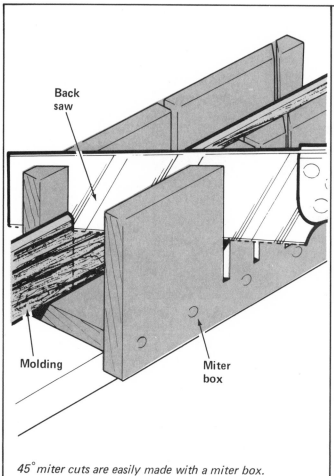

Back saw

Molding

Miter box

45° miter cuts are easily made with a miter box.

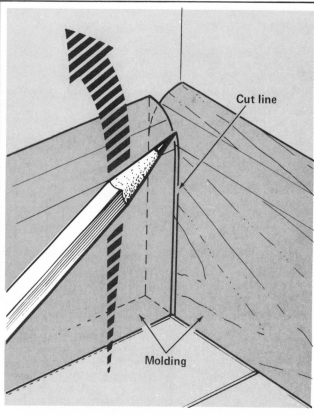

Cut line

Molding

Coped joints are cut with a special coping saw. To outline the cut area, butt the two molding pieces together and pencil in a cut line, as shown above. After the area is cut out, the one piece of molding will fit snugly in the other.

Miscellaneous Trimming and Installation

Invariably, each job presents a number of different odds and ends that you have to take care of to complete the bulk of the finish work. For example, interior doors usually need to be put in, because they weren't installed along with the frames and casings. There's a long list of different types of prefinished and unfinished doors—hollow-core, solid core, solid wood, French, Dutch, and cafe types are only a few examples—and there are many ways of installing them.

Also, appliances such as dishwashers, ranges, laundry equipment, water heater, and the main heating unit must be put in. Electrical devices—such as convenience outlets and switches—must be installed,

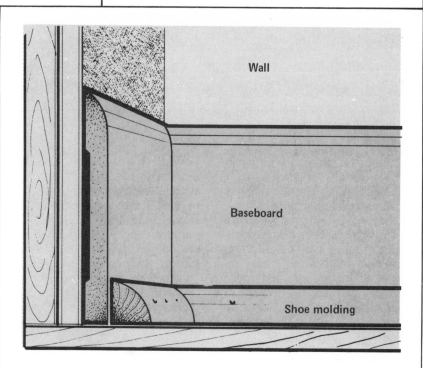

Wall

Baseboard

Shoe molding

Baseboard and shoe moldings, with a coped joint, are illustrated above.

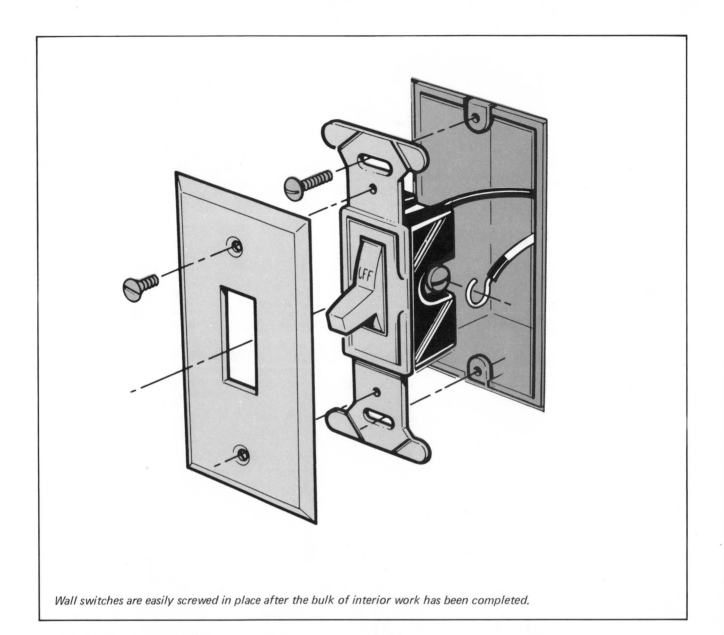

Wall switches are easily screwed in place after the bulk of interior work has been completed.

checked out, and their trim covers put on. Lighting fixtures must be hung, connected, and checked; drapery rods put up; banisters and balustrades set, and staircases trimmed out. And plumbing fixtures not previously installed can now be placed, connected, and tested.

In short, all the bits and pieces that go into the final finish and ultimate decor of the addition must now be fitted in place.

Applied Finishes

Except, perhaps, for wall-to-wall carpeting, a few trim plates, fixture canopies, or other trim

hardware, applied finishes are the last to be applied. They include paints, varnishes, synthetic finishes such as polyurethane, wax and stain-waxes, stains, and similar materials. Finish wall coverings, such as wallpaper and coated fabrics, are also sometimes considered applied finishes.

The procedures for applying these finishes varies by type and even by brand. Some work well under certain conditions, while others don't. Flat-white latex paint, for instance, wouldn't be a good choice for kitchen walls because it stains easily and can't be scrubbed satisfactorily. But it

would be fine for a bedroom ceiling. In all cases, apply any applied finish exactly the way the manufacturer suggests. It's the best way to get good results.

You must use some common sense when arranging the work flow for these left over finish items. For example, paint casing and trim moldings before applying wallpaper, so you don't get paint on the new paper. Similarly, the finish sanding of a wood cabinet shouldn't be done while the varnish on the next cabinet in line is still wet. Thinking out the job sequence in advance can save a lot of time and extra work.

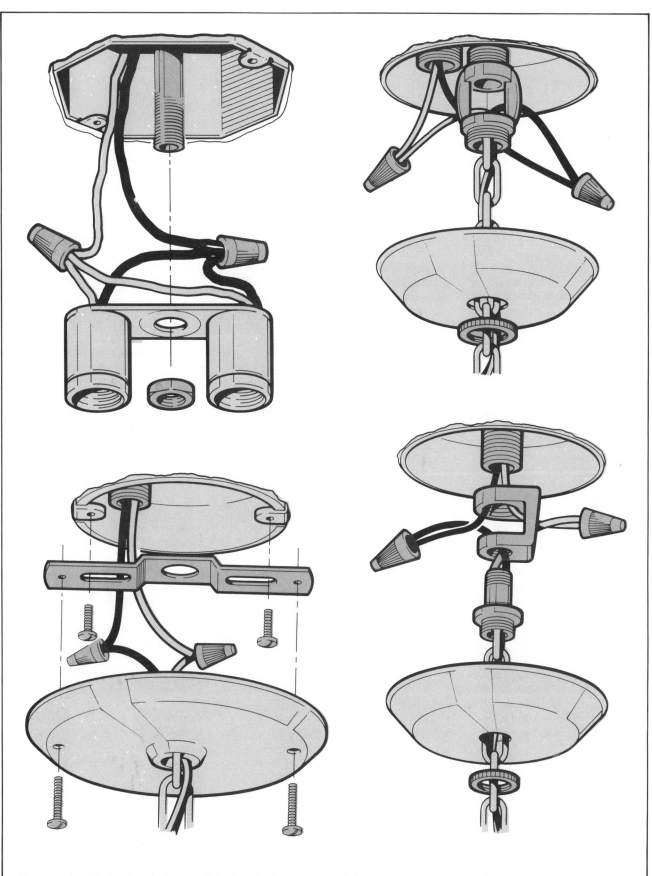

There are hundreds of variations on light installations. Some of the more common ceiling fixtures are illustrated above.

Converting Existing Living Space

Converting space in your home to more suitable living quarters can involve an infinite number of construction and reconstruction details. However, the basic principles and procedures of construction and decorating, and the various tools and materials, are the same as those used for building an addition.

Space conversion requires remodeling work, which alters the existing structure in some way. This can be as simple as removing a partition wall or changing the location of a doorway, or it can be as complex as completely gutting and rebuilding the entire interior.

A large part of the work involved in space conversion consists of dismantling the original structure and joining the new to the old properly. Much of this work, especially the dismantling, can be tackled with impunity by the do-it-yourselfer. The homeowner can do the job methodically to minimize damage. Then he can clean up and save some of the old material for reuse, to reduce overall costs. A contractor is unlikely to bother, and if he does, the cost will be higher.

Removing Existing Coverings

One of the first steps in remodeling is to remove existing interior finish coverings, sheathings, and trim. The job can be easy or ridden with problems, depending upon the circumstances. Here are a few suggestions.

Trimwork

Removing trimwork is the first, and probably the easiest, part of the demolition job. It must be done to clear the way for removal of structural framework, and can be done in a way that saves the material for reuse. Small moldings, like baseshoe, base, and quarter-round are best removed with a wide, flat tool that can be used as a pry. A stiff putty knife or fine-bladed pry bar works well. A wide wood chisel sometimes works, but a screwdriver is much too narrow and blunt. To remove a molding, you start at a joint or at one end and cautiously work a bit of the piece free. Then, the piece is bowed out from its mounting surface. A slight amount of outward pressure is kept on it, and the piece is pried loose in a continuous movement toward a joint or the opposite end. The thin finish nails that secured the molding should pull through with little trouble. If neither end of the molding is accessible, because the piece has two inside miter-cut corners, you must start in the middle and work in both directions. Moldings covering a joint between a horizontal and vertical surface are frequently nailed to both surfaces, which makes removal more difficult. In this case, you pick a likely looking spot and carefully work the piece free by joggling it outward; the nails should bend and finally pull free.

Flat trimwork—such as window or door casings, and baseboards—is easier to remove because it's stiffer, heavier, and less likely to break. Such pieces can be removed with a short, thin-bladed pry bar. The blade should be inserted under the end of a piece, rather than along its side. And the head of the pry bar should be jammed against a solid surface, rather than against an unsupported expanse. Successive bites with the bar will free the piece. When stripping a window assembly or other item with complex trim, the job is easier if you first determine the original sequence of installation. Then you start by removing the trim piece that was put on last, and work backwards through the sequence to the first piece installed. This reverse sequence method is also used for large trimwork, like box beams and boxed sills, which can be more difficult to remove. Usually the best course is to determine how and with what kind of fasteners the piece was installed. Then the process is reversed, starting with the last piece installed, and prying loose nailed pieces, removing hidden screws, and taking out bolts or lags.

Most trimwork is merely nailed in place, but occasionally some is glued. Depending upon the quality of the job and the age of the glue, such pieces may not be removable without damage. All you can do is try breaking the piece free with a wood chisel and mallet. Large trim pieces that were installed with screws, lags, anchors, or other types of threaded fasteners, cannot be pried loose

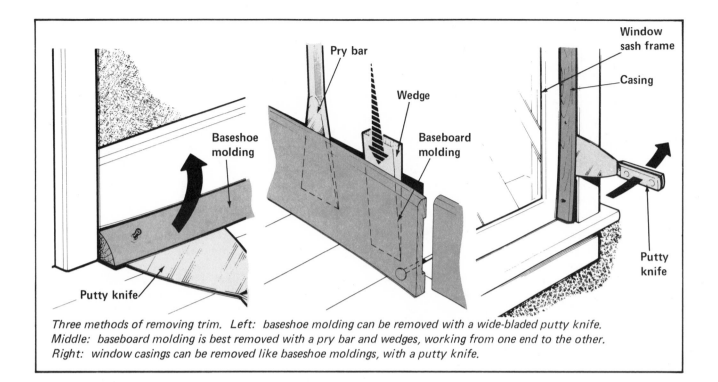

Three methods of removing trim. Left: baseshoe molding can be removed with a wide-bladed putty knife. Middle: baseboard molding is best removed with a pry bar and wedges, working from one end to the other. Right: window casings can be removed like baseshoe moldings, with a putty knife.

without ruining something. You can try to find the fasteners and remove them first. Failing that, all you can do is rip and tear.

Windows

Removing unwanted windows is frequently difficult, but the expensive units can often be salvaged for reuse or resale. There are two basic types of window units: premanufactured types that are installed in one piece, and the kind that's constructed on the job site as an integral part of the structure.

Commercial window units are installed in rough openings as the structure is built. Almost invariably they are held in place by long finishing or casing nails. You begin removing the unit by taking off all interior trimwork, including the interior stool. Next, you must find the nail locations. Most windows are nailed through the brickmold on the exterior. Field-built windows are nailed through the jambs. It's easiest to remove these nails by snipping them in half with wire cutters. If there isn't enough room to do this, you can cut them with a hacksaw. This is a two-man job, because someone

must hold the window unit secure while the last few nails are cut. Then the unit can be boosted out of the opening.

If you can't find the nails, you must remove parts of the window, such as the interior sash frame, window stop, or jamb moldings, to see if the nails are hidden beneath them. If they still aren't visible, you can try prying gently on various parts of the window with a pry bar. Tapping the window frame with a mallet will sometimes reveal hidden nails by popping out the filler used to plug the hole over the nail head. If you can't cut the nails off, you may still be able to grip the nail heads with the pointed jaws of a pair of electrician's diagonal wire cutters. Then you can lever the nails out by taking short bites on their shanks. This causes little, if any, damage to the woodwork.

Some newer, vinyl-clad factory-made window units have a nailing flange all around the window on the outside. It lies flat against the exterior wall sheathing beneath the finish siding. Consequently, it's necessary to remove sections of

the siding to reach the flange. Once exposed, however, the flange nails are easily removed, because they're usually broad-headed roofing nails.

Built-in, fixed windows are a different matter. These are made by nailing and sealing an exterior stop molding to a heavy, built-in wood frame. This frame may actually be part of the building framework itself. The fixed glass pane is cut to exactly fit the opening created by the frame. There may or may not be additional interior or exterior trimwork or molding installed for appearance.

First you take off any fancy trimwork, and then you remove the glass. If the pane is more than three or four feet square in size, insulating or heavy plate glass, you need to use two or more glaziers' suction-cup carrying handles. They should be fixed to the pane on the side toward which it will be removed. Either the interior or exterior set of stop moldings is then pried free of the frame, leaving the glass loose. If sealant or caulk keeps the pane in place, you may have to dig around the edges to free it up. A hot knife blade

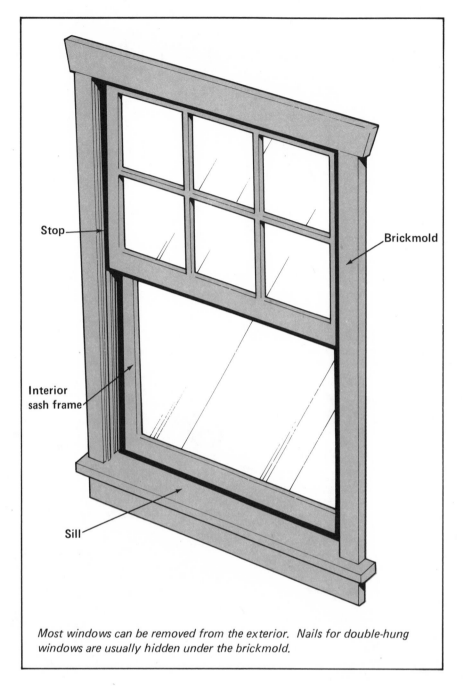

Most windows can be removed from the exterior. Nails for double-hung windows are usually hidden under the brickmold.

Labels on figure: Stop, Brickmold, Interior sash frame, Sill

works well on some kinds of sealant. In any case, you must be alert for a sudden freeing-up of the pane. And you should avoid removing windows on windy days; it can be dangerous.

Doors

Doors are expensive, and should be removed carefully so they can be used elsewhere or sold. The same goes for door hardware and trim. Doors usually have removable-pin hinges, making

removal a simple matter. You just set the tip of an old screwdriver at a sharp upward angle in the crack between the bottom of the hinge pin head and the top of the hinge barrel, and tap the screwdriver handle smartly with a mallet. The pin should move upward, and can be tapped clear of the hinge barrel to separate the two hinge leaves. Then you can remove the hinge halves from the door and frame by removing the screws. If the

door has fixed-pin hinges, tapping with a screwdriver won't work. Instead, you must jam shims beneath the bottom of the opened door to bear its weight, and remove the hinge mounting screws.

Both prehung and built-on-site door frames are installed much like a factory-made window unit. Removing the casings from both sides of the frame may reveal the nails that hold the frame in place. If they're visible, you can cut them easily. However, they're most likely to have been driven through shim stock installed to align the frame. If there's no flooring material in the way, it may be possible to pry the bottoms of the side jambs away from the wall studs. Working upward carefully should loosen and remove most or all of the nails. Then it's just a matter of prying the entire frame free. Or you can use an old wood chisel and a mallet to chop away the shim material, which is often soft cedar shingle stock or pine blocks. This will expose the nails, which can then be cut off.

Exterior door frames are harder to remove. A heavy threshold is often secured directly to the sill or other structural members from beneath. The fasteners that attach the side jambs to the threshold ends are inaccessible. Usually, the easiest approach is to remove or cut all nails driven through the side and head jambs first, and then try to pry the threshold slightly upward, but mostly outward, to the outside of the wall. When the threshold is free, the rest of the frame will follow

Cabinetry

Cabinetry and built-ins, of course, must be removed before any other major work can proceed. Prefabricated cabinetry that is purchased and installed as individual units is not usually difficult to remove. This is especially true if the units were separately secured with screws,

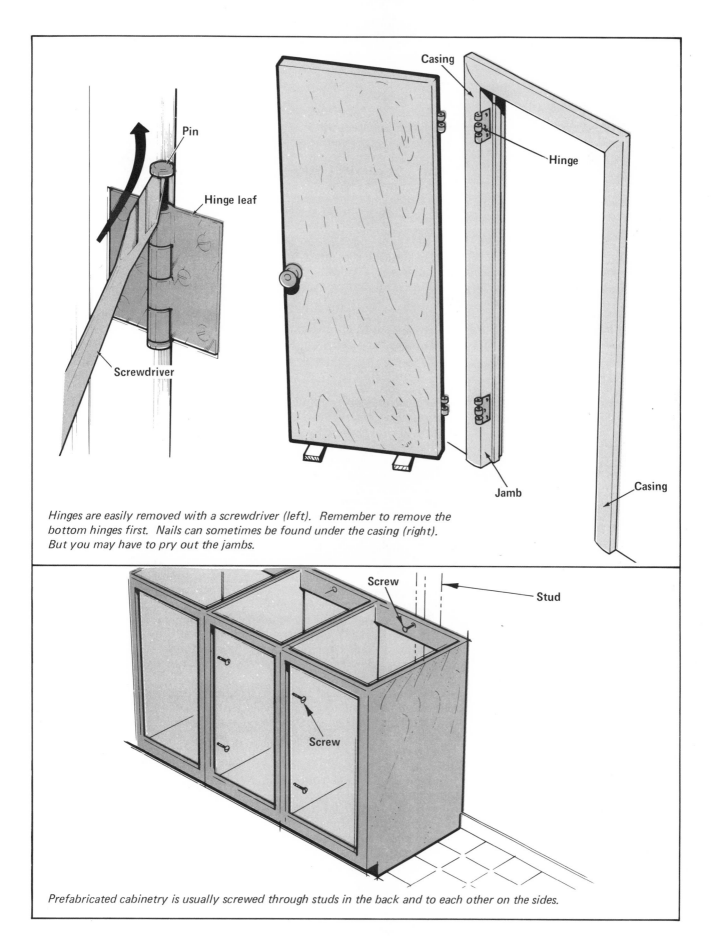

Hinges are easily removed with a screwdriver (left). Remember to remove the bottom hinges first. Nails can sometimes be found under the casing (right). But you may have to pry out the jambs.

Prefabricated cabinetry is usually screwed through studs in the back and to each other on the sides.

lags, or anchors. In the case of wall-hung cabinetry, however, it's a good idea to jam plenty of props or supports beneath the units before removing the fasteners. This will prevent the units from falling free unexpectedly.

There are two types of built-ins. Some are built on site as units and then installed. Others are constructed piece by piece on location and use the house as partial support. It's usually easy to remove the former intact by locating and removing the fasteners. The latter, however, is almost always impossible to remove in one piece. All you can do, especially with the better kinds of nailed and glued construction, is to take off or take apart whatever pieces come loose easily, and break or saw the remainder into pieces. It's often difficult to salvage much.

Ceilings

Tearing down old ceilings can be very unpleasant. There are only a couple types that are likely to be relatively clean and easy to remove. One is the suspended-grid ceiling, which can be readily dismantled and salvaged entirely. The job consists of merely lifting the loose finish ceiling panels out of the gridwork, and removing any lighting troffers or other fixtures. Then the gridwork is disassembled by popping apart the snap-together sections. The wall-angle members, which are nailed in place, can be carefully pried loose.

Removing a tile ceiling is another easy project. If glued to a solid backing, you can remove the tiles by prying carefully with a putty knife. If stapled to wood strips, you can dig the staples out with a small-bladed screwdriver. The first few tiles will probably have to be broken out, but the rest can usually be saved. You can wash some types of ceiling tiles, and almost all can be repainted and put back in service. However, painting most acoustical tile will reduce some

of its sound absorbing qualities.

Drywall ceiling removal is a tough, dirty job, and removing a lath-and-plaster ceiling is a nightmare of a task. Nothing can be salvaged, and the demolition is potentially dangerous. The usual inclination is to grab a wrecking bar and have at it, but this practice could rupture a hidden water pipe or split a buried electrical cable. **Caution:** Before proceeding with any demolition, you should turn off the water and electrical systems, and locate pipes, wires, and ductwork, if possible. There's also a danger of getting struck by a falling or flying piece of material. Old plaster lath in particular is often tough and springy, and can snap apart or fly off with considerable force. Wear safety goggles to protect your eyes and be wary.

In addition, above-ceiling areas of older houses tend to accumulate a variety of horribles—deep layers of house and coal dust, sawdust, mouse droppings, packrat nests, and other debris. Also, the older the ceiling, the more fine plaster dust it will generate during demolition. The result is a thick cloud of dust that can carry active germs, and act as a dangerous irritant, especially to people who have allergies or respiratory problems. Remember to seal all interior doors or door openings with tarps, and open all windows. Wear old clothes, long sleeves, gloves, a hat, a good dust respirator, and tight-fitting safety goggles. Change respirator filters often; wash your clothing and take a shower as soon as the job is over.

Old nails present a hazard, too. Chunks of drywall that come down will carry some nails, but many will remain in the framework. Plaster lath, however, usually comes away full of short and rusty nails. It's easy to step on one of these nails when your attention is focused on the work above. The best procedure is to keep the floor working area clear by moving

rubbish to one side. If you do step on a nail or scratch or cut yourself, seek medical attention. Tetnus is the danger.

Although unpleasant, the procedure for taking down a ceiling is simple enough. You remove all trim molding and lighting fixtures. Then find a likely spot out in the open and between joists and slam a hole through the material. From then on, it's just a matter of bashing and yanking everything down.

Walls

Removing old walls is similar to ripping down ceilings, only easier. If the finish wall covering is plywood or hardboard paneling, you can probably salvage most of the material by carefully working the panels away from the wall studs or backing with a broad-blade pinch bar. Solid wood planking can be stripped away in the same way, although the first board or two is usually ruined.

As with ceilings, there's little hope of salvaging any material from drywall or plaster walls. They're just torn down in whatever way is handiest.

Before you knock down any wall, you must be sure to first strip trimwork, dismantle lighting fixtures, and remove convenience outlet covers. Also, turn off electrical power and watch for hidden water pipes and ductwork.

Floors

There's seldom much hope of saving any old flooring material, but it's usually not worth saving anyway. Except for plank-type flooring, removal is a matter of hacking, bashing, and prying up chunks of finish covering, underlayment, and subflooring, too, if necessary. Glued-down floor coverings, like tile and linoleum, can sometimes be loosened with a torch, using a great deal of caution. Then you can scrape down the underlayment and prepare it for a new covering. Wood strips or plank flooring can often be lifted piece by piece, by judicious use of a broad-bladed pry bar or chisel. Old wall-to-wall carpeting can simply be yanked free of its moorings. The underlayment or sheathing below is almost always suitable for recovering with new material.

One good method of removing old flooring in chunks is to use a circular saw, equipped with a special flooring blade. The blade is durable enough to withstand occasional nail hits. You set the circular saw's shoe so the depth of cut equals the thickness of the flooring. Then you just run a series of cuts in a rectangle or square, pry the cut section free, and go on to the next.

Building New Partitions

Depending upon circumstances, an interior partition wall of a space conversion project may or may not be made using the platform framing method. If the finished wall will run parallel with the ceiling joists and fit either between them or directly underneath one joist, the platform framing technique can be used. Of course, there must be enough room on the floor to do it. Frequently, these interior partition walls are built with only a single top plate. Usually the frame is installed, and then the coverings are put on. But it's possible to cover one side of the framework, while it's still laying on the floor.

In the case of a wall frame erected directly beneath a parallel ceiling joist, the top plate is first nailed to the joist and the sole plate to the flooring or floor joists. One or both end studs are anchored to a wall, although occasionally both ends are free. If the new wall frame position lies between parallel joists, nailing blocks made of lengths of 2 x 4's must be secured between the joists, and the wall top plate nailed to them.

When the partition frame is to run at an angle to the ceiling joists, a different construction method must be employed. The

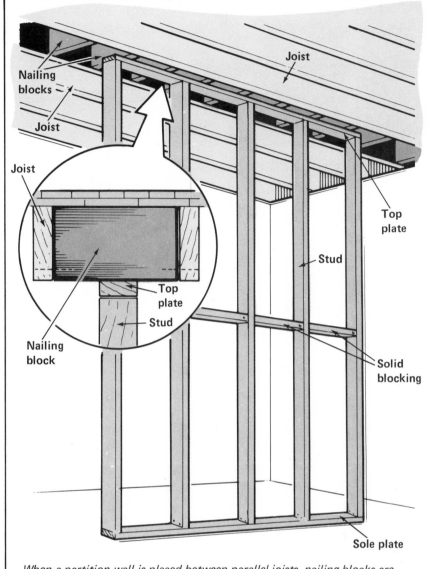

When a partition wall is placed between parallel joists, nailing blocks are necessary for construction. Solid blocking may be required by code.

problem is that if the frame is built on the floor, it cannot be raised into position; the diagonal of the frame in cross section from top to bottom is greater than the overall height from top to bottom. So, it must be built in place. The first step is to nail the single top plate in position to the ceiling joists. The sole plate position is lined up by a plumb bob or a series of measurements (the former is better and easier), and nailed to the floor. Stud center locations are next marked out on both sole and top plates, and the studs

successively toenailed into place. This is the method to use, too, in a situation where the original ceiling is left undisturbed.

An alternative method is to build the frame on the floor with a single top plate, but lacking full wall height by an amount equal to the thickness of the top plate. A second top plate is nailed to the joists in the correct position. You stand up the wall frame and slide it into place directly beneath the upper top plate, and the two are nailed together.

Though not essential unless

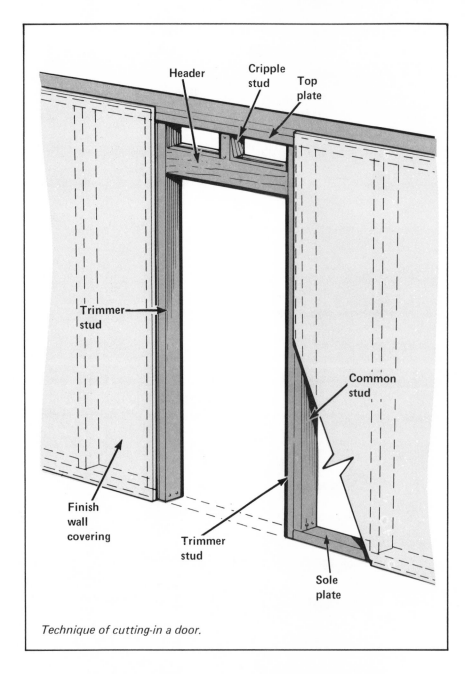

Technique of cutting-in a door.

remove the lower portions.

The new door rough opening is framed up in the usual fashion. A common stud running from sole plate to top plate must be put in on each side of the opening; sometimes an existing common stud can serve this purpose on one side or the other. A header, comprised of two pieces of dimension stock stood on edge with a spacer of appropriate thickness sandwiched between them, is nailed between the two common studs to form the top of the door opening. The short piece of unneeded existing sole plate between the two common studs can now be sawed out, and the cut ends of the remaining sole plate sections toenailed to the floor to keep them immovable. Then trimmer studs are nailed to the inside face of each common stud from floor to header bottom. The remaining cut-off pieces of common studs, which now become cripple studs, are toenailed to the header top and jambs.

If the door opening is less than three feet wide, as is usually the case, two pieces of 2 x 4 are adequate for a header, but larger stock will certainly do no harm. Sometimes it is easier, in fact, to entirely remove intermediate common studs and extend the header from the top of the door opening to the bottom of the top plate, eliminating the small cripple studs. In many cases, a 2 x 12 will work perfectly. If dimension stock does not fit the existing space perfectly, it can be shimmed with layers of additional wood stock laid flat, or a box header that will fit exactly can be made up of plywood.

Once the rough opening has been completed, the wall covering can be patched around it. This consists of cutting pieces of drywall, plywood, exterior fiberboard sheathing, or a similar suitable covering material of a thickness equal to the existing wall covering, and

required by local code, solid blocking in interior partition wall frames increases strength and rigidity and somewhat decreases potential stud warping. It also acts as a fire stop. The drawback is that it makes future fishing of television or electrical wires next to impossible.

Cutting-In Doors

The first step in cutting-in and installing a new door in a wall is to mark the door location on the wall. The second is to remove the finish wall covering. Sometimes it is not necessary to remove the wall covering beyond the door rough opening outline. Cut the covering material off flush with the stud faces, and allow enough room for nailing in the new framing members that will form the door rough opening. Any studs that lie within the door opening—there will probably be only one or two—must be removed. Cut these studs off at a point equal to the top of the header of the new door frame assembly, and nailing the pieces to the framework. In some cases, it may be necessary to secure wood nailing strips to the sides of studs or other structural members to provide a nailing surface for the new wall covering. Then the door frame and casings can be installed and the door hung in the same manner as with new construction.

Cutting-In Windows

Cutting-in windows is the process of installing windows in an existing wall. The procedure is much the same as for installing a new door. The first step is to locate the hidden studs in the wall; the next is to mark out the window outline on the wall. From this point, you can proceed in several ways. One good method is to remove the interior wall covering from floor to ceiling and beyond the outermost wall studs of the window location. The insulation is removed, but the exterior sheathing and siding are left intact. Portions of the studs that fall within the window rough opening are cut away, and new, full-length common studs are installed at the outsides of the opening. An existing stud can be used for one side, sometimes for both. A header is installed between these studs. You butt it tight against the bottom of the top plate, then nail a trimmer stud to each inside face of the common studs from sole plate to header bottom. Then the horizontal sill is nailed between the trimmer studs so the sill top is at the correct height for the bottom of the rough opening. The sill should also be nailed to the cut-off portions of the original common studs, which now become cripple studs.

Depending on the window's height, the bottom of the header may serve as the top of the rough opening. But, if the window is shorter than this measurement, a horizontal member needs to be nailed between the trimmer studs to

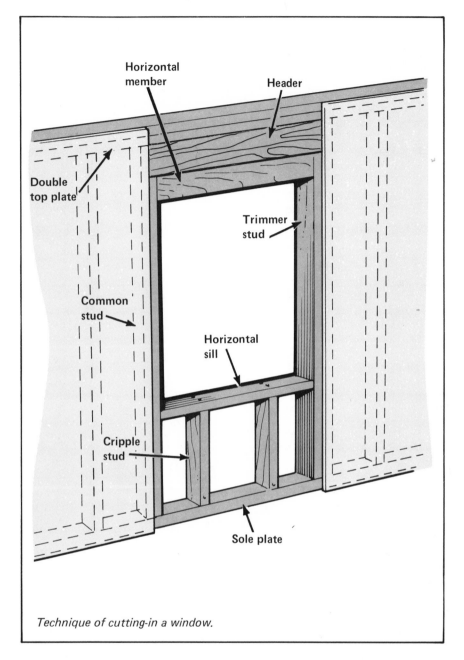

Technique of cutting-in a window.

finish boxing out the rough opening. Cripple studs aren't necessary between this member and the header. Dimensions of the completed rough opening should match those recommended by the manufacturer of the window unit to be installed.

The rough opening completed, exterior siding and sheathing can be sawed out, using the framing members as a guideline. Some types of siding permit installing the window unit so that the exterior window casing

lies over the siding—providing that the proper window jamb width has been specified. With others, the window unit must lie flush against the exterior sheathing. This requires removing portions of the siding back away from the rough opening. The finish siding must then be pieced back in. If the old siding can't be used for this purpose, new stock must be installed. The interior wall covering can be replaced after the window installation. Placing the window itself is done just like in new construction, by following the manufacturer's suggestions.

Reframing

Besides that for new doors, windows, and partitions, other types of reframing may be necessary. For instance, a floor frame might need reinforcing to bear a heavy load. Or, a series of heavy cabinets might require the installation of additional structural members to provide solid anchoring points and additional load-bearing strength. This happens frequently in old homes with nonmodular construction, structural members of odd sizes, or post-and-beam, or other types of construction.

The specifics of reframing depend upon the individual situation. But basically, the procedure begins with removing sheathings or coverings wherever necessary, fully exposing the existing framework. Then, more or less standard platform-framing techniques are used with materials that are matched closely to those used in the original framework. Usually, new members are added to the old, rather than ripping out the old ones and replacing them.

If the sizes, spacing, and placement of the original framing members is odd compared to current-day practices, all you can do is cut, fit, and shim, using as many

structural members as seems reasonable—then fasten everything securely. Beyond that, there aren't any rules to follow. It is just a question of "cobbling up" the best framing arrangement possible in the situation.

Working With Load-Bearing Walls

This is one of the trickiest parts of some remodeling jobs. All houses have load-bearing walls, which bear a portion of the weight of the structure that lies above them. All exterior walls bear a certain amount of weight. In a conventionally built gable-roof house, for example, the exterior walls running parallel

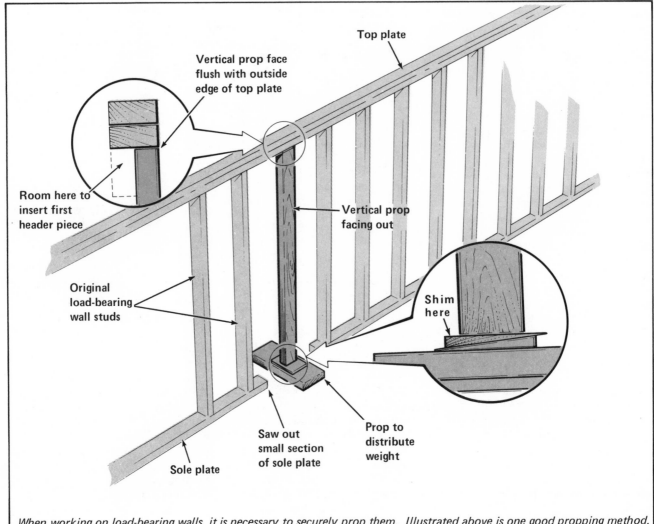

Top plate

Vertical prop face flush with outside edge of top plate

Room here to insert first header piece

Vertical prop facing out

Original load-bearing wall studs

Shim here

Sole plate

Saw out small section of sole plate

Prop to distribute weight

When working on load-bearing walls, it is necessary to securely prop them. Illustrated above is one good propping method.

with the roof ridge bear a substantial amount of weight, while the end walls hold up considerably less. Interior partition walls may also bear a heavy load. A longitudinal center partition running parallel with the roof ridge in a gable-roof house, for instance, may bear twice the load of each parallel exterior wall. And other partitions may support a certain amount of weight as well.

Caution: You must exercise a great deal of care when remodeling or cutting into such walls. There are many dangers—excessive settling and structural damage; doors sticking shut or open; windows jamming or actually bursting out of their frames; and even structural

collapse of part of the house. In addition, the last one or two remaining structural members of a virtually unsupported load-bearing wall can suddenly shatter into lethal projectiles. You can usually determine if a wall is load-bearing by finding out if other structural members rest on it. But sometimes construction complexities make this determination difficult. Whenever there is *any* doubt whatsoever, seek professional help or treat a wall as load-bearing.

The first step in reworking a load-bearing wall is to remove the covering or sheathing, preferably on both sides. This gives you plenty of room in which to work. An important

point to remember is that any permanent structural support or load-bearing capability removed has to be replaced with new load-bearing capacity at least equal to the original. Meantime, you have to provide temporary support to bear the load as you work. There are a number of ways to do this.

A series of 2 x 4's or 2 x 6's, spaced about three feet apart, works well, particularly with interior walls. These props should be canted at a very slight angle with their wide faces parallel with the wall and sides facing outward. They should be jammed against the top plate at one end and a pad of scrap wood at the floor. Partially driven toenails hold the props in place,

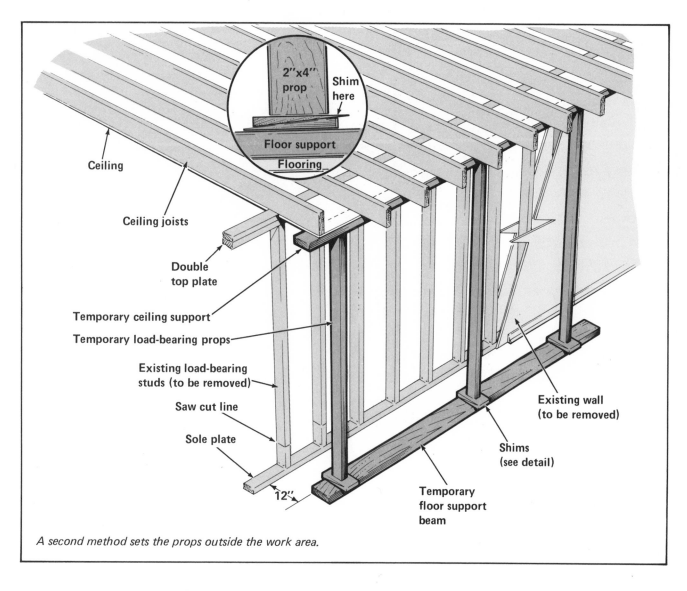

A second method sets the props outside the work area.

and they are set so that the tops leave the greater part of the top plate clear and the bottoms are slightly away from the sole plate.

Another possibility—useful for outside walls—makes use of props positioned slightly outside the work area and away from the wall being removed. First, you place a two-inch plank on the floor, preferably at an angle to the floor joists or directly over a parallel joist. Then you wedge another plank against the ceiling directly above the first plank. Both planks should be located a short distance from the wall, about two feet or so. Finally, you jam a series of temporary studs between the two planks, preferably in such a way that they are nearly or fully plumb, but very snug. This can be accomplished with 2 x 2's, 2 x 6's, or 4 x 4's set vertically with opposing shim-shingle wedges worked beneath them to drive them upwards. Adjustable steel columns with screw-thread tops work even better. The trick is to adjust the props so they withstand the downward pressure when the load-bearing members are removed, without driving the floor down or the ceiling up. It's a good idea to take floor-to-ceiling measurements both before and after, so if any settling or bulging does occur, adjustments can be made.

There are many other ways of installing temporary props, too, and easier or more practical methods may suggest themselves, depending on the project. The main object, of course, is to make sure there's ample solid support before you begin working. When this is done, ductwork, piping, and electrical wiring can be taken from the cavities. Then the load-bearing studs can be taken out by cutting them off and working the pieces free or by belting them out with a hand sledge. However, you should be careful when sawing through a stud under load, because it can pinch the saw blade and cause serious injury. Nails protruding from the sole and top plate can be cut off with a hacksaw or wire cutters.

Exterior corner posts should not be removed except to replace them with other permanent load-bearing members, perhaps of a different style. This can be done, but it requires a certain amount of tricky engineering and rebuilding. Success depends largely on the existing structural configuration.

Now a header—sometimes called a lintel—must be put in to replace the load-bearing studs. This header is built in the same way as a window or door header, and butts up tight against the bottom of the top plate. If the opening spans three feet or less, double 2 x 4's standing on edge are used. For an opening up to six feet wide, double 2 x 8's are called for, and if the opening is 10 feet wide, double 2 x 10's are used. Of course, these are minimum stock sizes, and larger sizes can always be installed. Clear openings of more than 10 to 12 feet usually require the installation of a support truss or some similar arrangement, or steel beam or steel flitch plates. Details should be worked out by an architect or structural engineer.

If the temporary props are clear of the top plate, the header can be made up of the two pieces

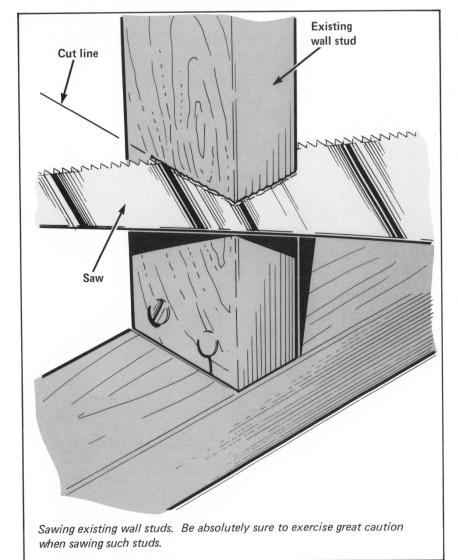

Cut line

Existing wall stud

Saw

Sawing existing wall studs. Be absolutely sure to exercise great caution when sawing such studs.

of dimension stock with a filler piece sandwiched between them to make up the full thickness of the wall. This is boosted into place and propped temporarily, while being end-nailed through each outside common stud in the wall sections that remain.

When the temporary support props rest against the top plate, the header is installed in three pieces. The first length of dimension stock is placed between the two outermost common studs. Then it's end-nailed with its outer face flush with the outer edges of the studs and top plate. You must also toenail through the face of the header piece into the top plate

about every 18 inches. Once this is done, you can remove the temporary support props; the half-header will provide sufficient support for the moment. The filler stock must be nailed to the inside face of the installed header half, and the second header half is installed in the same manner as the first.

To finish the job, you nail a trimmer stud to the inside of each outboard common stud, running from sole plate to header bottom. The exposed and now unnecessary section of the sole plate is cut flush with each trimmer stud and removed.

If the opening is to be left as is, you can now apply the wall

covering, leaving just the rough opening, which is later framed, cased, and trimmed with finish stock. In the case of an interior partition, wall covering can be installed as soon as the rough opening is complete. If the opening is for an oversize door assembly like a large sliding patio door, the opening width and height is framed to suit the specified rough-opening size of the door assembly. Window installations require some additional framing in the way of a sill, cripple studs, and perhaps a false header to achieve the proper rough-opening size. Exterior sheathing and siding is reinstalled as noted previously.

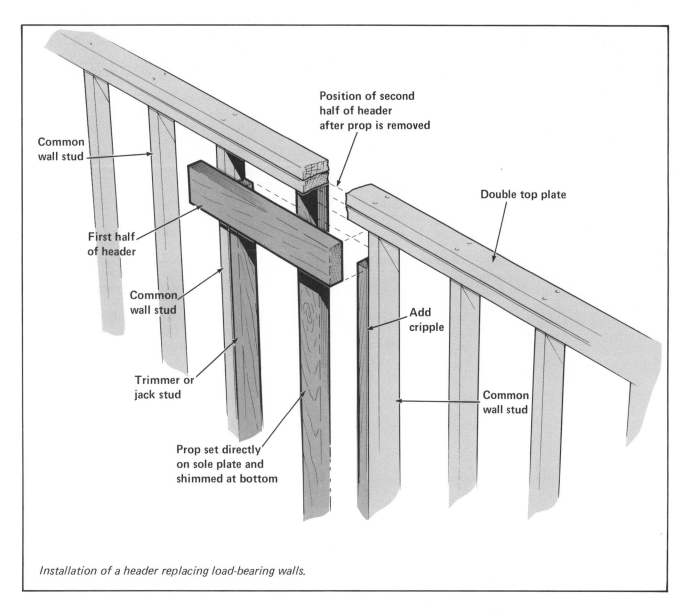

Common wall stud

Position of second half of header after prop is removed

Double top plate

First half of header

Common wall stud

Trimmer or jack stud

Prop set directly on sole plate and shimmed at bottom

Add cripple

Common wall stud

Installation of a header replacing load-bearing walls.

Reworking Utilities

Almost invariably, remodeling requires altering the utilities systems. Equipment such as lavatories, heat registers or baseboard units, lighting fixtures, receptacles and wall switches usually need to be repositioned or even eliminated entirely. Utility lines may have to be shortened, extended, rearranged or removed.

Whenever possible, a plan should be formed for moving utility lines around in the easiest way. Often, however, there's no way to tell how to do the job until the project is underway and utility lines are exposed to view. Electrical circuits are generally the easiest to change. **Caution:** Power to the affected circuits should be turned off. And before working on them, you should double-check to make certain they are off. Then you can remove fixtures and devices from their boxes. Often, you can pull the existing electrical cables free and reroute them. If the cables are too short or too old, they must be replaced all the way back to the nearest junction box, load center, entrance panel, or other source. Unless outmoded or in poor condition, boxes, switches, outlets, and lighting fixtures can be reused. However, you should make sure that the new installation follows the local electrical code requirements in all respects.

Changing or extending the plumbing is usually much more of a chore. Generally, the old piping must be removed piecemeal. Sometimes, certain parts can be salvaged or reused. There are occasions, though, when it's easier to disconnect the old system and just leave it in place, buried within the structure, and install new piping from the nearest convenient takeoff points. The most practical way to reroute or extend hot and cold water supply pipes and drainage piping is to install new runs of plastic tubing or pipe—where permitted by local code—and make up joints and connections with new adapter fittings. Where this is not allowable, copper tubing or pipe is a good alternative, though galvanized steel pipe is also sometimes used. Heating systems are generally reworked with copper pipe. Usually, work of this sort is best done by professional plumbers. They have the experience and knowledge that allows them to overcome the assorted problems that invariably pop up.

Rerouting and extending heating, ventilating, or air conditioning ductwork is likewise a job for a sheet metal professional, because most of this tinwork is bulky and difficult to work with. Not only must the best route be planned, but also many of the ductwork pieces must be custom-made from scratch to properly fit into place.

Reworking auxiliary systems such as telephones, fire/intrusion alarm systems, and the like is generally no problem. Existing stations, jacks, detectors, or what have you can be relocated, and new ones installed as necessary in the usual fashion. Wires and cables are easy to handle and can be rerouted or added to with no difficulties, and new connections made up as indicated. Except perhaps for telephone work, these jobs can be taken care of by the homeowner.

Matching-In

Once the basics just discussed have been completed, the sheathings, coverings, final finishes, and trimwork can be applied just as in new construction. However, during the process of putting things back together, there is an important consideration. This is a process of "matching-in," a general term that covers an incredible array of details and specifics. This is the business of conjoining the new to the old in such a manner that material dimensions match up, decors coordinate, and finishes and trim stock harmonize to hide all evidence of the remodeling process.

Sheathing

Often, exterior wall sheathing can be left intact by cutting away only the unneeded portions, as in a door or a window installation. When replacement sheathing must be pieced in, the new materials need not be identical to the old, but must be of the same thickness. Popular sheathing materials, such as plywood and fiberboard, can generally be directly matched. Substitutions can be easily made, too, and there are so many different kinds and thicknesses of sheathing materials available that making a reasonable match should not pose problems. However, corner locations that are susceptible to potential lateral stress should be sheathed with boards or plywood, rather than fiberboard.

Much of the same can be said of roof sheathing or decking. Various suitable sheathing materials are available in many thicknesses, so replacement is usually easy. Although thickness matching isn't as critical as in wall sheathing, the difference between old and new materials should not exceed $\frac{1}{8}$ inch. Sometimes, even that small difference will eventually show up as a ridge in the roofing, depending on the composition of the weather surface.

Plywood is the easiest material to use for replacement floor sheathing, because numerous thicknesses are available and it's easy to cut to fit the floor areas being repaired. Boards might also be used, despite their comparative lack of strength and stiffness. The thickness of the new and old sheathing should be exactly the same, so the finish flooring can be laid without difficulty or obvious transition. If necessary, you can adjust the floor level by using an underlayment material. This is particularly important

when you change from one type
of flooring to another. For
example, if hardwood flooring is
removed and replaced with
carpeting, subfloor levels often
must be adjusted to match up
with abutting original flooring.
When this is difficult or
impossible, special metal edging
strips or wedge-shaped
hardwood moldings can be
applied to break an abrupt
flooring-level change.

Exterior Siding

Matching-in replacement
exterior siding pieces is often
difficult. Some siding is
standardized, making it easy to
find matching material for
replacement. It may be hard to
find a match for older siding,
however, and old siding is often
weathered and worn, so patched-
in areas are quite noticeable.

By removing the old siding
carefully, you may be able to
reuse it for matching-in. Where
this isn't possible, the siding
pieces should be carefully
removed back to the nearest
joints, or cut away at suitable
points where there is an
adequate nailing surface for the
replacement pieces. Cutting lines
should be staggered to lessen
their obviousness. Then new
pieces of matching material can
be nailed up. If the siding has a
finish like paint or stain, the
entire wall will probably have to
be refinished. It's usually
impossible to match-in such
finishes successfully.

If you can't find a close match
for the old siding, or if the
existing siding is so weathered
that patching would be obvious,
you may have to replace all the
siding. Although expensive and
a lot of work, it's usually the
only solution if you want good
appearance. Sometimes,
however, you can redo only a
portion of the wall with
contrasting siding materials.

Wall Coverings

Drywall is easy to match-in, and
if done carefully, the joints are
invisible. The same is true of

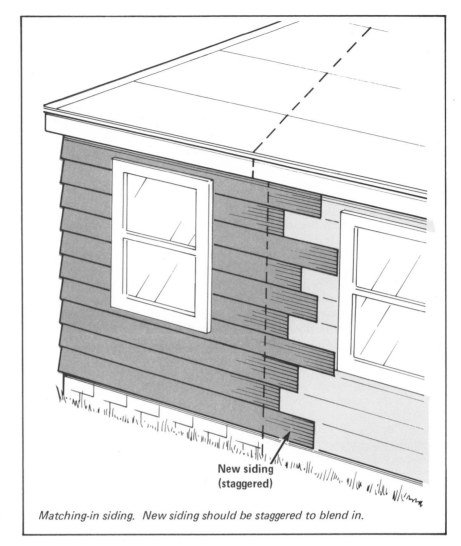

Matching-in siding. New siding should be staggered to blend in.

paneled or planked walls,
because of the wide variety of
matching and contrasting
materials available in identical
thicknesses. However, lath-and-
plaster walls present a lot of
problems. You can repair and
patch-in with more laths and
plaster. This is possible, but not
often practical. Usually lath-and-
plaster walls are dealt with by
using drywall of appropriate
thickness, and with plenty of
compound around the joints.
Often, extensive shimming is
necessary for a ripple-free wall,
and sometimes reframing or
additional framework is required
to provide ample drywall
support and nailing surfaces.

If matching-in seems to be too
difficult to be done successfully,
there are alternatives. You can

just remove all the old coverings
and replace them with new ones.
Or you can replace the torn-out
portions with pieces of drywall
of roughly similar thickness to
the original wall—then hide
everything with an entirely new
covering. Another possibility is
to work out a definite contrast
between the old and new
sections. This can be done by
installing a horizontal chair rail
molding with one finish above
and a false wainscoting below, or
by arranging a new decorative
paneled, planked, stone-veneered,
or similar section covering the
remodeled area.

Flooring

Unless the existing flooring is
either wood or masonry, it's
usually impossible to match-in

successfully. Sheet vinyl, asphalt, vinyl or vinyl-asbestos tile, and all types of carpeting can seldom be patched or pieced. All repairs will be obvious. Most often, the best course is to tear up the old floor covering and lay a new one, or to install new flooring directly on top of the old with the rebuilt area properly shimmed up to achieve a uniform surface.

There are a few alternatives to replacing the entire floor. For example, if half of a balanced or symmetrical section needs to be renewed it may be possible to escape the expense of a whole new floor. It might be possible to introduce a neutral border strip separating the sections, and then lay contrasting flooring of the same or a different type of material in the new section. Or, definite interfaces or breakpoints might be arranged, allowing the use of either nearly identical or totally different colors or designs in the same or some other flooring material. The most successful arrangement invariably involves a considerable degree of contrast.

Wood flooring, such as plain pine plank and hardwood strip types can usually be matched-in quite easily, although it is invariably necessary to sand and refinish the entire floor. Masonry floors, such as quarry tile, flagstone, or brick can be patched, realigned, or extended; the chief difficulty here is in matching the new mortar to the old in terms of color.

When matching-in any type of flooring, the surface levels of the new and old materials must be equal. This is easily accomplished by laying the correct thickness of sheathing or underlayments, and by providing edgings or wedge-moldings where necessary, as explained previously.

Ceilings

Drywall ceilings can be handled much like walls, and so can repairs to lath-and-plaster ceilings. As long as you match

the thickness of new and old materials, and there's plenty of space to smooth on patching plaster, you should get good results. Where ridges or seams are visible, they can often be hidden by applying a finish of heavy texture paint to the entire ceiling.

Tile ceilings are more of a problem, because new ceiling tiles will seldom match existing ones. Even if the imprints or patterns are identical, the color tones won't match due to discoloration and grime. However, if the old ceiling tiles are washable, you may be able to install new tiles of the same type, and then paint the entire ceiling a suitable color. With

this treatment, there should be no detectable difference between the old and new tiles.

Like wood flooring, wood paneled or planked ceilings present the problem of matching finishes. After installing a similar type of stock, complete repainting or restaining is generally necessary. For that matter, the same holds true for practically any interior paintwork; it cannot be patched-in, but must be redone.

As often as not, the most satisfactory solution to matching-in ceilings is to recover the entire ceiling with a fresh layer of thin drywall, new paint, paper, paneling, or some other material. Depending on the

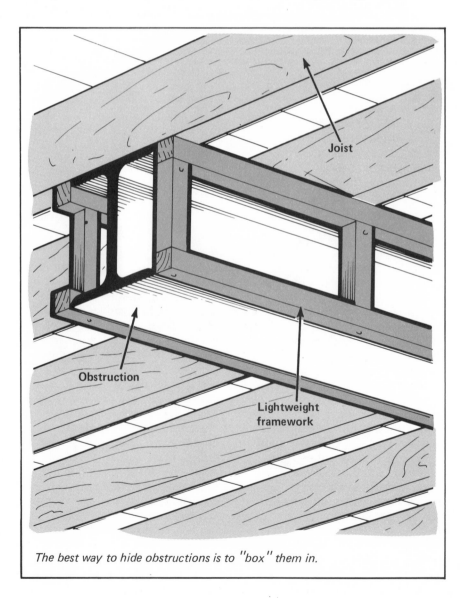

The best way to hide obstructions is to "box" them in.

nature of the room, installation of an entirely new dropped or suspended-grid ceiling may be a practical solution.

Boxing-in

In old houses, you may be forced to work around obstructions that cannot be easily removed or rebuilt. For example, in some post-and-beam constructions, the heavy beam sills extend up from the floor and out from the wall, or the heavy corner posts protrude into the living area. Surface-mounted piping may not lend itself to easy changing. Certain architectural features or structural members may obtrude, or integral masonry work not readily removable may be in the way. Rather than reengineering and trying to redo something that may lead to further difficulties and expense, the simplest way is often to cover up the obstructions.

This is usually done by a process called "boxing-in." The job is simple, and consists of disguising the structural members or whatever by enclosing them. Sometimes a lightweight framework must be built first, and then covered with plywood, wallboard, paneling, or other material. The boxed-in sections can be painted or stained to match the existing decor. Or they can be wallpapered or fitted out with trim stock in various attractive motifs. In most cases, simple construction turns out best, and when properly integrated with the remainder of the room or area, the boxing goes virtually unnoticed.

Where boxing-in is undesirable, you can hide the offending area with a built-in of some sort. Items like a windowseat, shelving, and cabinets make useful and attractive coverups.

Trimwork

Matching-in trim can pose problems. Items such as existing cove, base, baseshoe, and similar moldings, plus chair rails and door and window casings, should be duplicated exactly. However, if there are definitive breaks between the remodeled area and existing space—such as new partition walls, storage walls, or cabinetry—new moldings and materials can be used. When existing trim can't be matched, it should be replaced.

Often, it's possible to match old moldings with current-day production stock, in which case old and new can be joined by making a 45-degree splice and painting over. If moldings can't be duplicated from stock, they can often be customed-milled on a shaper or router with the proper cutter blade or blade combination. Even the blades can be custom-made, if you can't locate production models. However, this might cost more than replacing all the trim.

Plain, flat trim stock, as often found as mopboards or door and window casings, is usually easy to duplicate in appearance. Ornate casings that have been carved or routed in decorative patterns are more difficult, but can be matched by routing a duplicate pattern in raw stock. Where flat stock dressed up with applied molding is present, you can match the molding and attach it to similar flat stock. Of course, if you don't like the appearance of the trim in the first place, you can easily and inexpensively replace it with new trim of your choice.

Whenever you do match trim, all the old trim must be repainted, or stripped and stained with the same type of applied finish you use on the new trim. It's almost impossible to match applied finishes by just applying a finish coat to the new trimwork.

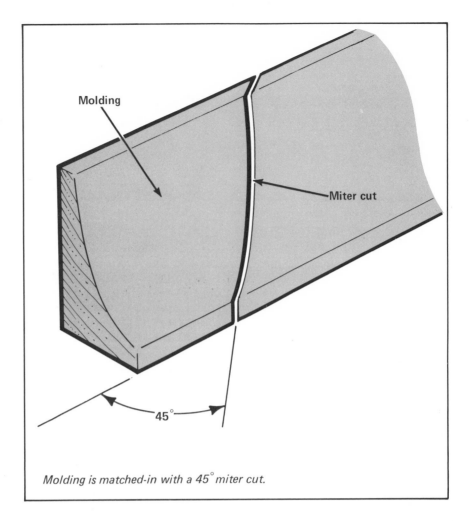

Molding is matched-in with a 45° miter cut.

Building an Outdoor Room

A deck is designed to conform with the surrounding topography. The above deck utilizes a simple post construction.

Most older homes, and many new ones, do not offer indoor/outdoor living facilities. But, through either conversion or addition, nearly all homes can provide practical, comfortable, and stylish indoor/outdoor living areas. And, if even just rudimentary facilities exist, they can be improved to meet a homeowner's needs.

Conversions

Depending upon the house's design, a relatively simple conversion can often create an enjoyable indoor/outdoor living space. There's no pat formula for working out such an arrangement; each home presents a different situation. There are, however, three basic approaches: indoor room conversions, outdoor conversions, and a combination of the two.

Indoor Room Conversions

An indoor room conversion can "bring the outdoors in" by way of strategically located, large picture windows. More often, however, one or two walls are fitted with floor-to-ceiling expanses of glass. A common arrangement is a combination of sliding glass patio doors, large fixed glazing panels, and a series of casement or other types of window sash that can be opened.

Here's an example of what can be done. Let's suppose that a house has a fairly large, but ineffectively utilized back hall that adjoins a kitchen. A rear outside door enters the hall and an interior door leads into the kitchen. One or two small windows, placed high in the hall, admit a modest amount of light and allow no view. An indoor/outdoor conversion could be arranged like this: the entire partition wall between the

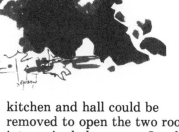

kitchen and hall could be removed to open the two rooms into a single large one. Load-bearing support columns would have to be substituted if the partition wall is a load-bearing one. Rearrangement of the kitchen counter, cabinetry, appliances, and furnishings would have to be done to suit the new space. To bring fresh air and sunshine into the kitchen, you could replace the rear outside door with a sliding patio door and rebuild the exterior hall wall with large expanses of glazing, including openable sash. The hall space itself could be used to expand the kitchen, or to make a cheerful laundry area, dining nook, solarium, or a plant room. If the roof design were suitable, skylights could be installed.

Outdoor Conversion

Many houses have porches, verandas, or decks that are seldom used. This could be owing to drawbacks like inconvenient access from the house; lack of screening, lighting fixtures, or furnishings. Whatever the problem is, it can usually be solved. It's simply a matter of repairing, rebuilding, or enlarging as necessary—then installing lighting receptacles and fixtures, glazing or screening, furnishings and accessories. Many times, it's desirable to at least partially open the house interior into the area. If the area is weatherproofed and heated, as in the case of an enclosed porch, it can be completely opened to the house. Otherwise doors (patio or otherwise) and glazing can be installed to achieve a similar goal.

Combinations

In most cases, an indoor/outdoor conversion job involves both opening the home interior to the outdoors, and providing a readily accessible outdoor living area. The adjoining outdoor area might be a patio, deck, balcony, courtyard, porch, or combination of areas and focal points. When these areas are built or rebuilt, you must pay a lot of attention to the overall design—even though the project may continue to develop over a long time span.

Building Indoor/Outdoor Living Areas

The best way to plan an indoor/outdoor area is to first envision the ideal one for you. Then alter the plan according to the house design, available space, climate, landscaping, terrain contour, and other factors. There can be one or more basic elements in any plan. The following are some major components that can be used individually or in combination, to be an indoor/outdoor living area's focal point.

Decks

A deck is basically a platform, supported above grade level by props. The deck platform can be only a few inches above grade, or it can be substantially elevated, as when built as a second-floor extension, or out over a steep banking or drop-off. A deck is usually, but not always, attached directly to a house. On a hillside site, for example, you could construct two or more decks at different levels, and join them with steps or staircases.

Basic deck construction is simple, although topography and other factors may present difficulties. In the most straightforward design, construction starts with setting the supports. If the deck is built almost on-grade, these supports may consist of "sleepers"— railroad ties or other treated wood beams—laid directly on the ground. They should never be laid on sod or topsoil. And although they're sometimes placed on topsoil, it's best to bed the beams in gravel and carefully level them. The sleepers should be 4 x 4's, and preferably larger. Spaced at 16 inches on center, you can nail nominal one-inch decking planks directly to them. When nominal two-inch planks are used, the sleepers can be moved out to 32 inches on centers. This is also a popular method for making walkways.

You can also space the sleepers farther apart and build a floor frame of dimension stock directly on them. The frame is built just like a house floor frame, with header joists around the perimeter and common joists between. Assuming one-inch deck planking and 16-inch joist spacing, 2 x 6's would serve for sleeper spans of up to 12 feet, 2 x 8's up to 14 feet, and 2 x 10's up to 22 feet. However, such long spans would be somewhat springy; the shorter the span, the more solid the deck becomes. Whatever the spacing, the deck planking is nailed to the joist tops as the final step.

Often, decks are supported by posts. Smaller decks are often set on 4 x 4's, especially if the elevation above grade level is only a foot or two. For higher, larger decks, 6 x 6's and 8 x 8's are commonly used. Often, though, the larger posts are chosen more for visual impact than strength. A six-foot 4 x 4 of almost any type of wood can hold up a direct load of more than three tons! And diagonal braces can be added to any size of deck posts to increase rigidity and stability. In any case, the object is to choose posts and construction methods that will result in a well-supported deck which is not wobbly.

Deck posts are generally spaced at least six or eight feet apart, and often more; spacing is governed by both appearance and the intended size of the floor frame joists. Posts can be set directly in the ground by digging a small hole to a depth of 2½ to 3 feet, dropping in the post and aligning it, and tamping earth in around it. Or, you can dig a larger hole that's 18 to 24 inches deep, set the post, and surround it with fresh concrete. A prepared, bagged concrete mix works well. Posts set in concrete tend to last longer than those set in earth. In either case, posts should be treated with a wood preservative, preferably by a commercial pressure method, unless they're made of a decay-resistant wood like redwood. Also, you should plan the setting of the posts carefully, and align and adjust them so they're all true and in perfect position.

Once the posts are set, the floor frame of dimension stock can be attached to them. If the deck is a freestanding unit, header joists are nailed around the perimeter posts, and the common joists are set between the headers. The common joists can either be end-nailed directly through the headers or can be mounted on metal joist hangers attached to the headers.

In many cases, one side or end of the deck is attached directly to the house. This requires removal of a certain amount of exterior siding, and nailing or lagging a dimension-stock ledger plate to the sill or wall studs of the house. If the deck joists run perpendicular to the house walls, they can be attached to the ledger plate with metal joist hangers. If the deck joists run parallel with the house walls, the ledger plate serves only as a nailing strip for the ends of the decking planks. In that case, a 2 x 4 plate is sufficient; otherwise, the ledger plate is usually the same size as the joists.

Numerous materials can be used for decking. Redwood and teak are excellent, and fir, spruce, and treated or stained pine work well. Nominal one- or two-inch thick and four- to eight-inch wide boards are laid as decking. The one-inch size is popular because it's inexpensive and easy to handle, but nominal four-inch wide boards are preferred because they are less susceptible to cupping.

The usual procedure is to space the planks from $\frac{1}{16}$ to $\frac{1}{4}$ inch apart to allow room for expansion and contraction, and so that rainwater and snowmelt will drain away. Certain types of exterior-grade plywood can also be used for solid decking, but they are usually less satisfactory. For quick water runoff, the deck must be pitched outward and downward, and decking must be laid evenly to prevent puddles. The deck frame should be heavy and solid if built in regions that experience heavy snows or high winds, especially if the deck is a considerable distance above ground level.

Decks, particularly those of redwood, are often left unfinished so they will weather to a pleasing silver-gray color. You can, however, successfully apply many finishes to these platforms. But, finishes should only be applied for appearance sake. They won't substantially lengthen the deck's life, and once you apply a finish, the process must be repeated at least every two years to maintain a fresh appearance. Commonly, owners stain or paint deck posts and framework, and perhaps the railing, but leave the decking unfinished.

Many low decks don't have railings, and if only a foot or two above ground level, steps are often fitted to the open edges. Higher decks, however, usually have railings for safety and appearance. You can install metal or wood railings by attaching railing posts to either the outside or inside of the outermost floor-frame structural member. When attached to the inside, the decking must be fitted around the railing posts. Often, the deck support posts are extended above floor level to become the primary anchoring points for the railing assembly. Railing posts are also attached to the deck frame at intermediate points. They can be secured with nails, but this results in flimsy construction. Railings should be anchored as securely as possible. Bolts are best, and heavy lag screws are a good alternative. Sometimes both must be used. In any case, be sure to check local codes.

Porches

Basically, a porch is just a roofed-over deck attached to a house. Floor and support assembly construction can be the same as for a deck, with one end or side secured to the house frame. The porch floor can be level with the interior floor of the house, or it can be adjusted one or two steps lower. A porch roof frame is constructed just like any other of the same style. A shed-style roof, pitched down and away from the house, is perhaps the most common, but gable and other styles are possible. The pitch of the roof is largely determined by the porch's size, shape, dimensional parameters, and what looks the best. However, you do have to consider the type of roofing to be used.

In simplest form, the roof is supported by a ledger plate, secured to the house wall at one side or end. The remainder is supported by a series of posts or columns, which extend from the porch floor to the underside of the roof frame. Support posts should be set directly atop the floor-frame support posts to eliminate sagging and to hold the roof up solidly. Or, a stronger method is to run the posts from small concrete foundation pads in the earth, directly to the roof frame. The porch frame is then attached to the support posts. Posts can be made of wood 6 x 6's or larger stock, heavy box beams, round wood columns made for the purpose, or even peeled logs. Spacing of the support columns can range from 4 to 12 feet, depending upon the design of the porch, size of the roof, and size of the columns.

This basic porch configuration can be modified in many ways. For example, instead of constructing the roof of standard building materials, the framework might be covered with a translucent, heavy plastic sheeting. Many styles, colors, and patterns are available. The openings between support posts might be partly enclosed with a low stud wall with glass or screening above. Also, by building a full wall framework between the support posts, windows and patio doors can be installed. And, if the porch is weathertight and is constructed with solid flooring instead of planking, it can be finished and furnished to closely resemble an interior room. However, without a lot of glazing or screening, skylights or translucent roofing, and immediate access to the grounds, such a porch doesn't make an indoor/outdoor living area. Such features should therefore be incorporated into the design.

Patios

Designed and built properly, a patio can be a very inviting indoor/outdoor living area. In essence, a patio is a flat leisure area, built on one or several levels. It's usually at least partially paved, and fitted with outdoor furnishings. Most are fully open, but some are partially or entirely roofed over.

One common method of patio construction is to lay out a substantial area, build forms around the perimeter, and pour a concrete slab. Sod and topsoil should be removed first, and the level built up if necessary with a cushion layer of sand or gravel. As with all exterior slabs, the patio slab should be five inches thick. Wire reinforcement mesh is bedded in the concrete which can be plain or colored. Then the concrete is steel-trowelled to a plain, but slightly rough finish, or broomed or otherwise treated for a textured finish. Sometimes, stone slabs or fist-sized cobblestones are bedded in the fresh concrete, or a particular finishing process can be used to produce an exposed-aggregate surface.

A do-it-yourselfer can also use a bagged concrete mix to build a poured patio. First, you lay out the patio area and remove sod, vegetation, and topsoil. Once the area is rough-leveled, a gridwork of 2 x 4's—redwood is best—is built. The grid squares can be any size, but two to four feet is most suitable. This gridwork is supported above the rough grade with stones, stakes, or chunks of brick and carefully leveled. The next step is to fill the area with clean sand, tamped firm and leveled to within about three inches of the top of the gridwork. Reinforcing mesh placed in the squares at mid-depth will reduce surface damage and keep the concrete at an even plane. The concrete is mixed in a wheelbarrow a few sacks at a time, and emplaced square by square. Each square should be screeded, darbied,

finished, and moist-cured until the patio is finished. If desired, the job can be done piecemeal over a lengthy period of time.

Another good way to construct a patio is to use masonry units. This kind of patio is easy to design and build by the do-it-yourselfer. It can also be made expandable and constructed over a long period of time. The masonry units used might be brick pavers laid straight or in various patterns; ordinary weatherproof brick; concrete pavers (which come in many shapes and several colors) or flagstones. There are several varieties of flagstones—slate in any of several colors, marble, granite, sandstone, or precast poured-concrete flags. You can cast the latter right in the backyard, by making either rectilinear or free-form forms and pouring them full of bagged concrete mix.

A masonry-unit patio can be built many ways, but the sand-bed method is one of the simplest. Sod, vegetation, and topsoil are removed from the patio area. The site is then rough-leveled and filled with sand; a depth of three inches or so is ample. The sand cushion should be dampened—but not soaked—tamped firm, and leveled. The height of the sand surface should be adjusted to the paver thickness, so the finish patio surface will be at the proper level, at or above grade. Then you just set one masonry unit at a time on the sand surface in whatever pattern is desired. They're usually set with open $\frac{1}{16}$- to $\frac{1}{4}$-inch joints, though some pavers are designed to interlock and fit tightly together. Joint cracks are filled by shoveling sand onto the pavers and sweeping it into the joints. Finally you settle the sand down with a fine mist of water and add more sand as necessary to fill the cracks. This type of patio is subject to some settling and heaving in areas of harsh winter weather because of frost action. However, the

The design of your patio is limited only by your imagination. One or several masonry treatments can be combined for the final affect. This patio uses a simple combination of poured concrete and brick.

effects are seldom severe, and in any event, repairs are easy to make.

There are some other more difficult and expensive methods of laying a masonry-unit patio. While they do result in a longer-lasting patio that remains relatively flat, level, and unaffected by weather, many homeowners feel that they are not worth the extra cost and effort. For example, the patio base may be made of four to six

inches of crushed rock or road-base compacted with a four-ton (or heavier) roller. This is topped by two to four inches of compacted sand, with the pavers laid atop the sand. The joints are filled with a dry sand-mortar mix. After being dampened, the mix hardens and stabilizes the pavers. Or, a six-inch base of gravel can be laid and topped with one to two inches of hot-mixed, hot-laid asphalt. The pavers are laid on the asphalt in a thin coating of fresh hot tar, and the joints filled with either wet mortar or a dry sand-mortar mix. Another possibility is to lay the pavers in a mortar bed, with mortared joints, on top of a three- to five-inch poured-concrete slab.

There is another way to build a patio that, with imagination

and careful design, makes a most attractive outdoor living area. This combines several elements, like a series of different planter boxes, meandering gravel or marble chip walkways, and plant groupings with small areas of open space. These areas might be comprised of redwood-bordered geometric shapes with grass in some, plantings or driftwood in others, flagstone in a few, and so forth. You could also place lawn furnishings and garden ornaments, like birdbaths or fountains, in some of the forms. Railroad ties can sometimes be used to good effect, as can wood walkways, outdoor lighting, and various patio accessories.

Atriums and Courtyards

An atrium is an outdoor living area enclosed by the walls of a house, so its shape depends on the house's design. For maximum effect, all exterior house walls that face the atrium should have large expanses of glass. Also, each individual room should have direct access, perhaps by way of sliding patio doors. The atrium may include decking, patio area, lawn, plantings and planters, and assorted furnishings in various combinations. Certain focal points, such as a pool, hot tub, greenhouse, barbeque, fireplace or similar items, can be included, too. The most important factor is careful planning and design.

The situation is much the same for a courtyard. In this case, the house itself provides only a portion of the courtyard boundary; the rest is formed by fencing, walls, outbuildings, embankments, or natural topographical features. Generally, courtyards have several major elements that meld into an overall landscaping plan. As with atriums, the principal components may consist of some combination of decking, patio area, perhaps one or more porches, greenhouse, or other outbuildings. Focal points like a hot tub, fountain, gazebo, or playhouse may be included. Large courtyard areas may also have gardens, driveway and parking areas, service yards, maintenance equipment, and work areas.

Carports

A carport is an open-sided shelter that's large enough to accommodate one or more vehicles. Whether freestanding or attached to an existing building, it can serve as part of an outdoor living area if designed properly.

The simplest form of carport is a roof section supported by at least four heavy columns, if freestanding, or by a pair of columns on one side if attached to an existing building's wall on the opposite side. But most carports have one or more sides partially or wholly enclosed by simple panels, masonry screening, grillwork, or some similar arrangement. Often the back end of the carport is built in the form of a storage wall for lawn and garden equipment. A barbeque or outdoor cooking and dining center might also be built in. Actually, though, to be a pleasant outdoor living area, a carport should be made integral with surrounding landscaping, and perhaps near a patio, deck, or other outdoor living space.

One of the easiest ways to build a carport is to buy a kit. Many different kits are available, and most are easy to build and modify to meet various needs. Such modifications range from adding screening, lighting fixtures, cabinets and storage racks to partial enclosure and building in a complete outdoor dining or gardening center.

Alternatively, you can build a carport rather easily from scratch. All it takes is to construct a lightweight roof frame and attach it to the wall of the house. Whether or not the roof should be pitched depends upon local wind and snow

Carports are usually built when a garage has been converted to living space. The carport itself can become an attractive outdoor addition. The above utilizes a partial masonry wall as a background for landscaping.

conditions. The outer edge of the roof can be supported by a series of wood posts set in concrete. You can use either a conventional roof surface, like board or plywood sheathing, roofing felt underlayment, and asphalt or wood shingles. Or, sheets of metal or translucent plastic can be used to cover the roof frame. As with a carport kit, various additions could then be made to the basic structure.

Carport floors are often made of poured concrete, but there are alternatives. For example, it might be constructed patio-style by laying flags or pavers, or a

layer of gravel, marble chips, or cinders.

Solariums

Building a solarium is a matter of arranging glazing and furnishings to provide a convenient and comfortable spot for sunbathing. A southern exposure is best, but any area that's sunny during the day can be satisfactory.

A number of different constructions are possible. One is to replace a suitable existing section of the house wall with glass panels to admit sunlight. Under the right circumstances,

you could also glass-in a portion of a low roof, or fit it with skylights or roof windows. A large bathroom is an ideal location for this treatment. You can also convert a porch to a sunporch by glassing-in the porch wall with either plate-glass sheets or commercial window units. Here too, part or even all of the porch roof might be fitted with glass or plastic panels or skylights. In both situations, construction is a matter of reframing the wall structure as necessary to receive

the glazing, and decorating and furnishing the area.

A solarium might also be constructed by attaching a relatively small shed, or arched-roof section, comprised primarily of glazing panels, to some convenient wall of the house. Access could be gained from both the house and grounds. A small greenhouse kit, designed to attach to an existing structure, is a good starting point. You just place the structure on a permanent foundation and install a conventional floor—dispensing with plant-growing facilities. All that's left to make a solarium is

to put in suitable furnishings.

Outdoor solarium areas are popular, too, and they're easy to make. A small section of deck, patio, or even lawn is just enclosed with wood-and-glass walls to make a small, private, windproof enclosure. The height of the walls, which can be from four to eight feet, depends upon existing view planes from outside the immediate area. There's no roof, but sometimes polished aluminum reflectors are mounted at appropriate points along the tops of walls. These can redirect and intensify the sunlight entering the enclosure to make the solarium delightfully comfortable, even in mid-winter. This is especially true at higher altitudes.

The greenhouse is a must for many plant lovers. This greenhouse is based on a brick foundation.

Greenhouses

If you like plants and gardening, a greenhouse makes an enjoyable indoor/outdoor living area. Building one from scratch, however, is a complex subject that is well beyond the scope of this book and the skills of most homeowners. The easiest course is to purchase a kit. A homeowner can erect the structure himself or have the job done by a contractor. Kit greenhouses are available in many sizes and designs that can be adapted to fulfill practically any need. Prices range from a few hundred to thousands of dollars.

The structure may be freestanding, attached to an existing building, or made integral with the structure of a house. It can even be built with only the roof and about two feet of the wall extending above ground.

A typical framework is made of wood, aluminum, steel, or structural plastic. Glass, plastic film, plastic sheet, or fiberglass panel, all of special types, can be used for glazing. Complete utilities systems are often built into larger units.

Hot-Tub Areas

A hot-tub area can be either an entity in itself, or part of a larger indoor/outdoor living area.

Hot-tubs—in many sizes and styles—come ready-made and in kit form, with instructions for assembly usually included. The tubs are set on the ground or a substantial foundation base (concrete or gravel pad, etc.) at grade level. Pumps, heaters, and other equipment are generally placed beside the unit; plumbing and electrical connections are also required. All of this can be left exposed, but more often it's covered and concealed by planters, landscaping, or a deck that surrounds the tub. Sometimes a small bath house is included on the surrounding deck.

The popular hot tub can adapt to a variety of surroundings. The deck surrounding this hot tub hides the bulky pumps and heaters.

Pergolas

True pergolas are structures seldom seen in the United States, because of their large, heavy, formal characteristics. However, derivitives of the pergola—arbors, trellises, sunscreens, and sungrids—have been popular for many decades. Usually they support vines and climbing plants, although sungrids are often built only to partially screen direct sunlight, and are unadorned by plants.

An arbor can be arched or flat-topped, and consists primarily of side posts and top bars or rails to form a canopy. A trellis is a vertical structure that supports climbing plants. Sunscreens, or sungrids, are generally flat or slightly sloping, rectilinear assemblies, much like a roof frame. But, they're topped with slats instead of roofing. These structures are generally attached to an existing building at one end and supported by posts at the other, and they often cover a deck or patio.

There are dozens of ways to build an arbor. The traditional, arched rose arbor consists of a pair of wood arches, much like long-legged horseshoes, set in the ground. They're two or more feet apart and connected with strips of wood laths set ladder-fashion. A modern counterpart employs two or more sets of 2 x 4 or 4 x 4 posts, placed in the ground and connected with cross-beams overhead and lighter laths from set to set. Also, some arbors are made simply by setting posts and attaching trelliswork to them on both sides.and top. A more complex, but beautifully rustic arbor, can be made by arranging logs, poles, driftwood pieces or "dry-ki" (long-dead, naturally weathered, but unrotted trunks or limbs) in a geometric structure of interconnected posts, supports, and cross rails.

Likewise, there are many pattern possibilities for trellises. The trellis body itself contains the principal pattern. It's usually made of interwoven or cross-lapped strips of laths or lattice, both of which are generally available at most well-stocked lumber yards. The trellis' outside frame is made of more substantial wood to provide a solid and sturdy framework for the body. This framework is often made of 1 x 2's, 1 x 3's and 1 x 4's, but may be built of dadoed 2 x 4 stock as well. Trellises can be made in rectangular, curved, or other geometric shapes. The fan pattern is popular; other patterns include grid, diamond, and basketweave types.

Sunscreens and sungrids are generally larger and more substantially constructed than arbors or trellises. But, building them is usually no more difficult. A simple sungrid is composed of a series of beams, like 4 x 4's. These are secured at one end to the house wall, and extend outward, either level or pitched slightly downward, for as much as 20 feet. The free ends of the beams are supported ,by posts set firmly into the ground. Smaller beams or dimension stock, or sometimes laths or narrow boards are attached—often on edge—to the main beam tops. They're spaced and positioned so the sun is partly filtered through them. You can calculate the spacing so that when the summer sun is lowering, the area beneath the sungrid is almost completely in shade. If vines are grown on the sungrid, the spacing can be considerably wider.

Sunscreen construction is simple, but sturdy. It must be able to withstand the ravages of wind and weather, as well as the prying forces of fast-growing vines. The posts should be set deep in the ground and well-anchored, preferably in concrete. Overhead beams should be secured to the posts with long lag screws, or better yet, steel saddle plates and bolts. Smaller cross-beams may be nailed or bolted on, depending on their size. And the beam ends that are anchored to the house must also be securely attached—either individually with anchor plates and bolts, or to a header plate that's solidly lagged or bolted to the house frame. The posts and beams can be of any size and spaced at considerable distances, unless the sungrid will be overgrown with large and heavy vines in an area where high summer winds are common.

Gazebos and Belvederes

The traditional gazebo style is octagonal, and more ornate models sport a matching octagonal cupola. The hexagonal form is another favorite, but a gazebo can be built square or rectangular, or in some other regular polygonal form. It can be any size that's in proportion to the surroundings and other structures in the immediate area. Above all, a gazebo should be light and airy in form and construction—never bulky, squat, or heavy-looking. Traditional gazebos are almost entirely open at the sides, with at most a low railing between the support posts—generally fashioned of light, thin rails and uprights. However, the structure could be partly or wholly enclosed. It can also be built permanently, or in take-apart sections.

The usual construction method is simple post-and-beam. A series of full-height posts is set in the ground, preferably in concrete, to mark the perimeter of the gazebo. If it is particularly large, midpoint posts may also be necessary to help support the floor frame. Floor posts can be made from 4 x 4's, though 6 x 6's could also be used. The floor joists, usually 2 x 6's or 2 x 8's, come next. End and header joists enclose the perimeter; common joists are set between them and toenailed or secured with metal hangers. Then deck planking of 1 x 4's is nailed to the joist tops. So far, construction is almost exactly like building a deck, except that the support posts extend upward

and will hold the roof assembly as well.

The roof assembly is built next, and exactly how this is done depends on the gazebo's shape and the roof style. Rafters can be made of 2 x 4's, especially if they are doubled, though 2 x 6's might be necessary for a large gazebo. The rafters extend from a band beam or ledger plate secured to the support posts at an appropriate height to a common joint at the roof peak. The rafters may be joined at the peak by toenailing, by metal joiner plates, or by making a header box. If a header box is used, the box must be supported with temporary props while the rafters are fastened to it. Then the props can be removed. The roof can be sheathed with spaced 1 x 3's or 1 x 4's, with edge-butted planks or plywood sheets. Although unnecessary, a roofing underlayment could be used. In either case, the weather surface can be any common residential type. Or translucent fiberglass sheets could be attached to the roof rafters without sheathing.

Railings can be put in next; 2 x 4's are often used as rails, with uprights made of 2 x 2's. Small gazebos usually have built-in bench-type seating, but larger ones can accommodate lightweight lawn furniture. Heavy, bulky furniture, however, looks out of place in a gazebo. The finish can be whatever is appealing and blends in with other nearby structures. Either exterior paint or exterior stain is a good choice, although redwood and cedar are often left unfinished.

The modern term for a belvedere is a garden shelter. Although there's sometimes a fine line between a garden shelter and a gazebo, the former almost always looks different and serves different purposes. In addition to providing shelter from the elements, a garden shelter might be fitted with work areas, dining facilities, lighting fixtures, changing room, planters, barbeque units and such.

Construction is usually post-and-beam, with a more or less conventional deck platform for a base. Considerable openwork roofing, latticing and trelliswork, railings, built-in seating, planters, and cabinetry are common. About the only common denominator among garden shelters is that they're sturdily built of heavy materials for longevity and minimum maintenance.

Glossary

A

Access Hatch: An opening, usually in a floor or ceiling, that allows entrance into a storage or unused area, such as a ceiling or crawl space.

All-Weather Wood Foundation (AWWF): New type of foundation utilizing wood instead of masonry. Has FHA approval.

Anchor Bolts: Required by code for certain connections, especially wooden walls to masonry foundations. Width is usually ½ inch; length determined by materials being connected, or by code ordinance.

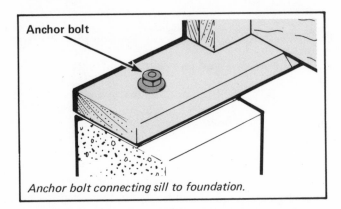

Anchor bolt connecting sill to foundation.

Angle Brackets: "Z" shaped metal forms, good for connecting poured concrete to concrete block.

Applied Finishes: Final touches of interior and exterior work. Includes paint, varnish, wallpaper, wax, etc.

Apron: (1) Bottom-most trim on a window, directly underneath sill; (2) Concrete extension on exterior of a garage door.

Arbor: Outdoor structure that supports vines or climbing plants.

Architect: Professional person licensed to practice architecture and protect public health and safety. Able to completely control the entire construction project. Specific skills include designing entire project, drawing up legal plans, obtaining building permits, and supervising or inspecting construction.

Architectural Control Committee *(legal):* Usually a neighborhood organization. Concerned with the exterior appearance of the house (color, design, etc.). Its main concern is to protect community architectural integrity.

Atrium: A courtyard-type area open to the sky within a building from which living space usually opens. Possibilities for passive solar heating are good.

B

Backfill: Earthen material removed for the purpose of installing a building foundation which is then replaced.

Balcony: A cantilevered or overhanging deck.

Band Board: Exterior trim piece hiding the joint between wall and roof, where the soffit hits the exterior wall.

Baseboard Heating Unit: Electrical, hot water, or steam heating device, able to fit along baseboard moldings. Can be installed at any convenient time.

Baseboard Molding: Interior trim piece of wood or vinyl, hiding joint between floor and wall.

Batt Insulation: Comes in rolls. Easy to fit between joists or studs. Usually made with fiberglass.

Batter Board: Temporary members used to outline foundation excavation at exterior corners.

Belvedere: A large outdoor living area. Usually includes some feature such as barbeque or workshop.

Bids: Contractors and subcontractors will cite a price for the execution of specified work. This price becomes legally binding to both parties when executed by both.

Bird's Mouth Cut *(roofing)*: A vertical and horizontal cut in the tail of a rafter that fits over the top plate of the wall.

Blanket Insulation: Large sheets of insulation. Especially useful when large areas need to be covered at one time.

Blind Nailing: Nailing in such a way that the head of the nail is invisible. The head of the nail is usually countersunk in the wood and then covered with a plug or filled.

Blocking *(Fire Blocking):* Horizontal wood strips placed between structural members to limit fire spread.

Blueprints: Standard copies of architectural plans. Adherence to blueprints is legally binding if so stated in a contract.

Board-And-Batten Siding: Vertical siding system with boards spaced slightly apart and wood strips, or battens, nailed to conceal the joints.

Box Cornice: An exterior trim method that usually closes up the rafter overhang with vertical and horizontal sheets of material.

Boxing-In: Method of hiding exposed pipe or other obstruction with a lightweight wooden framework, or box. (Sometimes referred to as "soffits").

Box Sill: The perimeter of the structural deck at the floor line. Contains header, sill, and sole plate.

Bracing *(Wind or Corner):* Extra support given to walls. Braces usually fit diagonally across wall

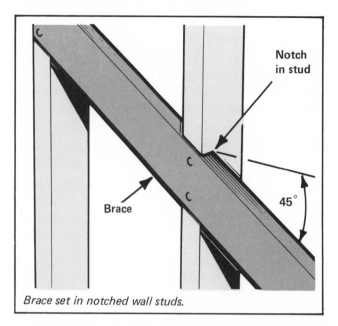

Brace set in notched wall studs.

studs, which are notched to hold the brace. Are required by most codes at all corners (exterior).

Breezeway: A passageway connecting two structures. Always covered, it may or may not have walls and windows.

Bridging: Technique of strengthening floor by adding wood or metal in between floor joists. Main purpose is to keep joists from twisting.

BTUs: British Thermal Units. Standard measurement for heat. Helpful when determining heater strength. One BTU is approximately equivalent to the heat caused by burning one wooden match stick.

Builder's Risk Insurance: Supplement to homeowner's insurance policy.

Building Codes *(legal):* Vary from state to state, and even from town to town. Specify types of materials and construction techniques. Check local building department for latest local code information, and the code adopted by that community.

C

Cantilever: A method of extending a structure substantially beyond its vertical support, such as a balcony.

Carport: Roofed structure with open walls, usually attached directly to house.

Casings: Trim pieces used to finish off doors and windows. Casings cover the rough-opening gap between the wall and window or door frames.

Caulk: To seal the joint between two materials, making it watertight.

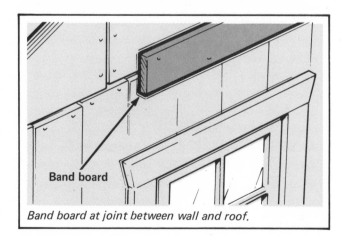

Band board at joint between wall and roof.

Ceramic Tile: Durable, attractive finish material. Especially good for bathrooms.

Clamshell Molding: Simple door casing technique. Clamshell moldings attach to the door jambs like a picture frame.

Clapboards: Popular horizontal exterior siding. Clapboards overlap one another, giving a rippled affect to the homes exterior.

Close Rake: Exterior trim method used on rafter ends when there is no overhang.

Cluster Home: Type of construction that adds identical structure(s) to existing one(s).

Collar-Beam Ties: Structural members tying a roof together in an "A" form. Collar-beam ties add considerable strength and stiffness to the roofing assembly.

Common Joist: A consistently spaced structural member, in a floor or ceiling.

Common Rafter: A consistently spaced structural member in a roof.

Composition Board: Sheathing material, applied like plywood with roofing nails. Material is often asphalt impregnated for moisture resistance.

Concrete Block: Usually 8x8x16 sized blocks of concrete-like material, used in construction.

Continuous Wall Foundation: A foundation wall of either poured concrete or concrete block that continues uninterrupted around the foundation.

Convenience Outlet *(electrical):* Generally, a duplex receptacle.

Corner Boards: Special trim to smooth over the corner breaks in exterior siding.

Covenants *(legal):* Typically general regulations found where zoning regulations are weak or nonexistant. Covers legalities such as property line setbacks, and garage size.

Crawl Space: A small area, usually about three feet high, within the foundation, under the house.

Cripple Jack *(roofing):* Rafters that run between valley jacks and hip rafters.

Cripple Studs: Used to support headers over windows or doors.

Crown: The natural bow or peak on a rafter or joist. Always set rafter or joist with the crown up.

Curing: The hardening process of concrete. It is best to keep concrete wet to slow the evaporation of surface water and yield better concrete.

Cutting-In: The process of making a hole in an existing wall to fit door or window.

D

Darby: A tool with two handles used by masons to finish concrete.

Daylight Basement: Basement with at least one wall completely exposed. Large windows could be installed in such a wall, letting in the sun.

Deck: An outdoor area, usually a few feet above ground, supported by piers. Most decks are connected to the house.

Device Box *(electrical):* Component that transmits electricity, but does not utilize it, such as a receptacle or wall switch.

Dimension Stock: Standard sized lumber.

Door Stop: A device or piece of finished hardware used to prevent a door from opening to a point to which it will cause damage.

Dormer: Extension from roof, usually with its own roof. Usually contains at least one window.

Doubled Joist: Two joists nailed together or set slightly apart. Used to support exceptionally heavy loads, such as partition walls.

Double-Span Joists: A single joist over two consecutive bearing points.

Drain, Waste, and Vent (DWV) Lines *(plumbing):* Plumbing pipes designed and constructed to carry drainage from a plumbing system.

Drywall: Popular finish material for walls and ceilings consisting of a layer of gypsum sandwiched between two layers of special paper.

E

Edging *(roofing):* Metal pieces bent slightly downward and outward into a lip, diverting moisture from roof sheathing.

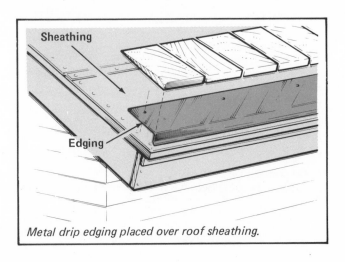

Metal drip edging placed over roof sheathing.

Elastomeric Compound: Special flexible material needed when making an expansion joint.

Excavation: An area that has been dug out, usually to accept foundation materials. Excavations can be the entire foundation area or merely the hole that a pier will sit in.

Expansion Joint: A joint provided to allow materials to expand and contract without breaking the integrity of the material. Expansion joints may be waterproof.

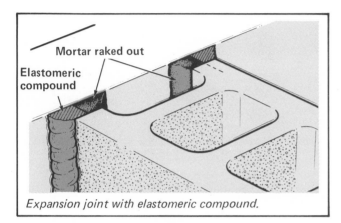

Expansion joint with elastomeric compound.

F

Finish Fascia *(roofing):* Long horizontal flat board, usually nailed to rafter tails. Trimwork.

Fixture: Final finishing appliance, securely attached, such as faucet, ceiling light, etc.

Flashing *(roofing):* Pieces of metal used to cover exterior joints and angles. Aids in waterproofing house.

Footings: Concrete pads set at base of foundation wall. Footings are usually set to a minimum of 36 inches below grade level, or below local frost line. Their purpose is to distribute concentrated wall loads on undisturbed base material, usually earth or clay.

Forms: Usually wooden and metal pieces set up to frame concrete wall area. Once concrete has cured, forms can be stripped away.

Foundation Drains: Usually set next to footing. Attached to sewer or drainage system.

Frieze Blocks *(roofing):* Wood blocks placed between top plate of wall and rafters, to fully enclose interior area.

Frost Line: Differs between locals. Foundation need only be dug below the local frost line.

Furring Strips: Strips of wood, or similar material, attached to a wall or floor and providing even support for an interior wall or floor surface.

G

Gable Roof: Method of roofing in which two sides meet at a high center ridgeboard, then slope off.

Garden Shelter: Large outdoor living area. Usually incorporating barbeque, work area, or dining facilities.

Gazebo: Small outdoor living area. May include benches or swing.

General Contractor: A contractor who takes on the responsibility of securing subtrades for a fee. Capable of seeing the project through completion. Duties include hiring labor, buying materials, arranging for inspections, obtaining permits, and doing the job to the homeowner's satisfaction.

Girder: Support placed strategically to help carry heavy loads.

Grade Level: The top-most surface of ground around a building where it strikes the foundation wall.

Greenhouse: A special structure designed to capture light in a way that plants best grow.

Grout: A bonding and leveling material used on masonry materials such as block, brick or tile.

H

Header Joists: Also known as "headers." These main joists are what the common joists are nailed into. Headers are usually attached to sill plates or around openings.

Hinge: A connecting piece of metal, usually with two leafs, that attaches a door to a door frame.

Hip Jack *(roofing):* A rafter that extends from the top plate to a hip rafter.

Hip Rafter *(roofing):* Rafter installed when roof changes direction. Runs diagonally from ridgeboard to top plate at an outside corner.

Hot Tub: A wooden, usually round tub of extremely hot water. Used for therapeutic and recreational purposes.

I

Indoor/Outdoor Living Facilities: Areas designed to tie the shelter of the indoors with the nature of the outdoors. Decks, patios, and porches are popular examples.

Insulation: Special material, such as fiberglass, made to keep heat and cold from entering or leaving a dwelling.

J

Jack Rafter: Shorter, secondary rafter extending from one principal member to another.

Jamb: The vertical members in a door or window frame.

Joist: Horizontal member. Used in the basic framing of floors and ceilings.

Junction Box *(electrical):* A closed metal box in which different circuits combine.

K

Keyway: Recessed area in foundation footing, made with a 2x4, to prevent lateral slippage of a foundation wall due to earth pressure.

L

Lag Screws: Heavy screws used for wood. The screws are usually driven in with a wrench.

Load-Bearing Walls: Walls which help transmit vertical loads to the ground.

Lookout Ladder *(roofing):* Area where rafter tails overhang top plate. Usually brought together with a frieze board.

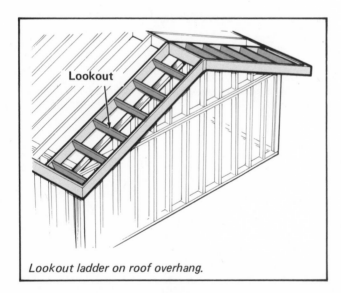

Lookout ladder on roof overhang.

M

Masonry: Material constructed by a mason. General term used primarily for stone work—brick, stucco, concrete, etc.

Mastic: A special adhesive prepared to secure tile, flooring, and other finishes. Different mastics are used for different purposes.

Matching-In: The technique of securing old finish to new in a clean, professional manner.

Materials-Flow Chart: Time chart made up by contractor determining which materials are needed when.

Metal Bridging: Special metal placed between joists to help prevent twisting of joists.

Miter Joint: A 45 degree cut used to join two pieces of trim, such as molding.

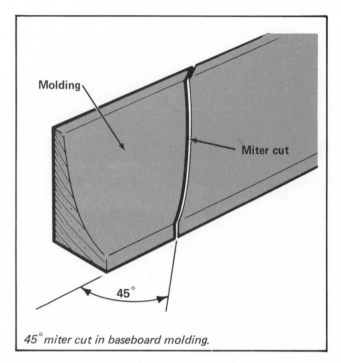

45° miter cut in baseboard molding.

Molding: Trim pieces used to cover interior joints between floor and wall, and wall and ceiling.

Monolithic Concrete Pour: Method of pouring foundation. Footing and forms are dug and set. Then concrete is poured at once. Used primarily for detached buildings.

Mud Room: An entrance room where boots can be removed and coats hung.

O

O.C.: On Center. Term used to designate spacing between studs or joists. 16 inches o.c. means 16 inches from the center of one member to the center of the other.

Open Cornice *(roofing):* Simple technique that doesn't apply exterior trim to overhang, leaving the rafter tails "open."

Overload *(electrical):* An amperage load greater than the electrical device capacity, causing the safety device to open.

P

Parquet Flooring: Wood strips, usually in tiles, in patterns on the floor.

Partition: An interior wall used to divide rooms into two sections.

Patio: An outdoor area, made of masonry, used for recreation.

Pergola: An outdoor structure topped with horizontal trellis work, supported by posts.

Perimeter Foundation: Foundation with a concrete wall of varying height set continuously around the house area.

Piers: Structural pieces used to support stress points. At times, piers can be used in construction of foundation.

Pitch (roofing): The amount of slope a roof section has. Can be calculated in terms of fraction (¼ pitch) or formula (1 in 1 pitch).

Plaster Lath: A thin strip of wood. Used to support plaster or stucco.

Platform Framing: Common method of framing floors, walls, and ceilings. Framework sections are assembled on a platform and set into place as the job goes along.

Polyethylene Film: Vinyl waterproof plastic sheet. Good as a vapor barrier.

Porch: An enclosed outdoor area, usually attached to the house.

Punch List: List of undone items prepared by the architect, contractor, or homeowner in construction. Items in Punch List must be remedied to the homeowners satisfaction before job is complete.

R

Rafter: Principal roofing member, used to frame the actual roof.

Rafter Tail: Part of rafter that overhangs top plate.

Receptacles (electrical): Also known as outlets. Current passes through and is made available for electrical appliance or fixture.

Ridgeboard (roofing): The highest member of a roof, set at angle to the rafters, but perpendicular to the ground. All common rafters attach to the ridgeboard.

Ridgepole: See ridgeboard

Rigid Insulation: Hard insulation used primarily for foundation or roof.

Rise (roofing): Height of the ridgeline above the top of the plate, measured from plate top to ridgeboard centerboard.

Roofing Felt: Underlayment for roof or wall finish. Applied over roof or wall sheathing.

Roughing-In: The technique of placing an opening in a wall to fit a door or window.

Run (roofing): Measured in different ways for different roof constructions. Basically, the distance between the outside top plate and the ridgeline.

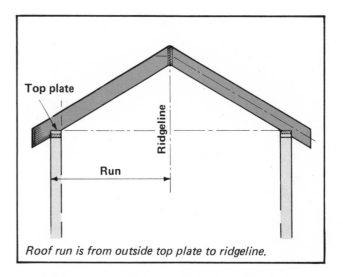

Roof run is from outside top plate to ridgeline.

R-Value: Measurement of insulation ability. Higher R-value is better insulation.

S

Screed: A tool, such as a board, used to level concrete slabs.

Setback Requirements: The distance to which you can build on your own property. Usually determined by local ordinances.

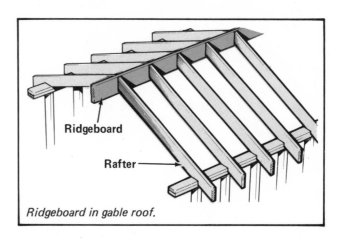

Ridgeboard in gable roof.

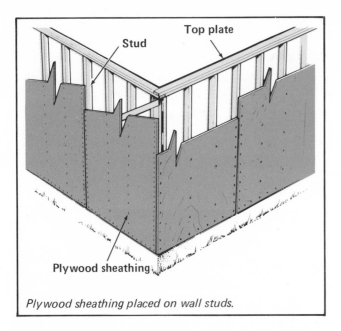

Plywood sheathing placed on wall studs.

Sheathing: The initial covering of studs or rafters on a house. Sheathing is placed over joists, studs, and rafters.

Shed Roof: Type of roof with only one slope.

Shell: Composed of all the elements that make up the basic structure of a house or addition, plus items like unfinished stairways, fireplaces, chimneys, doors, and porches.

Shimming: The technique of wedging one element up slightly to make it align properly, such as shimming the hinges of a door.

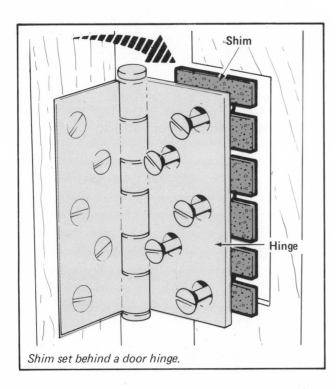

Shim set behind a door hinge.

Shingles: Finishing material used for roofs and siding.

Shoe Molding: Interior trim pieces used with baseboard molding along joint between baseboard and the floor.

Shutoff Valve *(plumbing):* Manually operated valve used to regulate water supply.

Siding: The finishing material used for the exterior of the building. Aluminum, brick, and shingles are examples.

Sill: (1) Window—the horizontal piece of wood resting at the bottom of the window frame; (2) Shell—structural piece of wood, set immediately on foundation, serves as base on which headers and joists are set.

Sill Plate: See sill (2)

Sill Seal: Usually a thin strip of fiberglass insulation placed between foundation and sill plate.

Skylights: Openings placed directly in roofing, letting in light.

Slab-On-Grade Foundation: Foundation type utilizing flat pad of poured concrete with its top surface set at least six inches above grade level.

Soffit Board: Used primarily on roofs with long overhang. A piece of wood nailed under the rafter tails.

Soil Stack *(plumbing):* A vertical pipe that carries human waste. Can also serve as main pipe for both human and nonhuman wastes in close-knit group of plumbing fixtures, such as bathroom.

Solar Heating: Heat obtained from the sun. Solar panels attached to the roof are a popular solar heating technique.

Solarium: Glassed-in room designed primarily for sunbathing.

Sole Plate: The horizontal bottom member of a wall.

Spacer Block: 2x4 block of wood, used to make corners in wall framing.

Span *(roofing):* Distance the roof covers from wall to wall in direction of rafter lie. Measured from the insides of the wall top plates.

Stool: Interior sill of a window.

Storage Walls: Cabinets, shelves, and such forming a wall.

Structural Engineer: Professional person able to work with homeowner throughout project. Specific skills include drawing up plans, evaluating structural needs, obtaining permits, and inspecting project.

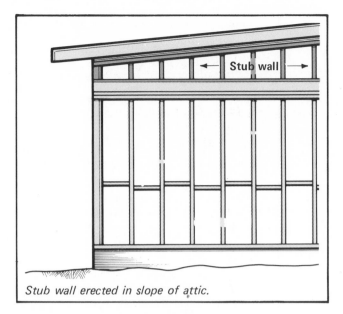

Stub wall erected in slope of attic.

Stub Wall: Short wall, usually sloped, as in the wall of an attic.

Stud: Wooden member used to construct wall frame.

Stud Wall: A wall with studs nailed to top and sole plates.

Subcontractor: Usually specialized contractor, able to complete, for example, roofing or electrical work.

Subflooring: Rough flooring material placed directly over floor joists.

Suspended Ceiling: Ceiling tiles placed on metal grids set below the ceiling structure.

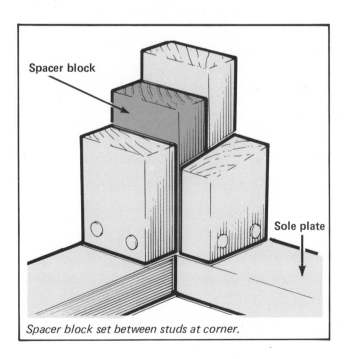

Spacer block set between studs at corner.

T

Toenail: Method of nailing where the nail is driven at a 60 degree angle, or slant.

Tongue and Groove Boards: Boards that fit together by design. One board has a lengthwise projection, or tongue, that fits into a groove on the other.

Top Plate: The top horizontal member of a wall.

Trap *(plumbing):* A "U" shaped piece of pipe under every fixture. It holds a plug of water, preventing sewer gases from entering the house.

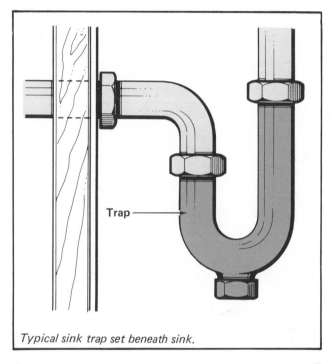

Typical sink trap set beneath sink.

Trellis: An outdoor framework used to support vines and plants.

Trimmer Joists: Special cut joists added to rough window or door opening.

Trimming-Out: Includes all the finishing touches in the final decor. Includes molding, painting, etc.

Trimwork: All the final finishing applications, such as casing, molding, etc.

2•4•1 Subfloor/Underlayment: Special plywood system that uses plywood as both subfloor and underlayment for non-structural flooring, such as tile or carpet.

U

Underlayment: Floor material positioned between subfloor and finished floor.

V

Valley Jack *(roofing):* Member that runs between valley rafter and ridgeboard.

Valley Rafter *(roofing):* Member that runs from top plate to ridgeboard at inside corner.

Vapor Barrier: Material, such as polyethylene film, used to prevent moisture penetration from insulation.

Vent Stack *(plumbing):* Vertical pipe providing air to the drainage system. It allows air to get into the system so that liquids will flow.

Vent stack placed on roof.

Vent: Opening that allows air to circulate in structure.

W

Wall Cavity: Opening in wall, ceiling, or floor, such as a space between joists, in which pipes or wire can run.

Weatherstripping: Material used around doors and windows to keep air from entering or escaping.

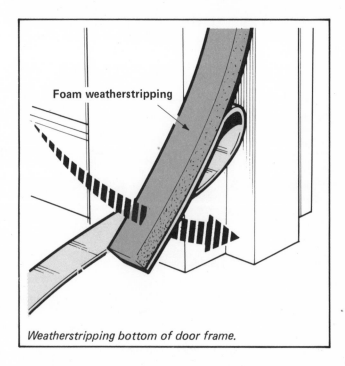

Weatherstripping bottom of door frame.

Work-Flow Chart: Time table kept by contractor to determine when various types of help (roofers, electricians) will be needed.

Workers Compensation Insurance: Special insurance, mandatory for employers, that covers injuries on the job.

Index